Sparse Coding and its Applications in Computer Vision

Sparse Coding and its Applications in Computer Vision

Zhaowen Wang (Adobe Systems, Inc., USA)

Jianchao Yang (Snapchat, Inc., USA)

Haichao Zhang (Amazon.com, Inc., USA)

Zhangyang Wang (University of Illinois, Urbana-Champaign, USA)

Yingzhen Yang (University of Illinois, Urbana-Champaign, USA)

Ding Liu (University of Illinois, Urbana-Champaign, USA)

Thomas S Huang (University of Illinois, Urbana-Champaign, USA)

World Scientific

NEW JERSEY · LONDON · SINGAPORE · BEIJING · SHANGHAI · HONG KONG · TAIPEI · CHENNAI · TOKYO

Published by

World Scientific Publishing Co. Pte. Ltd.

5 Toh Tuck Link, Singapore 596224

USA office: 27 Warren Street, Suite 401-402, Hackensack, NJ 07601

UK office: 57 Shelton Street, Covent Garden, London WC2H 9HE

British Library Cataloguing-in-Publication Data

A catalogue record for this book is available from the British Library.

SPARSE CODING AND ITS APPLICATIONS IN COMPUTER VISION

ISBN 978-981-4725-04-0

Preface

Sparse coding is an important model to represent visual information. By exploiting the latent structure of natural images in low-dimensional subspaces, sparse coding has achieved great success in many image processing and understanding tasks. In this monograph, we have an in-depth analysis of the working mechanism of sparse coding based on the prior theoretical and empirical studies. We also overview various applications of sparse coding including object recognition, sensor fusion, super-resolution, de-blurring and hyper-spectral signal processing, with special emphasis on learning the sparse representation in specific task domain. Also discussed is the connection between sparse coding and deep networks - which are currently the best performers in computer vision. Such connection sheds some light on the future direction of using sparse coding in problems with larger scale and higher complexity.

The main features of this book include:

- explanation of sparse coding from both theoretical and practical point of views;
- comprehensive review of the applications of sparse coding in both low-level and high-level vision problems;
- inspiration on future research directions of sparse coding by making connection with modern machine learning algorithms including deep neural networks.

In writing this book, we have tried to simplify the mathematics and place more emphasis on the concepts and applications, in the hope that it can reach a broader audience.

Authors

Contents

Chapter 1

Introduction

1.1 Background

Representing a signal in an accurate, compact and meaningful form has always been the cornerstone of digital signal processing. Although sparse coding has become a dominant approach for signal representation, its way has been paved by numerous previous efforts in related fields.

The classical way to represent a multi-dimensional signal x is to express it as the linear combination of the components in an orthonormal basis D:

$$x = D\alpha, \tag{1.1}$$

where α is the linear combination coefficient and it can be efficiently obtained as $\alpha = D^T x$. Famous examples of orthonormal basis D include Fourier basis [Proakis and Manolakis (2006)] and wavelet basis [Mallat (1999)]. When D is properly chosen, α often exhibits some desired characteristics for signals such as speech and natural image, which lays the foundation for various signal processing tasks. In some cases, the constraint to have an orthonormal basis may be too strong. Biorthogonal bases [Cohen *et al.* (1992)] were thus proposed where two different basis matrices are used in signal synthesis and analysis. Representations with orthogonal bases were prevalent due to their mathematical simplicity and computational efficiency.

The goal of linearly transforming a signal x with respect to D is to have a more predictable pattern in the resultant coefficient α. To capture such prior knowledge of x, we do not have to explicitly transform the signal into another domain, or limit the transform to linear form. For natural signals, "smoothness" (in spatial/temporal/spectral domain) is often a good prior to use, which has motivated many signal processing techniques such as anisotropic filtering [Perona and Malik (1990)] and total variation

[Rudin and Osher (1994)]. From a generative perspective, probabilistic models have also been extensively studied to learn signal representations from observed data, with Gaussian [Tipping and Bishop (1999); Vincent *et al.* (2008)], Gibbs [Smolensky (1986)] and non-parametric [Buades *et al.* (2005); Jojic *et al.* (2003)] ones as the most common priors. More recently, learning signal representation using neural networks with deep architecture [Ranzato *et al.* (2007a); Krizhevsky *et al.* (2012); Bengio *et al.* (2013)] has achieved great success in practical applications. Each layer in the network is usually defined according to a conventional shallow representation. The relation between neural networks and sparse coding is discussed in Section 3.2 and [Gregor and LeCun (2010)].

1.2 Basic Formulation

One important observation of (1.1) is that, for most natural signals such as image and audio, most of the coefficients in $\boldsymbol{\alpha}$ are zero or close to zero if $\boldsymbol{D}$ is properly selected. To make better use of this "sparseness" property, people have used overcomplete frames, which are also called dictionaries, in place of the complete and orthogonal bases. As there are more atoms than the dimension of signal in an overcomplete dictionary $\boldsymbol{D}$, we can represent a wider range of signal phenomena in a more compact form [Rubinstein *et al.* (2010)]. Specifically, we model a signal $\boldsymbol{x}$ of K-sparsity as

$$\boldsymbol{x} = \boldsymbol{D}\boldsymbol{\alpha}, \ \|\boldsymbol{\alpha}\|_0 \ll K, \tag{1.2}$$

with the $\boldsymbol{\alpha}$ here being the sparse coefficient vector, or sparse code, for $\boldsymbol{x}$. $\|\cdot\|_0$ denotes the ℓ^0-norm which is used to count the number of non-zero elements, or sparsity, in the sparse code $\boldsymbol{\alpha}$. Sparse representation assumes that, for any signal of our interest, its corresponding sparse code has a sparsity far less than the total number of atoms in $\boldsymbol{D}$.

To find the sparsest $\boldsymbol{\alpha}$, we need to solve the following ℓ^0 minimization problem:

$$\min_{\boldsymbol{\alpha}} \|\boldsymbol{\alpha}\|_0, \ \text{s.t.} \ \boldsymbol{x} = \boldsymbol{D}\boldsymbol{\alpha}. \tag{1.3}$$

Unfortunately, solving (1.3) requires intractable combinatorial optimization when the linear constraint is underdetermined. Approximate solutions can be found using greedy basis pursuit algorithms [Mallat and Zhang (1993); Tropp (2004)], whose accuracy cannot be guaranteed. Alternatively, the ℓ^1-norm is commonly used in place of the ℓ^0-norm to obtain a convex relaxation of (1.3), which, according to the compressive sensing theory [Candès (2006);

Donoho (2006b)], is known to give the same solution under broad conditions for sparse enough α. In many cases, the strict constraint of $x = D\alpha$ also needs to be relaxed to account for noise contamination, which results in the ℓ^1-norm regularized minimization problem:

$$\min_{\alpha} \|x - D\alpha\|_2^2 + \lambda \|\alpha\|_1, \qquad (1.4)$$

where $\lambda > 0$ is a regularization parameter to balance between reconstruction error and sparsity.

Besides the formulation in (1.4), a variety of other sparse coding methods have been proposed, which are going to be introduced in Chapter 2. It remains an open and active research problem to solve sparse code α efficiently and design dictionary D effectively.

1.3 Important Applications

In various image processing and computer vision problems, visual signal representations based on sparse coding formulation (1.4) and its variants have been widely used and led to state-of-the-art results in general [Wright *et al.* (2010)]. Famous examples include denoising [Elad and Aharon (2006); Mairal *et al.* (2009b)], inpainting [Mairal *et al.* (2008c)], super-resolution [Yang *et al.* (2010a); Adler *et al.* (2010)], face recognition [Wright *et al.* (2009)], motion segmentation [Elhamifar and Vidal (2009)], action recognition [Qiu *et al.* (2011)], sensor fusion [Zhang *et al.* (2012b,a)], *etc.* In the following, we briefly discuss how the mathematical model of sparse coding can be used to solve some of these real world problems.

Restoration In image super-resolution (SR), an unknown high-resolution (HR) image x is related to the observed low-resolution (LR) image y through a linear transform in a noise-free situation:

$$y = SHx, \qquad (1.5)$$

where S and H are downsampling and blurring operators, respectively. The linear system in (1.5) is heavily ill-posed and extra regularization is necessary to get a stable solution of x. Sparse coding effectively offers such a regularization as shown in [Yang *et al.* (2008)], where both x and y are sparely encoded according to (1.4) with respective to their individual dictionaries D_x and D_y. The sparse code robustly inferred from y can then be used to recover x. Ideally, two dictionaries should satisfy the relationship $D_y = SHD_x$ so that any HR and LR image pair have the same sparse representation. However, the filters S and H are often unknown. Therefore, the dictionaries are learned in the joint space of x and y [Yang *et al.* (2010a, 2012a)]. The sparse coding algorithm has also been integrated with recurrent neural network [Wang (2014)] and self-similar examples [Wang *et al.* (2014b)] to further improve SR quality.

For other image restoration tasks such as deblurring, the sparse coding formulation can be applied similarly [Zhang *et al.* (2011c,d, 2013b)].

Association   Sparse coding have been shown to be robust to noise and capable of handling high dimensional data [Wright *et al.* (2009)]. Therefore, it fits naturally to clustering problems where data samples within a cluster display large variation but reside in a low-dimensional subspace. To capture the local subspace property, an ℓ^1-graph [Cheng *et al.* (2010)] can be built by reconstructing each data point with other data in its local neighborhood as the selected dictionary atoms. Then a spectral clustering algorithm [Ng *et al.* (2002)] is carried out based on the graph matrix constructed by the sparse codes. In [Sprechmann and Sapiro (2010); Chen *et al.* (2013)], dictionary learning is combined with the clustering process, by Lloyd's-type algorithms that iteratively re-assign data to clusters and then optimize the dictionary tied with each cluster. In [Zheng *et al.* (2011)], the authors learned the sparse codes that explicitly take into account the local data manifold structure, indicating that encoding geometrical information will significantly enhance the learning performance. Other extensions of ℓ^1-graph in clustering have been proposed by [Yang *et al.* (2014c,d); Wang *et al.* (2015b)].

Sparse coding can not only associate data points of the same kind, but also data of multiple modalities arising due to the same event. Structured sparsity prior can be used in such cases to help deal with challenges such as the ill-posedness of inverse problems, curse of dimensionality, as well as feature and variable selection. This is due to the fact that many real world problems have intrinsic low degrees of freedom with structures. By exploiting the structural prior on non-zero sparse coefficients, we can greatly reduce the degrees of freedom of the problem, thus may potentially avoid the risk of over-fitting and reduce the number of observations/measurements required for a proper model estimation. The structural sparsity priors that have been previously investigated include clustering prior sparsity [Tibshirani *et al.* (2005); Zou and Hastie (2005); Huang *et al.* (2009); Liu and Ye (2010); Baraniuk *et al.* (2010); Faktor *et al.* (2012)], group/block sparsity [Yuan and Lin (2006); Eldar and Mishali (2009)] and joint sparsity [van den Berg and Friedlander (2009); Cotter *et al.* (2005); Duarte *et al.* (2005); Mishali and Eldar (2008, 2009)]. In many situations, the sparse coefficients tend to cluster and a clustering prior exploiting correlations between neighboring coefficients is enforced in the optimization algorithms in order to obtain a better representation. In group sparsity, the data is inherently represented by a small number of pre-defined groups of data samples, thus a sparsifying term over the groups is used to promote this property. In the case of multiple measurements, a specific group sparsity called joint structured sparsity is explored for joint sparse representation and heterogeneous feature fusion [Zhang *et al.* (2012b,a)], where not only the sparsity property for each measurement is utilized, but the structural information across the multiple sparse representation vectors for the multiple measurements is exploited as well.

Discrimination Although sparse coding was originally proposed as a generative model, it also performs surprisingly well in many classification problems. The Sparse Representation-based Classification (SRC) proposed in [Wright *et al.* (2009)] is a pioneering work in this direction. In SRC, a signal x from class c is assumed to lie in or near a low-dimensional subspace spanned by the atoms in the class-specific dictionary D_c. If we try to represent x using the composite dictionary $D=[D_1, ..., D_C]$ for all the C classes, the resulting sparse code $\alpha=[\alpha_1; ...; \alpha_C]$ is supposed to have non-zero coefficients concentrating in α_c, which is associated with its class.

In the original work of [Wright *et al.* (2009)], D_c consists of all the training samples from class c, which is not practical if the total class number or the training set is large. There are quite a few recent papers trying to learn dictionaries with a more compact form and a better discriminative capability by augmenting the reconstruction objective in (1.4) with additional discrimination terms such as Fisher discriminant criterion [Yang *et al.* (2011c)], structural incoherence [Ramirez *et al.* (2010)], class residual difference [Mairal *et al.* (2008b); Yang *et al.* (2011b)] and mutual information [Qiu *et al.* (2011)]. Sparse codes generated by discriminative dictionaries are also used as the input features of general classification models other than SRC [Bradley and Bagnell (2008); Yang *et al.* (2010b); Jiang *et al.* (2011); Mairal *et al.* (2012)]. In addition to natural images, discriminative sparse representation learning has also been actively applied in other imageries such as hyperspectral classification [Wang *et al.* (2014a, 2015a)].

1.4   Organization

In the remainder of this book, we will first discuss the theoretical foundation of sparse coding in Chapter 2, and then delve into the details of its applications in super-resolution, deblurring, fusion, clustering, image recognition and hyper-spectral classification through Chapters 3 to 8. Concluding remarks are made in Chapter 9.

Chapter 2

Theories of Sparse Coding

2.1 Fundamentals

We start with a general formulation for sparse coding, and discuss some popular realizations and solutions in the subsequent sections in this chapter.

Assume our signal $\boldsymbol{x}$ lies in the high dimensional space $\mathbb{R}^m$, and it is to be represented using a dictionary $\boldsymbol{D} \in \mathbb{R}^{m \times n}$ with n atoms. The corresponding representation coefficient vector $\boldsymbol{\alpha}$ lies in space $\mathbb{R}^n$. When $m = n$, $\boldsymbol{D}$ has to be a complete basis to represent any signal in the space. To describe a signal with a sparse subset of atoms in $\boldsymbol{D}$, we can use an overcomplete dictionary such that $n > m$. However, this may result in an infinite number of $\boldsymbol{\alpha}$s that can perfectly reconstruct $\boldsymbol{x}$. To resolve this ambiguity, people have commonly formulated sparse coding as the following optimization problem:

$$\min_{\boldsymbol{\alpha}, \boldsymbol{D}} \quad \mathcal{L}_1(\boldsymbol{x}, \boldsymbol{\alpha}, \boldsymbol{D}) + \lambda \mathcal{L}_2(\boldsymbol{\alpha}), \tag{2.1}$$

where the first loss function $\mathcal{L}_1$ measures the reconstruction error of signal $\boldsymbol{x}$, and the second loss function $\mathcal{L}_2$ penalizes the sparsity of sparse code $\boldsymbol{\alpha}$. While the linear ℓ^2 reconstruction loss $\|\boldsymbol{D}\boldsymbol{\alpha} - \boldsymbol{x}\|_2$ is usually adopted as $\mathcal{L}_1$, there are more variations exist for $\mathcal{L}_2$. When $\boldsymbol{D}$ is predefined, Eq. (2.1) is optimized solely with respect to $\boldsymbol{\alpha}$, which is a sparse code inference problem. When $\boldsymbol{D}$ is unknown (and hence also $\boldsymbol{\alpha}$), Eq. (2.1) becomes a dictionary learning task. We will discuss each of these problems in the following.

2.2 Sparse Priors

As we have already seen in Chapter 1, ℓ^0-norm is the most straightforward choice for $\mathcal{L}_2$ to find the most sparse $\boldsymbol{\alpha}$. In practice, ℓ^1-norm has been more widely used as the convex relaxation for the intractable ℓ^0-norm, inducing the objective function in (1.4). It is ensured by theories from compressive sensing [Donoho (2006b,a); Candes *et al.* (2006); Candès (2006)] that, under certain favorable conditions, the solutions obtained using ℓ^0-norm and ℓ^1-norm are exactly the same or within bounded difference in noisy environment. These conditions mainly depend on the characteristics of D, such as null space property, restricted isometry property (RIP), spark and coherence. An intuitive understanding can be developed from Fig. 2.1 for the equivalence between the two sparse regularizers. Interested readers are referred to [Fornasier and Rauhut (2011)] and the references within for a more comprehensive and in-depth review.

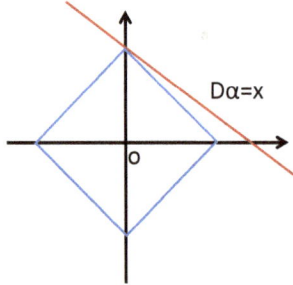

Fig. 2.1 The ℓ^1 plane (blue diamond) coincides with the linear system solution space (red line) at a coordinate axis, generating a sparse solution.

Besides the ℓ^1-norm sparse penalty, there have been other forms of $\mathcal{L}_2$ proposed to find a better tradeoff between promoting sparsity and reducing computation. A differentiable sparse coding model was developed in [Bradley and Bagnell (2008)], which employs smoother sparse priors such as KL divergence and ℓ_p^p-norm ($p \leq 1$). It has been shown that smoother priors can preserve the benefits of sparse priors while adding prediction stability when the sparse codes are inferred using maximum a posteriori (MAP) estimate. With similar probabilistic formulation, sparse representation has also been obtained using relevance vector machine (RVM) [Ji *et al.* (2008)], tree-structured graph model [He *et al.* (2010)] and Bernoulli distribution [Zhou *et al.* (2009a)]. In [Ling *et al.* (2013)], a deterministic sparse regularization based on the sum-log of ℓ^q-norm was used (with q being 1 or 2), which has the advantage of decentralized joint optimization.

2.3 Sparse Solvers

The past decade has seen great process in the development of efficient solvers for various sparse prior models. As finding the exact solution with ℓ^0-norm constraint has combinatorial complexity, algorithms to find approximated solutions have been proposed. Greedy approaches, such as matching pursuit (MP) [Mallat and Zhang (1993)], iteratively select dictionary atom with the largest correlation with the current reconstruction residual until the required sparsity is reached. Orthogonal matching pursuit [Tropp *et al.* (2007)] makes extension by updating residual using orthogonal projection. In this way, an atom will only be selected once at the cost of more computation.

More attention has been attracted to solve the ℓ^1-norm regularized problem in (1.4). In statistics literatures, this model is conventionally called LASSO and its optimal property has been studied for long [Zou *et al.* (2007)]. The ℓ^1-constrained optimization can be cast as a general linear programming problem, which cannot be solved very efficiently in large scale. Homotopy methods, *e.g.*, least angle regression (LARS) [Efron *et al.* (2004); Osborne *et al.* (2000)], start from a trivial solution and follow the regularization path of the LASSO, which may take a simple form like piecewise linear and make the search of solution space more efficient.

Coordinate descent can generally provide a quick solution to LASSO, and converge to a global minimum. A number of soft-thresholding based methods [Fu (1998); Daubechies *et al.* (2003); Friedman *et al.* (2007); Nesterov *et al.* (2007)] have been proposed following this direction. The convergence speed may be slowed down if there exists heavy correlation among the dictionary atoms.

Another important category of algorithms to solve Eq. (1.4) is the proximal method [Combettes and Pesquet (2011)]. In each iteration, a proximal method optimizes a proximal problem, which is a local approximation of the original objective function but takes a simpler form such as smooth and linear functions. The principle of proximal methods is similar to subgradient descent, however, it is demonstrated in [Mairal (2010)] that proximal methods have faster convergence rates both theoretically and practically.

Just as the counterpart of OMP in the ℓ^1 case, active set methods [Lee *et al.* (2006); Roth and Fischer (2008); Bach (2009)] solve a sequence of reduced sub-problems where only a small subset of active variables are considered. The active set is augmented at each iteration while the global optimality condition is ensured.

The analysis of other sparse coding solvers, such as the reweighted ℓ^2 method [Daubechies *et al.* (2010)], can be found in [Mairal (2010)] together with a comprehensive performance comparison.

2.4   Dictionary Learning

How to obtain a good overcomplete dictionary D is the most intriguing as well as challenging problem in sparse coding. Some early work tries to analytically define D with tight frames in the hope that they can preserve some of the nice properties presented in complete bases. In recent years, with more data and computation resources being available, data-driven dictionary learning approaches have become increasingly popular. When the size of training data is of high quality and moderate size, stacking them together directly to form D proves to be an effective approach [Wright *et al.* (2009)]. Clustering algorithms such as k-means can be used to produce a more compact dictionary.

To learn dictionary D in a more systematic way, the original objective of sparse coding in (1.4) is optimized with respect to D. As sparse code α depends on D, optimization is usually carried out in an alternative way until convergence. It should be noted that even with ℓ^1-norm regularization, the sparse coding objective is not convex with respect to both D and α. Fortunately, solutions obtained at local minimum generally work well in practice. Well-known examples along this direction include the K-SVD method [Aharon *et al.* (2006)] for ℓ^0-norm and the efficient least squares method [Lee *et al.* (2006)] for ℓ^1-norm. To learn dictionaries with varying sizes *in situ*, a Bayesian non-parametric method based on beta process was explored in [Zhou *et al.* (2009a)].

All the aforementioned methods learn a dictionary by minimizing representation error. However, when sparse coding is used for prediction or discrimination, dictionaries with different structures or characteristics are desired. In the classical work where sparse representation is applied to face recognition [Wright *et al.* (2009)], a dictionary $D=[D_1, ..., D_C]$ is composed of sub-dictionary blocks for all C classes. The sparse representation based classifier (SRC) then makes prediction of input x based on the dictionary block yielding the smallest reconstruction error:

$$\hat{c} = \arg\min_c \|x - D_c \alpha_c\|_2. \tag{2.2}$$

Each block of the SRC dictionary can be further trained using different criteria, such as block incoherence [Ramirez *et al.* (2010)], fisher discrimination [Yang *et al.* (2011c)], mutual information [Qiu *et al.* (2011)] and margin maximization [Wang *et al.* (2013)]. Sparse coding for other supervised learning tasks [Mairal *et al.* (2012); Wang *et al.* (2015a)] can also benefit from joint representation and task-oriented learning.

Chapter 3

Image Super-Resolution

Sparse representation has been successfully applied to single image SR, with the fundamental framework first proposed in [Yang *et al.* (2010a)]. A LR image $\boldsymbol{Y}$ is commonly modeled as a blurred and downsampled version of its corresponding HR image $\boldsymbol{X}$:

$$\boldsymbol{Y} = SH\boldsymbol{X} + \epsilon, \tag{3.1}$$

where S and H are downsampling and blurring operators, respectively, and ϵ is a Gaussian noise. Solving $\boldsymbol{X}$ directly from (3.1) is a highly ill-posed problem. For SR, the unknown variables in $\boldsymbol{X}$ significantly outnumber the known variables in $\boldsymbol{Y}$, not to mention that we usually do not have precise knowledge about the linear operators S and H. Therefore, an additional regularization is imposed on each local patch $\boldsymbol{x}$ in image $\boldsymbol{X}$ such that

$$\boldsymbol{x} \approx \boldsymbol{D}_x \boldsymbol{\alpha}, \quad \text{for some } \boldsymbol{\alpha} \in \mathbb{R}^K, \ \|\boldsymbol{\alpha}\|_0 \ll K, \tag{3.2}$$

where $\boldsymbol{x} \in \mathbb{R}^{d_1}$ represents a HR image patch with its pixels stacked in a vector form, $\boldsymbol{D}_x \in \mathbb{R}^{d_1 \times K}$ is the overcomplete dictionary for HR image patches with $K > d_1$ basis atoms, and $\boldsymbol{\alpha}$ is the sparse code for $\boldsymbol{x}$. The sparsity prior imposed by (3.2) is a common property of most natural images, and it serves as the cornerstone for SR reconstruction here.

Since the degradation model in (3.1) also applies to local patches, we can express the LR patch $\boldsymbol{y}$ corresponding to the HR patch $\boldsymbol{x}$ as follows:

$$\boldsymbol{y} \approx SH\boldsymbol{x} \approx SH\boldsymbol{D}_x \boldsymbol{\alpha} = \boldsymbol{D}_y \boldsymbol{\alpha}, \tag{3.3}$$

where $\boldsymbol{y} \in \mathbb{R}^{d_2}$, and $\boldsymbol{D}_y = SH\boldsymbol{D}_x \in \mathbb{R}^{d_2 \times K}$ is the dictionary for LR patches. Therefore, the same sparse code $\boldsymbol{\alpha}$ can be used to represent both $\boldsymbol{x}$ and $\boldsymbol{y}$ with respect to the dictionaries $\boldsymbol{D}_x$ and $\boldsymbol{D}_y$, respectively. Note that since we do not know the operators S and H, both $\boldsymbol{D}_x$ and $\boldsymbol{D}_y$ are to be learned.

Now suppose the dictionaries $\boldsymbol{D}_x$ and $\boldsymbol{D}_y$ are given; for an input LR patch $\boldsymbol{y}$, what we need is just to find the sparse code $\boldsymbol{\alpha}$ for $\boldsymbol{y}$, and reconstruct its HR patch as $\hat{\boldsymbol{x}} = \boldsymbol{D}_x\boldsymbol{\alpha}$. According to the compressive sensing theories [Candès (2006); Donoho (2006b)], if the sparse code $\boldsymbol{\alpha}$ is sufficiently sparse, it can be efficiently recovered by solving the following ℓ^1 regularized minimization problem:

$$\min_{\boldsymbol{\alpha}} \|\boldsymbol{y} - \boldsymbol{D}_y\boldsymbol{\alpha}\|_2^2 + \lambda\|\boldsymbol{\alpha}\|_1, \tag{3.4}$$

where $\lambda > 0$ is a regularization parameter. Once all the HR patches $\{\boldsymbol{x}\}$ are obtained, the entire HR image $\boldsymbol{X}$ can be reconstructed by placing them at appropriate locations.

3.1 Learning Dictionary Pairs for Super-Resolution

The dictionary pair $\{\boldsymbol{D}_x, \boldsymbol{D}_y\}$ plays a crucial role in analyzing and reconstructing image patches. In the following, we will see how to learn the dictionary pair from training set using joint and coupled sparse coding methods.

3.1.1 *Joint Sparse Coding*

Unlike the standard sparse coding, joint sparse coding considers the problem of learning two dictionaries $\boldsymbol{D}_x$ and $\boldsymbol{D}_y$ for two coupled feature spaces with training pairs $\{\boldsymbol{x}_i, \boldsymbol{y}_i\}_{i=1}^N$. It is required that the paired samples $\boldsymbol{x}_i$ and $\boldsymbol{y}_i$ can be represented as the sparse linear combinations of atoms from their respective dictionaries $\boldsymbol{D}_x$ and $\boldsymbol{D}_y$ using the *same* sparse code $\boldsymbol{\alpha}_i$. In this way, the relationship between the two feature spaces is encoded in the corresponding atoms in the two dictionaries. Yang *et al.* [Yang *et al.* (2010a)] addressed this problem by generalizing the basic sparse coding scheme as follows:

$$\min_{\boldsymbol{D}_x,\boldsymbol{D}_y,\{\boldsymbol{\alpha}_i\}_{i=1}^N} \sum_{i=1}^N \left(\|\boldsymbol{x}_i - \boldsymbol{D}_x\boldsymbol{\alpha}_i\|_2^2 + \|\boldsymbol{y}_i - \boldsymbol{D}_y\boldsymbol{\alpha}_i\|_2^2\right) + \lambda\|\boldsymbol{\alpha}_i\|_1, \tag{3.5}$$

$$\text{s.t.} \quad \|\boldsymbol{D}_x(:,k)\|_2 \le 1, \quad \|\boldsymbol{D}_y(:,k)\|_2 \le 1.$$

The formulation above basically requires that the resulting common sparse code $\boldsymbol{\alpha}_i$ should reconstruct both $\boldsymbol{y}_i$ and $\boldsymbol{x}_i$ well. Grouping the two reconstruction error terms together and denoting

$$\bar{\boldsymbol{x}}_i = \begin{bmatrix} \boldsymbol{x}_i \\ \boldsymbol{y}_i \end{bmatrix}, \quad \bar{\boldsymbol{D}} = \begin{bmatrix} \boldsymbol{D}_x \\ \boldsymbol{D}_y \end{bmatrix}, \tag{3.6}$$

we can convert Eq. (3.5) to a standard sparse coding problem in the concatenated feature space:

$$\min_{\bar{D},\{\alpha_i\}_{i=1}^N} \sum_{i=1}^N \|\bar{x}_i - \bar{D}\alpha_i\|_2^2 + \lambda\|\alpha_i\|_1 \tag{3.7}$$
$$\text{s.t.} \quad \|\bar{D}(:,k)\|_2 \leq 1.$$

Therefore, such a joint sparse coding scheme can only be claimed to be optimal in the concatenated feature space, but not in each feature space individually.

In testing, given an observed signal y, we want to recover the corresponding latent signal x by inferring their common sparse code α. However, since x is unknown, there is no way to find α in the concatenated feature space as has been done in training. Instead, we can only infer the sparse code of y in its own feature space with respect to D_y, and use it as an approximation to the joint sparse representation for x and y, which is not guaranteed to be consistent with the sparse code of x with respect to D_x. Consequently, the accuracy of recovering x may be undermined using the above jointly learned dictionaries.

3.1.2 *Coupled Sparse Coding*

A better way to construct dictionary pair for coupled feature spaces was developed in [Yang *et al.* (2012a)], where the sparse representation of a signal in one feature space is optimized to well reconstruct its corresponding signal in the other space. Formally, an ideal pair of coupled dictionaries D_x and D_y should satisfy the following equations for any coupled signal pair $\{x_i, y_i\}$:

$$z_i = \arg\min_{\alpha_i} \|y_i - D_y\alpha_i\|_2^2 + \lambda\|\alpha_i\|_1, \forall i = 1...N \tag{3.8}$$

$$z_i = \arg\min_{\alpha_i} \|x_i - D_x\alpha_i\|_2^2, \forall i = 1...N^1 \tag{3.9}$$

where $\{x_i\}_{i=1}^N$ are the training samples from $\mathcal{X}$, $\{y_i\}_{i=1}^N$ are the training samples from $\mathcal{Y}$ with $y_i = \mathcal{F}(x_i)$, and $\{z_i\}_{i=1}^N$ are the sparse representations.

Given an input signal y, the recovery of its latent signal x consists of two sequential steps: first to find the sparse representation z of y in terms

---

[1]Alternatively, one can require that the sparse representation of x_i in terms of D_x is z_i. However, since only the recovery accuracy of x_i is concerned, we directly impose $x_i \approx D_x z_i$.

of $\boldsymbol{D}_y$ according to Eq. (3.8), and then to estimate the latent signal as $\hat{\boldsymbol{x}} = \boldsymbol{D}_x \boldsymbol{z}$. Since the goal of our dictionary learning is to minimize the recovery error of $\|\boldsymbol{x} - \hat{\boldsymbol{x}}\|_2^2$, we define the following squared loss term:

$$L(\boldsymbol{D}_x, \boldsymbol{D}_y, \boldsymbol{x}, \boldsymbol{y}) = \frac{1}{2}\|\boldsymbol{x} - \boldsymbol{D}_x \boldsymbol{z}\|_2^2. \tag{3.10}$$

Then the optimal dictionary pair $\{\boldsymbol{D}_x^*, \boldsymbol{D}_y^*\}$ is found by minimizing the empirical expectation of (3.10) over the training signal pairs,

$$\min_{\boldsymbol{D}_x, \boldsymbol{D}_y} \frac{1}{N} \sum_{i=1}^{N} L(\boldsymbol{D}_x, \boldsymbol{D}_y, \boldsymbol{x}_i, \boldsymbol{y}_i)$$

$$\text{s.t.} \quad \boldsymbol{z}_i = \arg\min_{\boldsymbol{\alpha}} \|\boldsymbol{y}_i - \boldsymbol{D}_y \boldsymbol{\alpha}\|_2^2 + \lambda\|\boldsymbol{\alpha}\|_1, \text{ for } i = 1, 2, ..., N, \tag{3.11}$$

$$\|\boldsymbol{D}_x(:,k)\|_2 \le 1, \quad \|\boldsymbol{D}_y(:,k)\|_2 \le 1, \text{ for } k = 1, 2, ..., K.$$

Simply minimizing the above empirical loss does not guarantee that $\boldsymbol{y}$ can be well represented by $\boldsymbol{D}_y$. Therefore, we can add one more reconstruction term to the loss function to ensure good representation of $\boldsymbol{y}$,

$$L(\boldsymbol{D}_x, \boldsymbol{D}_y, \boldsymbol{x}_i, \boldsymbol{y}_i) = \frac{1}{2}\left(\gamma\|\boldsymbol{x}_i - \boldsymbol{D}_x \boldsymbol{z}_i\|_2^2 + (1-\gamma)\|\boldsymbol{y}_i - \boldsymbol{D}_y \boldsymbol{z}_i\|_2^2\right), \tag{3.12}$$

where γ $(0 < \gamma \le 1)$ balances the two reconstruction errors.

The objective function in (3.11) is highly nonlinear and nonconvex. We can minimize it by alternatively optimizing over $\boldsymbol{D}_x$ and $\boldsymbol{D}_y$ while keeping the other fixed. When $\boldsymbol{D}_y$ is fixed, the sparse representation $\boldsymbol{z}_i$ can be determined for each $\boldsymbol{y}_i$ with $\boldsymbol{D}_y$, and the problem in (3.11) reduces to

$$\min_{\boldsymbol{D}_x} \sum_{i=1}^{N} \frac{1}{2}\|\boldsymbol{D}_x \boldsymbol{z}_i - \boldsymbol{x}_i\|_2^2$$

$$\text{s.t.} \quad \boldsymbol{z}_i = \arg\min_{\boldsymbol{\alpha}} \|\boldsymbol{y}_i - \boldsymbol{D}_y \boldsymbol{\alpha}\|_2^2 + \lambda\|\boldsymbol{\alpha}\|_1, \text{ for } i = 1, 2, ..., N, \tag{3.13}$$

$$\|\boldsymbol{D}_x(:,k)\|_2 \le 1, \text{ for } k = 1, 2, ..., K,$$

which is a quadratically constrained quadratic programing that can be solved efficiently using conjugate gradient descent [Lee *et al.* (2006)].

When $\boldsymbol{D}_x$ is fixed, minimizing the loss function of Eq. (3.11) over $\boldsymbol{D}_y$ is a highly nonconvex bilevel programming problem [Colson *et al.* (2007)]. The upper-level optimization of (3.11) depends on the variable $\boldsymbol{z}_i$, which is the optimum of the lower-level ℓ^1-minimization. To solve this bilevel problem, we employ the same descent method developed in [Yang *et al.* (2010b)], which basically finds a descending direction along which the objective function will decrease smoothly with a small step. For easy of presentation, we drop the subscripts of $\boldsymbol{x}_i$, $\boldsymbol{y}_i$, and $\boldsymbol{z}_i$ in the following. Applying the chain rule, we can evaluate the descending direction as

$$\frac{\partial L}{\partial \boldsymbol{D}_y} = \frac{1}{2}\left(\sum_{j\in\Omega}\frac{\partial(\gamma R_x + (1-\gamma)R_y)}{\partial z_j}\frac{dz_j}{d\boldsymbol{D}_y} + (1-\gamma)\frac{\partial R_y}{\partial \boldsymbol{D}_y}\right), \qquad (3.14)$$

where we denote $R_x = \|\boldsymbol{D}_x\boldsymbol{z} - \boldsymbol{x}\|_2^2$ and $R_y = \|\boldsymbol{D}_y\boldsymbol{z} - \boldsymbol{y}\|_2^2$ as the reconstruction residuals with representation $\boldsymbol{z}$ for $\boldsymbol{x}$ and $\boldsymbol{y}$, respectively. z_j is the j-th element of $\boldsymbol{z}$, and Ω denotes the index set for j such that the derivative $dz_j/d\boldsymbol{D}_y$ is well defined. Let $\tilde{\boldsymbol{z}}$ denote the vector built with the elements $\{z_j\}_{j\in\Omega}$, and $\tilde{\boldsymbol{D}}_x$ and $\tilde{\boldsymbol{D}}_y$ denote the dictionaries that consist of the columns in $\boldsymbol{D}_x$ and $\boldsymbol{D}_y$ associated with indices in Ω. It is easy to find that

$$\frac{\partial R_x}{\partial \tilde{\boldsymbol{z}}} = 2\tilde{\boldsymbol{D}}_x^T(\boldsymbol{D}_x\boldsymbol{z} - \boldsymbol{x}),$$

$$\frac{\partial R_y}{\partial \tilde{\boldsymbol{z}}} = 2\tilde{\boldsymbol{D}}_y^T(\boldsymbol{D}_y\boldsymbol{z} - \boldsymbol{y}), \qquad (3.15)$$

$$\frac{\partial R_y}{\partial \boldsymbol{D}_y} = 2(\boldsymbol{D}_y\boldsymbol{z} - \boldsymbol{y})\boldsymbol{z}^T.$$

To evaluate the gradient in Eq. (3.14), we still need to find the index set Ω and the derivative $d\tilde{\boldsymbol{z}}/d\boldsymbol{D}_y$. Since there is no analytical link between $\tilde{\boldsymbol{z}}$ and $\boldsymbol{D}_y$, we use the technique developed in [Yang *et al.* (2010b)] to find the derivative as

$$\frac{\partial \tilde{\boldsymbol{z}}}{\partial \tilde{\boldsymbol{D}}_y} = \left(\tilde{\boldsymbol{D}}_y^T \tilde{\boldsymbol{D}}_y\right)^{-1}\left(\frac{\partial \tilde{\boldsymbol{D}}_y^T}{\partial \tilde{\boldsymbol{D}}_y}\boldsymbol{y} - \frac{\partial \tilde{\boldsymbol{D}}_y^T \tilde{\boldsymbol{D}}_y}{\partial \tilde{\boldsymbol{D}}_y}\tilde{\boldsymbol{z}}\right), \qquad (3.16)$$

where we assume the solution to Eq. (3.8) is unique and $(\tilde{\boldsymbol{D}}_y^T\tilde{\boldsymbol{D}}_y)^{-1}$ exists. (3.16) only gives us the derivative of $\tilde{\boldsymbol{z}}$ with respect to $\tilde{\boldsymbol{D}}_y$, which is associated the index set Ω. The other derivative elements of $\partial z_j/\partial\boldsymbol{D}_y$ required in (3.14) are simply set to zero, because it can be shown that the set Ω and the signs of $\tilde{\boldsymbol{z}}$ will not change for a small perturbation in $\boldsymbol{D}_y$ as long as λ is not a transition point of $\boldsymbol{y}$ in terms of $\boldsymbol{D}_y$ [Zou *et al.* (2007)]. As the chance for λ to be a transition point of $\boldsymbol{y}$ is low for any general distribution of $\boldsymbol{y}$, (3.14) can approximate the true gradient in expectation. A more rigid treatment of this issue has been provided by Mairal *et al.* [Mairal *et al.* (2012)] which leads to an identical way to calculate the sparse code derivative.

3.1.3 *Implementation Details*

Instead of directly working on raw pixel values, we extract simple features from HR/LR patches respectively as the signals in their coupled spaces. We extract gradient features from the bicubic-interpolated LR image patches as in Yang *et al.* [Yang *et al.* (2010a)], since the median frequency band in LR patches is believed to be more relevant to the missing high frequency information.

In the testing phase, the input LR image Y is first interpolated to the size of the desired HR image, and then divided into a set of overlapping LR patches of size $p \times p$. For each LR image patch, we extract its feature y as in the training phase, and compute its sparse code z with respect to the learned dictionary D_y. z is then used to predict the underlying HR image patch as $x = D_x z$. The predicted HR patches are tiled together to reconstruct the HR image X, where the average is taken for pixels in the overlapping region with multiple predictions.

The patch-wise sparse recovery approach can produce SR images of superior quality. However, the high computational cost associated with this approach has limited its practical use in real applications. To produce one SR image of moderate size, we need to process thousands of patches, each of which involves solving an ℓ^1-regularized minimization problem. Therefore, reducing the number of patches to process and finding a fast solver for the ℓ^1 minimization problem are the two directions for efficiency improvement. In [Yang *et al.* (2012a)], a selective patch processing strategy and a feed-forward sparse coding approximation model are used to speed up the algorithm without much compromise on SR performance.

3.1.4 *Experiments*

We apply coupled dictionary learning method to single image SR. For training, we sample 200,000 HR/LR 5×5 image patch (feature) pairs from a standard training set containing 91 images. For testing, the publicly available benchmarks Set5 [Bevilacqua *et al.* (2012)] and Set14 [Zeyde *et al.* (2012)] are used which contain 5 and 14 images respectively. All the LR images are obtained by downsampling and then upsampling the HR images by a desired upscaling factor. We use K=512 atoms in the learned coupled dictionaries unless otherwise stated.

We use the joint dictionary training approach by Yang *et al.* [Yang *et al.* (2010a)] as the baseline for comparison with our coupled training method. To ensure fair comparisons, we use the same training data for both methods, and employ exactly the same procedure to recover the HR image patches. Furthermore, to better manifest the advantages of our coupled training, we use the same D_x learned by joint dictionary training as our pre-defined

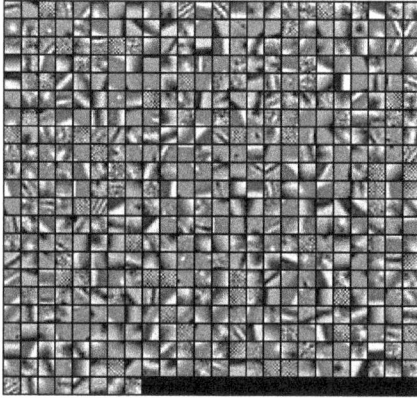

Fig. 3.1 The learned high-resolution image patch dictionary D_x.

dictionary for HR image patches, as shown in Fig. 3.1, and optimize only D_y to improve sparse recovery. This is clearly not the optimal choice, since D_x can be updated along with the optimization of D_y. The optimization converges very quickly, typically in less than 5 iterations.

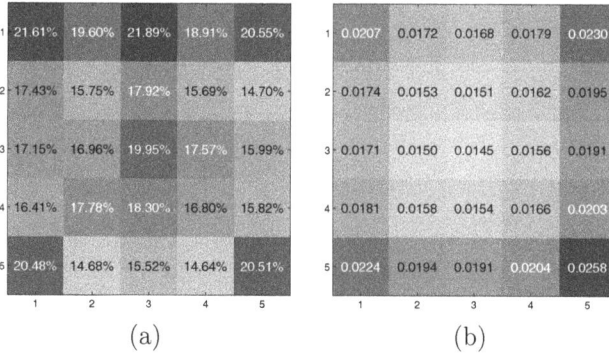

	1	2	3	4	5
1	21.61%	19.60%	21.89%	18.91%	20.55%
2	17.43%	15.75%	17.92%	15.69%	14.70%
3	17.15%	16.96%	19.95%	17.57%	15.99%
4	16.41%	17.78%	18.30%	16.80%	15.82%
5	20.48%	14.68%	15.52%	14.64%	20.51%

(a)

	1	2	3	4	5
1	0.0207	0.0172	0.0168	0.0179	0.0230
2	0.0174	0.0153	0.0151	0.0162	0.0195
3	0.0171	0.0150	0.0145	0.0156	0.0191
4	0.0181	0.0158	0.0154	0.0166	0.0203
5	0.0224	0.0194	0.0191	0.0204	0.0258

(b)

Fig. 3.2 (a) Percentages of pixel-wise RMSE reduced by our coupled training method compared with joint dictionary training method. (b) Pixel-wise RMSE of the recovered HR image patches (normalized and zero-mean) using our coupled dictionary training method.

To validate the effectiveness of our coupled dictionary training, we first compare the recovery accuracy of both dictionary training methods on a validation set, which includes 100,000 normalized image patch pairs sampled independently from the training set. Note that here we focus on evaluating the recovery accuracy for the zero-mean and normalized HR patch

Fig. 3.3 SR results upscaled by factor 2, using joint dictionary training (top row) and our method (bottom row). 0/1/2-pixel overlapping between adjacent patches are used for the Flower/Lena/Street image, respectively.

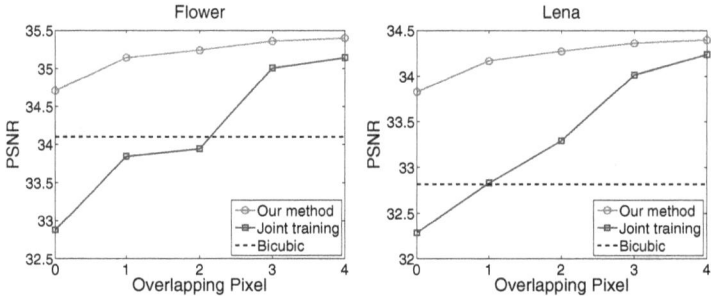

Fig. 3.4 The effects of pixel overlapping on PSNRs of the recovered images using different dictionary training methods. Our training method with 0-pixel overlapping can achieve the same level of performance as joint training with 3-pixel overlapping.

signals instead of the actual HR image pixels, thus isolating the affect of any application-specific technical details (*e.g.*, patch overlapping, contrast normalization, etc). Fig. 3.2 (a) shows the pixel-wise RMSE improvement using our coupled dictionary training method over the previous joint dictionary training method. It can be seen that our approach significantly reduces the recovery error in all pixel locations, which verifies the effectiveness of our training approach for sparse signal recovery.

For patch-based SR algorithms, the common practice is to recover each overlapping HR image patch independently, and then fuse the multiple pixel predictions in overlapping regions by simple averaging or other more sophisticated operation. Such a strategy is empirically supported by the error pattern observed in Fig. 3.2 (b): large recovery errors are most likely to occur at the corner and boundary pixels in a patch. Therefore, even with only one pixel overlapping between adjacent patches, the inaccurate predictions or outliers are expected to be suppressed significantly. However, such an improvement in accuracy is obtained at the cost of computation time, which increases almost quadratically with the amount of overlapping. In Fig. 3.3, the SR results by upscaling factor of 2 are compared on various real images between joint dictionary training and our coupled dictionary training with different amounts of patch overlapping between adjacent patches. As shown, the results by our method are free of artifacts no matter how much overlapping is used; in contrast, the artifacts introduced by joint dictionary training are always visible even up to 2-pixel overlapping. Actually, the artifacts of joint dictionary training will remain noticeable unless the overlapping increases to 3 pixels (note that the patch size is only 5×5).

Quantitatively, Fig. 3.4 shows the changes of the recovery PSNRs on both "Lena" and "Flower" as we increase the overlapping pixels between adjacent patches. For reference, we also show the PSNRs of the bicubic interpolation for both images with horizontal dashed lines. Our method outperforms bicubic notably even with 0-pixel patch overlapping, and continues to improve as overlapping increases. The PSNR for joint training is initially lower than bicubic, but increases substantially with more overlapping. One interesting observation is that our method does not benefit from pixel overlapping as much as joint dictionary training does; this is because our recovery is already close to the ground truth, and subsequently taking the average can not improve the accuracy too much. However, overlapping seems critical for the success of joint dictionary training for recovery. Another important observation is that the recovery using our training method with 0-pixel patch overlapping can achieve approximately the same level of performance as joint training with 3-pixel patch overlapping, with reduction in computation by more than 6 times. This advantage is crucial especially for real time applications and mobile devices.

Patch size is another important consideration in patch-based SR. When the patch is too small, the spatial correlation cannot be fully exploited. On the other hand, if the patch is too large, the signals become more diversified and the assumption of sparse representation cannot hold for a small dictionary. Table 3.1 shows that patch size of 5×5 is optimal for a dictionary with 512 atoms. But in any case, the dictionaries learned with

Table 3.1   PSNR of the SR result of the "Lena" image. Different patch sizes are tried with a fixed dictionary size of 512 and 2-pixel overlapping between patches.

Patch size	3×3	5×5	7×7
PSNR	34.03	34.67	33.97

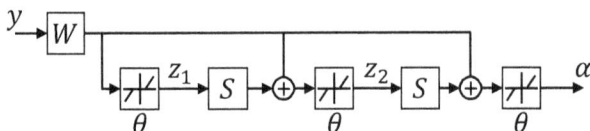

Fig. 3.5   A LISTA network [Gregor and LeCun (2010)] with 2 time-unfolded recurrent stages, whose output α is an approximation of the sparse code of input signal y. The linear weights $\mathbf{W}$, $\mathbf{S}$ and the shrinkage thresholds θ are learned from data.

coupled training has much higher PSNR than than bicubic interpolation.

3.2   From Sparse Coding to Deep Network

Recently, deep neural networks [Krizhevsky *et al.* (2012); Sermanet *et al.* (2013); Vincent *et al.* (2008)] have achieved great success in learning image representation for recognition related tasks. The key idea of end-to-end learning with deep architectures can also be applied to optimizing all the SR processing steps [Dong *et al.* (2014); Cui *et al.* (2014)]. However, it is not clear what kind of priors these deep networks have learned and enforced on HR images, since their structures are designed in a more or less intuitive way and have no correspondence to other shallow models.

In this section, we introduce a recurrent neural network (RNN), which closely mimics the behavior of sparse coding and at the same time benefits from end-to-end optimization over training data. We demonstrate through this novel network that a good model structure capturing correct image prior still plays a crucial role in regularizing SR solution even when we have sufficient modeling capacity and training data.

3.2.1   *LISTA Network for Sparse Coding*

One key building block in our RNN model is based on the work in [Gregor and LeCun (2010)], where a Learned Iterative Shrinkage and Thresholding

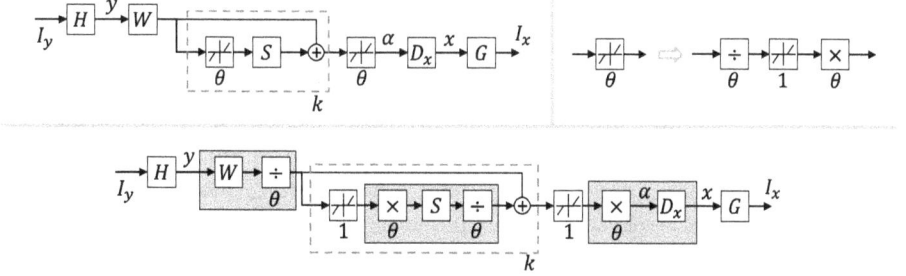

Fig. 3.6 Top left: the RNN network with a patch extraction layer **H**, a LISTA subnetwork for sparse coding (with k recurrent stages denoted by the dashed box), a HR patch recovery layer D_x, and a patch combination layer **G**. Top right: a neuron with adjustable threshold decomposed into two linear scaling layers and a unit-threshold neuron. Bottom: our RNN network re-organized with unit-threshold neurons and adjacent linear layers merged together in the gray boxes.

Algorithm (LISTA) is used to learn a feed-forward network to efficiently approximate sparse coding. As illustrated in Fig. 3.5, the LISTA network takes signal y as its input and outputs the sparse code α as it would be obtained by solving (3.8) for a given dictionary D_y. The network has a finite number of recurrent stages, each of which updates the intermediate sparse code according to

$$z_{k+1} = h_\theta(\mathbf{W}y + \mathbf{S}z_k), \qquad (3.17)$$

where h_θ is an element-wise shrinkage function defined as

$$[h_\theta(\mathbf{a})]_i = \text{sign}(a_i)(|a_i| - \theta_i)_+. \qquad (3.18)$$

Different from the iterative shrinkage and thresholding algorithm (ISTA) [Daubechies *et al.* (2004); Rozell *et al.* (2008)] which finds an analytical relationship between network parameters (weights **W**, **S** and thresholds θ) and sparse coding parameters (D_y and λ), the authors of [Gregor and LeCun (2010)] learn all the network parameters from training data using a back-propagation algorithm called learned ISTA (LISTA). In this way, a good approximation of the underlying sparse code can be obtained after a fixed small number of recurrent stages.

3.2.2 Recurrent Network for Image SR

Given the fact that sparse coding can be effectively implemented with a LISTA network, it is straightforward to formulate our RNN model that strictly mimics the processing flow of the sparse coding based SR method

[Yang *et al.* (2010a)] with multiple layers of neural networks. Same as most patch-based SR methods, our network takes the bicubic-upscaled LR image $\mathbf{I}_y$ as input, and outputs the full HR image $\mathbf{I}_x$. Fig. 3.6 shows the main network structure, and each of the layers is described in the following.

The input image $\mathbf{I}_y$ first goes through a convolutional layer $\mathbf{H}$ which extracts feature for each LR patch. There are m_y filters of spatial size $s_y \times s_y$ in this layer, so that our input patch size is $s_y \times s_y$ and its feature representation $\mathbf{y}$ has dimension m_y.

Each LR patch $\mathbf{y}$ is then fed into a LISTA network with k recurrent stages to obtain its sparse code $\boldsymbol{\alpha} \in \mathbb{R}^n$. Each stage of LISTA consists of two linear layers parameterized by $\mathbf{W} \in \mathbb{R}^{n \times m_y}$ and $\mathbf{S} \in \mathbb{R}^{n \times n}$, and a nonlinear neuron layer with activation function h_θ. The activation thresholds $\theta \in \mathbb{R}^n$ are also to be updated during training, which complicates the learning algorithm. To restrict all the tunable parameters in our linear layers, we do a simple trick to rewrite the activation function as

$$[h_\theta(\mathbf{a})]_i = \text{sign}(a_i)\theta_i(|a_i|/\theta_i - 1)_+ = \theta_i h_1(a_i/\theta_i). \tag{3.19}$$

Eq. (3.19) indicates the original neuron with adjustable threshold can be decomposed into two linear scaling layers and a unit-threshold neuron, as shown in the top-right of Fig. 3.6. The weights of the two scaling layers are diagonal matrices defined by θ and its element-wise reciprocal, respectively.

The sparse code $\boldsymbol{\alpha}$ is then multiplied with HR dictionary $\boldsymbol{D}_x \in \mathbb{R}^{m_x \times n}$ in the next linear layer, reconstructing HR patch $\boldsymbol{x}$ of size $s_x \times s_x = m_x$.

In the final layer $\mathbf{G}$, all the recovered patches are put back to the corresponding positions in the HR image $\mathbf{I}_x$. This is realized via a convolutional filter of m_x channels with spatial size $s_g \times s_g$. The size s_g is determined as the number of neighboring patches that overlap with a center HR patch in each spatial direction. The filter will assign appropriate weights to the overlapped pixels recovered from different patches and take their weighted average as the final prediction in $\mathbf{I}_x$.

As illustrated in the bottom of Fig. 3.6, after some simple reorganizations of the layer connections, the network described above has some adjacent linear layers which can be merged into a single layer. This helps to reduce the computation load as well as redundant parameters in the network. The layers $\mathbf{H}$ and $\mathbf{G}$ are not merged because we apply additional nonlinear normalization operations on patches $\boldsymbol{y}$ and $\boldsymbol{x}$, which will be detailed in Section 3.2.4.

Thus, there are totally 5 trainable layers in our network: 2 convolutional layers $\mathbf{H}$ and $\mathbf{G}$, and 3 linear layers shown as gray boxes in Fig. 3.6. The

k recurrent layers share the same weights and are therefore conceptually regarded as one. Note that all the linear layers are actually implemented as convolutional layers applied on each patch with filter spatial size of 1×1. Also note that all these layers only have weights but no biases (zero biases).

Mean square error (MSE) is employed as the cost function to train the network, and our optimization objective can be expressed as

$$\min_{\Theta} \sum_i \|RNN(\mathbf{I}_y^{(i)}; \Theta) - \mathbf{I}_x^{(i)}\|_2^2, \qquad (3.20)$$

where $\mathbf{I}_y^{(i)}$ and $\mathbf{I}_x^{(i)}$ are the i-th pair of LR/HR training data, and $RNN(\mathbf{I}_y; \Theta)$ denotes the HR image for $\mathbf{I}_y$ predicted using the RNN model with parameter set Θ. All the parameters are optimized through the standard back-propagation algorithm. Although it is possible to use other cost terms that are more correlated with human visual perception than MSE, our experimental results show that simply minimizing MSE also leads to improvement in subjective quality.

3.2.3 *Network Cascade for Scalable SR*

Like most SR models learned from external training examples, the RNN discussed previously can only generate HR images for a fixed upscaling ratio. A different model needs to be trained for each scaling factor to achieve the best performance, which limits the flexibility and scalability in practical use. One way to overcome this difficulty is to repeatedly enlarge the image by a fixed scale until the resulting HR image reaches a desired size. This practice is commonly adopted in the self-similarity based methods [Glasner *et al.* (2009); Freedman and Fattal (2011); Cui *et al.* (2014)], but is not so popular in other cases for the fear of error accumulation during repetitive upscaling.

In our case, however, it is observed that a cascade of RNNs (CRNN) trained for small scaling factors can generate even better SR results than a single RNN trained for a large scaling factor, especially when the target upscaling factor is large (greater than 2). The example shown in Fig. 3.7 tells part of the underlying reason. Here an input image (a) is magnified by $\times4$ times using a single RNN$\times4$ model (d), as well as using a cascade of two RNN$\times2$ models (e). It can be seen that the cascaded network generates a more natural-looking image for the complex object structures in the enlarged regions, while the single network produces notable artifacts. By further comparing the bicubic input to the single RNN$\times4$ (b) with the

(a) LR image

(b) bicubic×4

(c) RNN×2 & bicubic×2

(d) RNN×4

(e) RNN×2 & RNN×2

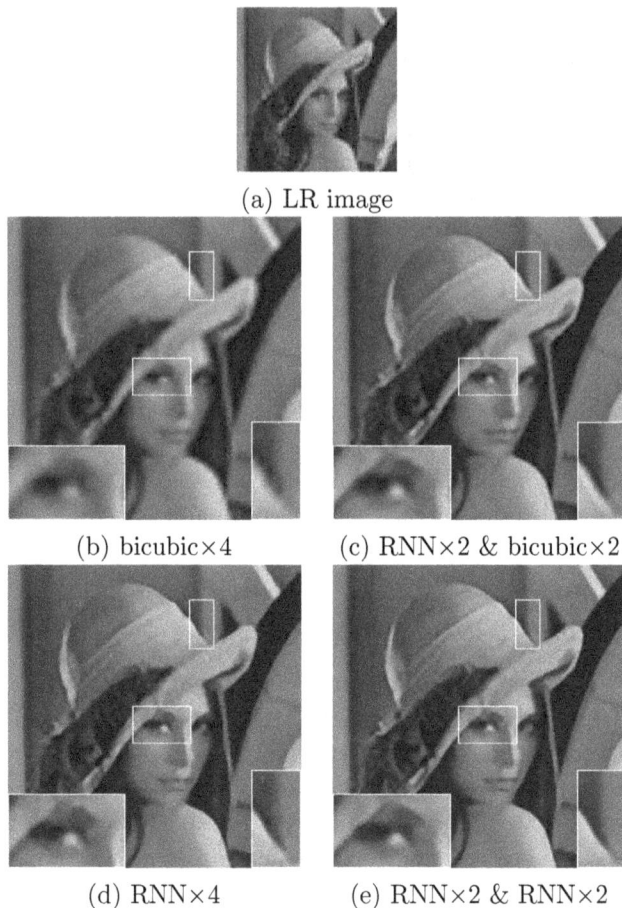

Fig. 3.7   SR results for Lena image upscaled by 4 times. (a) → (b) → (d) represents the processing flow with a single RNN×4 model. (a) → (c) → (e) represents the processing flow with two cascaded RNN×2 models.

input to the second cascaded RNN×2 (c), we find the latter one is much shaper and has much fewer artifacts along the edges. This indicates that (c) contains more relevant information but less noise than (b), and therefore it is easier to restore the HR image from (c) than from (b).

To get a better understanding of the above observation, we can draw a loose analogy between the SR process and a communication system. Bicubic interpolation is like a noisy channel through which an image is "transmitted" from LR domain to HR domain. And our RNN model (or any

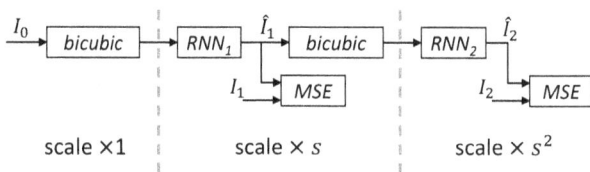

Fig. 3.8   Training cascade of RNNs with multi-scale objectives.

SR algorithm) behaves as a receiver which recovers clean signal from noisy observation. A CRNN is then like a set of relay stations that enhance signal-to-noise ratio before the signal becomes too weak for further transmission. Therefore, cascading will work only when each RNN can restore enough useful information to compensate for the new artifacts it introduces as well as the magnified artifacts from previous stages. This is why it will not help if we simply break a bicubic×4 operation into two sequential bicubic×2 operations.

The CRNN is also a deep network, in which the output of each RNN is connected to the input of the next one with bicubic interpolation in the between. To construct the cascade, besides stacking several RNNs trained individually with respect to (3.20), we can also optimize all of them jointly as shown in Fig. 3.8. Without loss of generality, we assume each RNN in the cascade has the same scaling factor s. Let $\mathbf{I}_0$ denote the input image of original size, and $\hat{\mathbf{I}}_j$ ($j>0$) denote the output image of the j-th RNN upscaled by a total of $\times s^j$ times. Each $\hat{\mathbf{I}}_j$ can be compared with its associated ground truth image $\mathbf{I}_j$ according to the MSE cost, leading to a multi-scale objective function:

$$\min_{\{\boldsymbol{\Theta}_j\}} \sum_i \sum_j \left\| RNN(\hat{\mathbf{I}}_{j-1}^{(i)} \uparrow s; \boldsymbol{\Theta}_j) - \mathbf{I}_j^{(i)} \right\|_2^2, \tag{3.21}$$

where i denotes the data index, and j denotes the RNN index. $\mathbf{I}\uparrow s$ is the bicubic interpolated image of $\mathbf{I}$ by a factor of s. This multi-scale objective function makes full use of the supervision information in all the scales, sharing a similar idea as the deeply supervised network [Lee *et al.* (2014)] for recognition. All the layer parameters $\{\boldsymbol{\Theta}_j\}$ in (3.21) could be optimized from end to end by back propagation. We use a greedy algorithm here to train each RNN sequentially in the order they appear in the cascade so that we do not need to care about the gradient of bicubic layers. Applying back propagation through a bicubic layer or its trainable surrogate will be considered in future work.

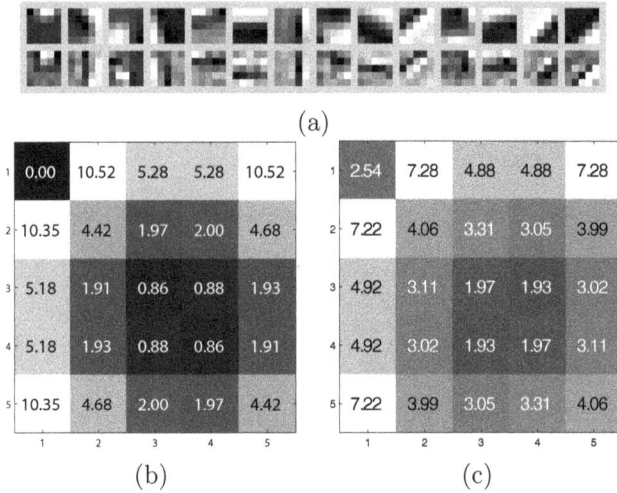

(a)

1	0.00	10.52	5.28	5.28	10.52
2	10.35	4.42	1.97	2.00	4.68
3	5.18	1.91	0.86	0.88	1.93
4	5.18	1.93	0.88	0.86	1.91
5	10.35	4.68	2.00	1.97	4.42

1	2.54	7.28	4.88	4.88	7.28
2	7.22	4.06	3.31	3.05	3.99
3	4.92	3.11	1.97	1.93	3.02
4	4.92	3.02	1.93	1.97	3.11
5	7.22	3.99	3.05	3.31	4.06

(b)   (c)

Fig. 3.9   Some 5×5 filters in layer D_x are shown in (a). Top row: initial filters from coupled dictionary; bottom row: trained filters in RNN. Power spectral densities (in percentage) averaged over all 512 filters before/after training are plotted in (b)/(c).

3.2.4   *Experiments*

The same data sets for training and testing are used here as the coupled dictionary learning. The RNN model is trained with the CUDA ConvNet package [Krizhevsky *et al.* (2012)]. All the experiments are run on a workstation with 12 Intel Xeon 2.67GHz CPUs and 1 GTX680 GPU.

3.2.4.1   *Analysis of RNN*

To illustrate the benefits of joint training in RNN, we examine how the filters learned by RNN have changed from their initial values given by coupled dictionary learning. Fig. 3.9 (a) visualizes some 5×5 filters in the layer of D_x. It is found that the learned filters (bottom row) still have similar structures as the initial ones (top row), but with thinner edges and finer details. The power spectral densities for the filters of coupled dictionary and RNN are plotted in (b) and (c) respectively, where spatial frequency increases from top-left to bottom-right in two directions. We can see there is a deficiency of energy in mid-band frequency for the initial filters, while the energy distribution is more balanced in RNN's filters. This indicates the potential of our RNN to recover a richer variety of signal patterns.

Table 3.2   Effect of training data augmentation on the performance of RNN on Set5 for scaling up by ×2 times.

training data	translation	+scaling	+rotation
PSNR	36.65	36.81	36.97

Table 3.3   Effect of dictionary size on the PSNR performances of sparse coding and RNN on Set5 for scaling up by ×2 times.

n	128	256	512
SC	35.61	35.74	35.95
RNN	36.87	36.93	36.97

Table 3.4   Effect of network structure on PSNR performance on Set5, for different SR scaling factors.

upscale factor	×1.5	×2	×3	×4
RNN×2, $k=1$	40.12	36.92	33.03	30.73
RNN×2, $k=2$	40.17	36.97	33.06	30.77
RNN×2, $k=3$	**40.19**	**37.01**	33.12	30.81
RNN×1.5, $k=2$	40.16	36.44	30.38	29.09
RNN×3, $k=2$	39.89	36.79	32.94	30.70
RNN×4, $k=2$	39.72	36.59	32.82	30.60
CRNN, $k=2$	40.17	36.97	**33.16**	**30.93**

Data augmentation plays an important role in training deep networks, especially when the training set is small as in our case. Three types of image transform are used to augment our training set: translation, scaling and rotation. We have about 0.18 million training samples generated from 91 images when all the augmentations are used. Table 3.2 shows that the PSNR of RNN on Set5 gets improved consistently as each of these augmentations is added in sequel.

Besides using a large dictionary of size $n=512$, we also train RNNs with smaller dictionaries and compare their performances with our sparse coding (SC) method in Table 3.3. For all the n's, RNN significantly outperforms SC from which it is initialized. And the PSNR achieved by RNN drops more gracefully than SC when n is reduced from 512 to 128.

In Table 3.4, the effect of different network structures is investigated. First, we compare different numbers of recurrent stages k for the RNN×2 model. As k increases from 1 to 3, the PSNR is slightly improved by less than 0.1dB. We fix $k=2$ in all the experiments below.

Table 3.5   Time consumption(s) for RNN to upscale the "baby" image from 256×256 to 512×512 under different settings.

	$n=128$	$n=256$	$n=512$
$k=1$	0.351	0.679	1.852
$k=2$	0.434	1.012	3.172
$k=3$	0.516	1.347	4.492

Second, we apply the same RNN×2 model one or more times for scaling factors other than 2, and compare it with the RNNs trained for a particular scale. It is observed such simple cascade (without training as a cascade network) can perform as well as the scale-specific model for small scaling factor (1.5), and much better for large scaling factors (3 and 4). Note that the cascade of RNN×1.5 does not lead to good results since artifacts quickly get amplified through many repetitive upscalings. Therefore, we use RNN×2 as the default building block for CRNN in the following, and drop the notation ×2 when there is no ambiguity.

Finally, the last row in Table 3.4 shows that a CRNN trained using the multi-scale objective in Eq. (3.21) can further improve the SR results for scaling factors 3 and 4, as the second RNN in the cascade becomes less sensitive to the artifacts generated by the first one.

The computation time of upscaling an image of typical size using our GPU implementation is listed in Table 3.5 for various network settings. The RNN model is efficient compared with most state-of-the-art SR algorithms, and its complexity can be reduced a lot by using smaller dictionary size n and fewer recurrent stages k, which cause little performance degradation as shown in Table 3.3 and 3.4. Note that without GPU parallelization, it takes 13.62s to upscale the same image using a network with $n = 512$ and $k = 1$.

3.2.4.2   Visual Comparison with State of the Arts

The SC and CRNN methods are compared with the Convolutional Neural Network (CNN) based SR method [Dong *et al.* (2014)], which is most related to our models among the exiting state-of-the-art methods. As can be seen from the testing results in Fig. 3.10, SC can generate plausible HR images and does a good job in homogeneous regions. CRNN produces much sharper edges and textures with finer details. CNN can also recover sharp edges, but introduces noticeable artifacts along long edges as shown in the

(a) SC   (b) CNN   (c) CRNN

Fig. 3.10   SR results given by (a) SC, (b) CNN [Dong *et al.* (2014)] and (c) CRNN. Each row from top to bottom: the "monarch" image upscaled by ×3; the "bird" image upscaled by ×4; the "zebra" image upscaled by ×3.

(a) ground truth   (b) CNN   (c) CRNN

Fig. 3.11   The "barbara" image upscaled by ×3 using (b) CNN [Dong *et al.* (2014)] and (c) CRNN.

enlarged areas.

The test image "barbara" in Fig. 3.11 is more challenging since it has many high frequency textures which neither CNN nor our CRNN can handle

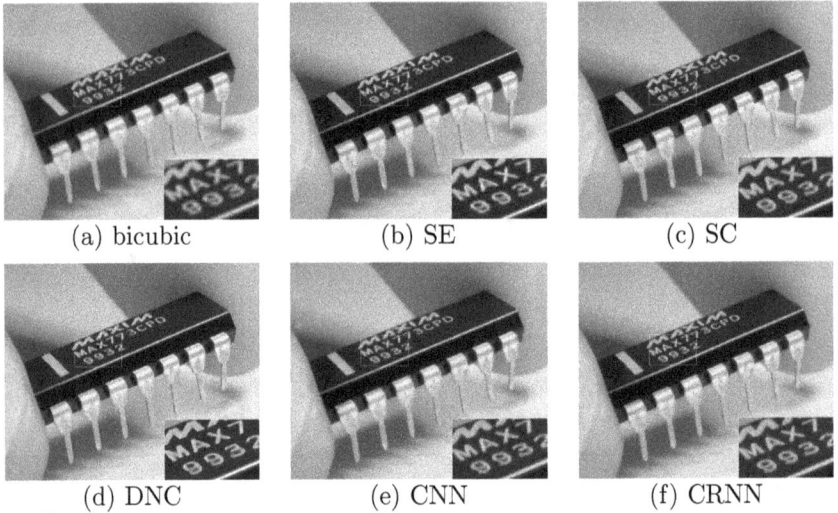

<table>
<tr><td>(a) bicubic</td><td>(b) SE</td><td>(c) SC</td></tr>
<tr><td>(d) DNC</td><td>(e) CNN</td><td>(f) CRNN</td></tr>
</table>

Fig. 3.12 The "chip" image upscaled by ×4 using: (a) bicubic; (b) SE [Freedman and Fattal (2011)]; (c) SC [Yang *et al.* (2010a)]; (d) DNC [Cui *et al.* (2014)]; (e) CNN [Dong *et al.* (2014)]; (f) CRNN [Wang (2014)].

well. Nevertheless, the textures generated by CRNN are visually more appealing and look more natural than those given by CNN.

Fig. 3.12 shows the SR results on the "chip" image produced by more methods including the basic bicubic interpolation, self-example based method (SE) [Freedman and Fattal (2011)], deep network cascade (DNC) [Cui *et al.* (2014)] and CNN [Dong *et al.* (2014)]. The SE method leads to sever artifacts when it fails to find good enough self examples. The DNC gives the sharpest edges but cannot recover the corners of the characters well. CRNN improves the sharpness of SC remarkably and can correctly recover all the details of complex patterns.

3.3 Learning Super-Resolution Jointly from External and Internal Examples

The most popular single image SR methods rely on example-based learning techniques. Classical example-based methods learn the mapping between LR and HR image patches, from a large and representative external set of image pairs, and is thus denoted as *external SR*. Meanwhile, images generally possess a great amount of self-similarities; such a self-similarity property motivates a series of *internal SR* methods. With much progress being made, it is recognized that external and internal SR methods each suffer from their certain drawbacks. However, their complementary properties inspire people to do the *joint super-resolution* (joint SR) [Wang *et al.* (2014b)], that adaptively utilizes both external and internal examples for the SR task. In this section, we present joint SR exploiting both external and internal examples, by defining an adaptive combination of different loss functions. The external part is essentially built on coupled sparse coding [Yang *et al.* (2012a)].

3.3.1 *A Motivation Study of Joint SR*

3.3.1.1 *Related Work*

The joint utilization of both external and internal examples has been most studied for image denoising [Zontak and Irani (2011)]. Mosseri et. al. [Mosseri *et al.* (2013)] first proposed that some image patches inherently prefer internal examples for denoising, whereas other patches inherently prefer external denoising. Such a preference is in essence the tradeoff between noise-fitting versus signal-fitting. Burger et. al. [Burger *et al.* (2013)] proposed a learning-based approach that automatically combines denoising results from an internal and an external method. The learned combining strategy outperforms both internal and external approaches across a wide range of images, being closer to theoretical bounds.

In SR literature, while the most popular methods are based on either external or internal similarities, there have been limited efforts to utilize one to regularize the other. The authors in [Dong *et al.* (2011)] incorporated both a local autoregressive (AR) model and a nonlocal self-similarity regularization term, into the sparse representation framework, weighted by constant coefficients. Yang et. al. [Yang *et al.* (2013)] learned the (approximated) nonlinear SR mapping function from a collection of external images with the help of in-place self-similarity. Despite the existing efforts, there is little understanding on how the external and internal examples interact with each other in SR, how to judge the external versus internal preference for each patch, and how to make them collaborate towards an overall optimized performance.

External SR methods use a universal set of example patches to predict the missing (high-frequency) information for the HR image. In [Freeman *et al.* (2002)], during the training phase, LR-HR patch pairs are collected. Then in the test phase, each input LR patch is found with a nearest neighbor (NN) match in the LR patch pool, and its corresponding HR patch is selected as the output. It is further formulated as a kernel ridge regression (KRR) in [Kim and Kwon (2010)]. More recently, a popular class of external SR methods are associated with the *sparse coding* technique [Lee *et al.* (2006)], [Yang *et al.* (2010a)]. The patches of a natural image can be represented as a sparse linear combination of elements within a redundant pre-trained dictionary. Following this principle, the advanced *coupled sparse coding* is further proposed in [Yang *et al.* (2012a)], [Yang *et al.* (2010a)]. External SR methods are known for their capabilities to produce plausible image appearances. However, there is no guarantee that an arbitrary input patch can be well matched or represented by the external dataset of limited size. When dealing with some unique features that rarely appear in the given dataset, external SR methods are prone to produce either noise or oversmoothness [Yang *et al.* (2011a)]. It constitutes the inherent problem of any external SR method with a finite-size training set [Dong *et al.* (2013)].

Internal SR methods search for example patches from the input image itself, based on the fact that patches often tend to recur within the image [Glasner *et al.* (2009); Mairal *et al.* (2009b); Yang *et al.* (2011a)], or across different image scales [Freedman and Fattal (2011)]. Although internal examples provide a limited number of references, they are very relevant to the input image. However, this type of approach has a limited performance, especially for irregular patches without any discernible repeating pattern [Chatterjee and Milanfar (2010)]. Due to the insufficient patch pairs, the mismatches of internal examples often lead to more visual artifacts. In addition, epitome was proposed in [Jojic *et al.* (2003); Ni *et al.* (2009); Chu *et al.* (2010)] to summarize both local and non-local similar patches and reduces the artifacts caused by neighborhood matching. We apply epitome as an internal SR technique in our model, and evidence its advantages by our experiments.

3.3.2   *Comparing External and Internal SR Methods*

Both external and internal SR methods have different advantages and drawbacks. See Fig. 3.13 for a few specific examples. The first row of images are from the $3\times$ SR result sof the *Train* image, and the second row from the $4\times$ SR results of the *Kid* image. The eight images form four pairs: the

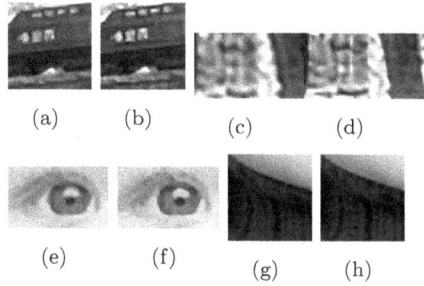

Fig. 3.13   (a) *Train*, carriage region by [Yang *et al.* (2012a)]; (b) *Train*, carriage region by [Freedman and Fattal (2011)]; (c) *Train*, brick region by [Yang *et al.* (2012a)], (d) *Train*, brick region by [Freedman and Fattal (2011)]; (e) *Kid*, Eye region by [Yang *et al.* (2012a)]; (f) *Kid*, eye region by [Freedman and Fattal (2011)]; (g) *Kid*, sweater region by [Yang *et al.* (2012a)], (h) *Kid*, sweater region by [Freedman and Fattal (2011)].

pair (a) (b) are cropped from the same spatial location, in the SR results of *Train* by external [Yang *et al.* (2012a)] and internal methods[Freedman and Fattal (2011)], respectively (similarly for (c)(d), (e)(f), and (g)(h)). In the first pair, the top contour of carriage (b) contains noticeable structural deformations, and the numbers "425" are more blurred than those in (a). That is because the numbers can more easily find counterparts or similar structure components from an external dataset; but within the same image, there are few recurring patterns that look visually similar to the numbers. Internal examples generate sharper SR results in images (d) than (c), since the bricks repeat their own patterns frequently, and thus the local neighborhood is rich in internal examples. Another winning case of external examples is between (e) and (f), as inconsistent artifacts along the eyelid and around the eyeball are obvious. Because the eye region is composed of complex curves and fine structures, external examples encompass more suitable reference patches and perform a more natural-looking SR. In contrast, the repeating sweater textures leads to a sharper SR in (h) than that in (g).

These comparisons display the generally different, even complementary behaviors of external and internal SR. Based on the observations, we expect that the external examples contribute to visually pleasant SR results for smooth regions as well as some irregular structures that barely recur in the input. Meanwhile, internal examples serve as a powerful source to reproduce unique and singular features that rarely appear externally but repeat in the input image (or its different scales). Note that similar arguments have been validated statistically in the the image denoising literature [Burger *et al.* (2013)].

3.3.3   *A Joint SR model*

Let $\mathbf{X}$ denote the HR image to be estimated from the LR input $\mathbf{Y}$. $\mathbf{X}_{ij}$ and $\mathbf{Y}_{ij}$ stand for the (i, j)-th $(i, j = 1, 2...)$ patch from $\mathbf{X}$ and $\mathbf{Y}$, respectively. Considering almost all SR methods work on patches, we define two loss functions $\ell_{\mathcal{G}}(\cdot)$ and $\ell_{\mathcal{I}}(\cdot)$ in a patch-wise manner, which enforce the external and internal similarities, respectively. While one intuitive idea is to minimize a weighted combination of the two loss functions, a patch-wise (adaptive) weight $\omega(\cdot)$ is needed to balance them. We hereby write the joint SR in the general form:

$$\min_{\mathbf{X}_{ij},\Theta_G,\Theta_I} \quad \ell_{\mathcal{G}}(\mathbf{X}_{ij}, \Theta_G|\mathbf{Y}_{ij})$$
$$+ \omega(\Theta_G, \Theta_I|\mathbf{Y}_{ij})\ell_{\mathcal{I}}(\mathbf{X}_{ij}, \Theta_I|\mathbf{Y}_{ij}). \quad (3.22)$$

Θ_G and Θ_I are the latent representations of $\mathbf{X}_{ij}$ over the spaces of external and self examples, respectively. The form $f(\mathbf{X}_{ij}, \Theta|\mathbf{Y}_{ij})$, f being $\ell_{\mathcal{G}}$, $\ell_{\mathcal{I}}$ or ω, represents the function dependent on variables $\mathbf{X}_{ij}$ and Θ (Θ_G or Θ_I), with $\mathbf{Y}_{ij}$ known (we omit $\mathbf{Y}_{ij}$ in all formulations hereinafter). We will discuss each component in (3.22) next.

One specific form of joint SR will be discussed here. However, note that with different choices of $\ell_{\mathcal{G}}(\cdot)$, $\ell_{\mathcal{I}}(\cdot)$, and $\omega(\cdot)$, a variety of methods can be accommodated in the framework. For example, if we set $\ell_{\mathcal{G}}(\cdot)$ as the (adaptively reweighted) sparse coding term, while choosing $\ell_{\mathcal{I}}(\cdot)$ equivalent to the two local and non-local similarity based terms, then (3.22) becomes the model proposed in [Dong *et al.* (2011)], with $\omega(\cdot)$ being some empirically chosen constants.

3.3.4   *Sparse Coding for External Examples*

The HR and LR patch spaces $\{\mathbf{X}_{ij}\}$ and $\{\mathbf{Y}_{ij}\}$ are assumed to be tied by some mapping function. With a well-trained coupled dictionary pair ($\mathbf{D_h}$, $\mathbf{D_l}$) (see [Yang *et al.* (2012a)] for details on training a coupled dictionary pair), the *coupled sparse coding* [Yang *et al.* (2010a)] assumes that ($\mathbf{X}_{ij}$, $\mathbf{Y}_{ij}$) tends to admit a common sparse representation $\mathbf{a}_{ij}$. Since $\mathbf{X}$ is unknown, Yang et. al. [Yang *et al.* (2010a)] suggest to first infer the sparse code $\mathbf{a}_{ij}^L$ of $\mathbf{Y}_{ij}$ with respect to $\mathbf{D_l}$, and then use it as an approximation of $\mathbf{a}_{ij}^H$ (the sparse code of $\mathbf{X}_{ij}$ with respect to $\mathbf{D_h}$), to recover $\mathbf{X}_{ij} \approx \mathbf{D_h}\mathbf{a}_{ij}^L$.

We set $\Theta_G = \mathbf{a}_{ij}$ and constitute the loss function enforcing external similarity:

$$
\begin{aligned}
&\ell_{\mathcal{G}}(\mathbf{X}_{ij}, \mathbf{a}_{ij}) \\
&= \lambda ||\mathbf{a}_{ij}||_1 + ||\mathbf{D_l}\mathbf{a}_{ij} - \mathbf{Y}_{ij}||_F^2 + ||\mathbf{D_h}\mathbf{a}_{ij} - \mathbf{X}_{ij}||_F^2.
\end{aligned} \tag{3.23}
$$

3.3.5 *Epitomic Matching for Internal Examples*

3.3.5.1 *The High Frequency Transfer Scheme*

Based on the observation that singular features like edges and corners in small patches tend to repeat almost identically across different image scales, Freedman and Fattal [Freedman and Fattal (2011)] applied the "high frequency transfer" method to searching the high-frequency component for a target HR patch, by NN patch matching across scales. Defining a linear interpolation operator $\mathcal{U}$ and a downsampling operator $\mathcal{D}$, for the input LR image $\mathbf{Y}$, we first obtain its initial upsampled image $\mathbf{X}^{'E} = \mathcal{U}(\mathbf{Y})$, and a smoothed input image $\mathbf{Y}' = \mathcal{D}(\mathcal{U}(\mathbf{Y}))$. Given the smoothed patch $\mathbf{X}_{ij}^{'E}$, the missing high-frequency band of each unknown patch $\mathbf{X}_{ij}^E$ is predicted by first solving a NN matching (3.24):

$$
(m, n) = \arg\min_{(m,n) \in \mathcal{W}_{ij}} ||\mathbf{Y}'_{mn} - \mathbf{X}_{ij}^{'E}||_F^2, \tag{3.24}
$$

where $\mathcal{W}_{ij}$ is defined as a small local searching window on image $\mathbf{Y}'$. We could also simply express it as $(m, n) = f_{NN}(\mathbf{X}_{ij}^{'E}, \mathbf{Y}')$. With the co-located patch $\mathbf{Y}_{mn}$ from $\mathbf{Y}$, the high-frequency band $\mathbf{Y}_{mn} - \mathbf{Y}'_{mn}$ is pasted onto $\mathbf{X}_{ij}^{'E}$, i.e., $\mathbf{X}_{ij}^E = \mathbf{X}_{ij}^{'E} + \mathbf{Y}_{mn} - \mathbf{Y}'_{mn}$.

3.3.5.2 *EPI: Epitomic Matching for Internal SR*

The matching of $\mathbf{X}_{ij}^{'E}$ over the smoothed input image $\mathbf{Y}'$ makes the core step of the high frequency transfer scheme. However, the performance of NN matching (3.24) is degraded with the presence of noise and outliers. Moreover, the NN matching in [Freedman and Fattal (2011)] is restricted to a local window for efficiency, which potentially accounts for some rigid artifacts.

Instead, we can use *epitomic matching* to replace NN matching in the above frequency transfer scheme. As a generative model, epitome [Chu *et al.* (2010); Yang *et al.* (2014a)] summarizes a large set of raw image patches into a condensed representation in a way similar to Gaussian Mixture Models. We first learn an epitome $\mathbf{e}_{\mathbf{Y}'}$ from $\mathbf{Y}'$, and then match each $\mathbf{X}_{ij}^{'E}$ over $\mathbf{e}_{\mathbf{Y}'}$ rather than $\mathbf{Y}'$ directly. Assume $(m, n) = f_{ept}(\mathbf{X}_{ij}^{'E}, \mathbf{e}_{\mathbf{Y}'})$, where

f_{ept} denotes the procedure of epitomic matching by $\mathbf{e_{Y'}}$. It then follows the same way as in[Freedman and Fattal (2011)]: $\mathbf{X}_{ij}^{E} = \mathbf{X}_{ij}^{'E} + \mathbf{Y}_{mn} - \mathbf{Y}'_{mn}$: the only difference here is the replacement of f_{NN} with f_{ept}. The high-frequency transfer scheme equipped with epitomic matching can thus be applied to SR by itself as well, named *EPI* for short, which will be included in our experiments in Section 3.3.8 and compared to the method using NN matching in [Freedman and Fattal (2011)].

Since $\mathbf{e_{Y'}}$ summarizes the patches of the entire $\mathbf{Y'}$, using epitomic matching benefits from non-local patch matching. In the absence of self-similar patches in the local neighborhood, epitomic patching weights refer to non-local matches, thereby effectively reducing the artifacts arising from local matching [Freedman and Fattal (2011)] in a restricted small neighborhood. In addition, note that each epitome patch summarizes a batch of similar raw patches in $\mathbf{Y'}$. For any patch $\mathbf{Y'}_{ij}$ that contains certain noise or outliers in $\mathbf{Y'}$, its has a small posterior and thus tends not be selected as candidate matches for $\mathbf{X}_{ij}^{'E}$, improving the robustness of matching.

Moreover, we can also incorporate Nearest Neighbor (NN) matching to our epitomic matching, leading to a enhanced patch matching scheme that features both non-local (by epitome) and local (by NN) matching. Suppose the high frequency components obtained by epitomic matching and NN matching for patch $\mathbf{X}_{ij}^{'E}$ are $\mathbf{H}_{ij,\mathbf{e}}$ and $\mathbf{H}_{ij,\text{NN}}$ respectively, we use a smart weighted average of the two as the final high frequency component $\mathbf{H}_{ij}$:

$$\mathbf{H}_{ij} = w\mathbf{H}_{ij,\mathbf{e}} + (1 - w)\mathbf{H}_{ij,\text{NN}} \qquad (3.25)$$

where the weight $w = p(\mathcal{T}_{ij}^{*}|\mathbf{X}_{ij}^{'E}, \mathbf{e})$ denotes the probability of the most probable hidden mapping given the patch $\mathbf{X}_{ij}^{'E}$. A higher w indicates that the patch $\mathbf{X}_{ij}^{'E}$ is more likely to have a reliable match by epitomic matching (with the probability measured through the corresponding most probable hidden mapping), thereby a larger weight is associated with the epitomic matching, and vice versa. This is the practical implementation of EPI that we used.

Finally, we let $\Theta_I = \mathbf{X}_{ij}^{E}$ and define

$$\ell_{\mathcal{I}}(\mathbf{X}_{ij}, \mathbf{X}_{ij}^{E}) = ||\mathbf{X}_{ij} - \mathbf{X}_{ij}^{E}||_F^2, \qquad (3.26)$$

where $\mathbf{X}_{ij}^{E}$ is the internal SR result by epitomic matching. A more detailed explanation of epitome can be found in A.1.1.

3.3.6   *Learning the Adaptive Weights*

In [Mosseri *et al.* (2013)], Mosseri et. al. showed that the internal versus external preference is tightly related to the Signal-to-Noise-Ratio (SNR) estimate of each patch. Inspired by that finding, we could seek similar definitions of "noise" in SR based on the latent representation errors. The *external noise* is defined by the residual of sparse coding

$$N_g(\mathbf{a}_{ij}) = ||\mathbf{D_1}\mathbf{a}_{ij} - \mathbf{Y}_{ij}||_F^2. \tag{3.27}$$

Meanwhile, the *internal noise* finds its counterpart definition by the epitomic matching error within f_{pet}:

$$N_i(\mathbf{X}_{ij}^E) = ||\mathbf{Y}'_{mn} - \mathbf{X}_{ij}^{'E}||_F^2, \tag{3.28}$$

where $\mathbf{Y}'_{mn}$ is the matching patch in $\mathbf{Y}'$ for $\mathbf{X}_{ij}^{'E}$.

Usually, the two "noises" are on the same magnitude level, which aligns with the fact that external- and internal-examples will have similar performances on many (such as homogenous regions). However, there do exist patches where the two have significant differences in performances, as shown in Fig. 3.13, which means the patch has a strong preference toward one of them. In such cases, the "preferred" term needs to be sufficiently emphasized. We thus construct the following patch-wise adaptive weight (p is the hyperparameter):

$$\omega(\alpha_{ij}, \mathbf{X}_{ij}^E) = \exp(p \cdot [N_g(\mathbf{a}_{ij}) - N_i(\mathbf{X}_{ij}^E)]). \tag{3.29}$$

When the internal noise becomes larger, the weight decays quickly to ensure that external similarity dominates, and vice versa.

3.3.7   *Optimization*

Directly solving (3.22) is very complex due to the its high nonlinearity and entanglement among all variables. Instead, we follow the coordinate descent fashion [Bertsekas (1999)] and solve the following three sub-problems iteratively.

3.3.7.1 $\mathbf{a}_{ij}$-*Subproblem*

Fixing $\mathbf{X}_{ij}$ and $\mathbf{X}_{ij}^E$, we have the following minimization w.r.t α_{ij}

$$
\begin{aligned}
\min_{\mathbf{a}_{ij}} \quad & \lambda||\mathbf{a}_{ij}||_1 + ||\mathbf{D_1}\mathbf{a}_{ij} - \mathbf{Y}_{ij}||_F^2 + ||\mathbf{D_h}\mathbf{a}_{ij} - \mathbf{X}_{ij}||_F^2 \\
& + [\ell_{\mathcal{I}}(\mathbf{X}_{ij}, \mathbf{X}_{ij}^E) \cdot \exp(-p \cdot N_i(\mathbf{X}_{ij}^E))] \cdot \exp(p \cdot N_g(\mathbf{a}_{ij})).
\end{aligned}
\tag{3.30}
$$

The major bottleneck of exactly solving (3.30) lies in the last exponential term. We let $\mathbf{a}_{ij}^0$ denote the $\mathbf{a}_{ij}$ value solved in the last iteration. We then apply first-order Taylor expansion to the last term of the objective in (3.30), with regard to $N_g(\alpha_{ij})$ at $\alpha_{ij} = \alpha_{ij}^0$, and solve the approximated problem as follows:

$$
\begin{aligned}
\min_{\mathbf{a}_{ij}} \quad & \lambda||\mathbf{a}_{ij}||_1 + (1+C)||\mathbf{D_l}\mathbf{a}_{ij} - \mathbf{Y}_{ij}||_F^2 \\
& +||\mathbf{D_h}\mathbf{a}_{ij} - \mathbf{X}_{ij}||_F^2,
\end{aligned}
\tag{3.31}
$$

where C is the constant coefficient:

$$
\begin{aligned}
C &= [\ell_{\mathcal{I}}(\mathbf{X}_{ij}, \mathbf{X}_{ij}^E) \cdot \exp(-p \cdot N_i(\mathbf{X}_{ij}^E)] \cdot [p \cdot \exp(p \cdot N_g(\mathbf{a}_{ij}^0)] \\
&= p\ell_{\mathcal{I}}(\mathbf{X}_{ij}, \mathbf{X}_{ij}^E) \cdot \omega(\alpha^0{}_{ij}, \mathbf{X}_{ij}^E).
\end{aligned}
\tag{3.32}
$$

(3.31) can be conveniently solved by the feature sign algorithm [Lee *et al.* (2006)]. Note (3.31) is a valid approximation of (3.30) since $\mathbf{a}_{ij}$ and $\mathbf{a}_{ij}^0$ become quite close after a few iterations, so that the higher-order Taylor expansions can be reasonably ignored.

Another noticeable fact is that since $C > 0$, the second term is always emphasized more than the third term, which makes sense as $\mathbf{Y}_{ij}$ is the "accurate" LR image, while $\mathbf{X}_{ij}$ is just an estimate of the HR image and is thus less weighted. Further considering the formulation (3.32), C grows up as $\omega(\alpha^0{}_{ij}, \mathbf{X}_{ij}^E)$ turns larger. That implies when external SR becomes the major source of "SR noise" on a patch in the last iteration, (3.31) will correspondingly rely less on the last solved $\mathbf{X}_{ij}$.

3.3.7.2 $\mathbf{X}_{ij}^E$-Subproblem

Fixing $\mathbf{a}_{ij}$ and $\mathbf{X}_{ij}$, the $\mathbf{X}_{ij}^E$-subproblem becomes

$$
\min_{\mathbf{X}_{ij}^E} \quad \exp(-p \cdot ||\mathbf{Y}'_{mn} - \mathbf{X}_{ij}'^E||_F^2)\ell_{\mathcal{I}}(\mathbf{X}_{ij}, \mathbf{X}_{ij}^E),
\tag{3.33}
$$

While in Section 3.3.5.2, $X_{i,j}^E$ is directly computed from the input LR image, the objective in (3.33) is dependent on not only $X_{i,j}^E$ but also $X_{i,j}$, which is not necessarily minimized by the best match $X_{i,j}^E$ obtained from solving f_{ept}. In our implementation, the K best candidates ($K = 5$) that yield minimum matching errors of solving f_{ept} are first obtained. Among all those candidates, we further select the one that minimizes the loss value as defined in (3.33). By this discrete search-type algorithm, $X_{i,j}^E$ becomes a latent variable to be updated together with $X_{i,j}$ per iteration, and is better suited for the global optimization than the simplistic solution by solving f_{ept}.

3.3.7.3 $\mathbf{X}_{ij}$-*Subproblem*

With both $\mathbf{a}_{ij}$ and $\mathbf{X}_{ij}^E$ fixed, the solution of $\mathbf{X}_{ij}$ simply follows a weight least square (WLS) problem:

$$\min_{\mathbf{X}_{ij}} \quad ||\mathbf{D_h}\mathbf{a}_{ij} - \mathbf{X}_{ij}||_F^2 + \omega(\mathbf{a}_{ij}, \mathbf{X}_{ij}^E)||\mathbf{X} - \mathbf{X}_{ij}^E||_F^2, \qquad (3.34)$$

with an explicit solution:

$$\mathbf{X}_{ij} = \frac{\mathbf{D_h}\mathbf{a}_{ij} + \omega(\alpha_{ij}, \mathbf{X}_{ij}^E) \cdot \mathbf{X}_{ij}^E}{1 + \omega(\mathbf{a}_{ij}, \mathbf{X}_{ij}^E)}. \qquad (3.35)$$

(a) BCI (25.29 dB)   (c) LSE (21.17 dB)   (e) IER (25.54 dB)

(b) CSC (26.20 dB)   (d) EPI (24.34 dB)   (f) JSR (27.87 dB)

Fig. 3.14   3× SR results of the *Temple* image and their recovery PSNRs.

3.3.8   *Experiments*

3.3.8.1   *Implementation Details*

We itemize the parameter and implementation settings for the following group of experiments:

- We use 5×5 patches with one pixel overlapping for all experiments except those on SHD images in Section 3.3.8.4, where the patch size is 25×25 with five pixel overlapping.
- In (3.23), we adopt the $\mathbf{D_l}$ and $\mathbf{D_h}$ trained in the same way as in [Yang *et al.* (2012a)], due to the similar roles played by the dictionaries in their formulation and our ℓ_G function. However, we are aware that such D_l and D_h are not optimized for this model,

and integrating a specifically designed dictionary learning part can be done in future work. λ is empirically set as 1.

- In (3.26), the size of the epitome is $\frac{1}{4}$ of the image size.
- In (3.29), we set $p = 1$ for all experiments. We also observed in experiments that a larger p will usually lead to a faster decrease in objective value, but the SR result quality may degrade a bit.
- We initialize $\mathbf{a}_{ij}$ by solving coupled sparse coding in [Yang *et al.* (2012a)]. $\mathbf{X}_{ij}$ is initialized by bicubic interpolation.
- We set the maximum iteration number to be 10 for the coordinate descent algorithm. For SHD cases, the maximum iteration number is adjusted to be 5.
- For color images, we apply SR algorithms to the illuminance channel only, as humans are more sensitive to illuminance changes. We then interpolate the color layers (Cb, Cr) using plain bi-cubic interpolation.

3.3.8.2   *Comparison with State-of-the-Art Results*

We compare the joint SR method with the following selection of competitive methods as follows,

- *Bi-Cubic Interpolation ("BCI" for short and similarly hereinafter)*, as a comparison baseline.
- *Coupled Sparse Coding (CSC)* [Yang *et al.* (2012a)], as the classical external-example-based SR.
- *Local Self-Example based SR (LSE)* [Freedman and Fattal (2011)], as the classical internal-example-based SR.
- *Epitome-based SR (EPI)*. We compare EPI to LSE to demonstrate the advantage of epitomic matching over the local NN matching.
- *SR based on In-place Example Regression (IER)* [Yang *et al.* (2013)], as the previous SR utilizing both external and internal information.
- *The joint SR (JSR)*.

We list the SR results (best viewed on a high-resolution display) for two test images: *Temple* and *Train*, by an amplifying factor of 3. PSNR measurements and zoomed local regions (using nearing neighbor interpolation) are available for different methods as well.

In Fig. 3.14, although greatly outperforming the naive BCI, the external-example based CSC tends to lose many fine details. In contrast, LSE brings

(a) BCI (26.14 dB)   (c) LSE (22.54 dB)   (e) IER (24.80 dB)

(b) CSC (26.58 dB)   (d) EPI (26.22 dB)   (f) JSR (28.02 dB)

Fig. 3.15   3× SR results of the *Train* image and their PSNRs.

out an overly sharp SR result with observable blockiness. EPI produces a more visually pleasing result, through searching for the matches over the entire input efficiently by the pre-trained epitome rather than a local neighborhood. Therefore, EPI substantially reduces the artifacts compared to LSE. But without any external information available, it is still incapable of inferring enough high-frequency details from the input solely, especially under a large amplifying factor. The result of IER greatly improves but is still accompanied with occasional small artifacts. Finally, JSR provides a clear recovery of the steps, and it reconstructs the most pillar textures. In Fig. 3.15, JSR is the only algorithm which clearly recovers the number on the carrier and the bricks on the bridge simultaneously. The performance superiorities of JSR are also verified by the PSNR comparisons, where larger margins are obtained by JSR over others in both cases.

Next, we move on to the more challenging 4× SR case, using the *Chip* image which is quite abundant in edges and textures. Since we have no ground truth for the *Chip* image of 4× size, only visual comparisons are presented. Given such a large SR factor, the CSC result is a bit blurry around the characters on the surface of chip. Both LSE and EPI create jaggy artifacts along the long edge of the chip, as well as small structure distortions. The IER result cause less artifacts but in sacrifice of detail sharpness, The JSR result presents the best SR with few artifacts.

The key idea of JSR is utilizing the complementary behavior of both external and internal SR methods. Note when one inverse problem is better

Table 3.6   Average PSNR (dB) and SSIM performances comparisons on the Set 5 and Set 14 datasets.

		BCI	Sparse Coding [Yang et al. (2010a)]	LSE [Freedman and Fattal (2011)]	A+ [Timofte et al. (2014)]	SRCNN [Dong et al. (2014)]	JSR
Set 5, $s_t=2$	PSNR	33.66	35.27	33.61	36.24	36.66	**36.71**
	SSIM	0.9299	0.9540	0.9375	0.9544	0.9542	**0.9573**
Set 5, $s_t=3$	PSNR	30.39	31.42	30.77	32.59	**32.75**	32.54
	SSIM	0.8682	0.8821	0.8774	0.9088	0.9090	**0.9186**
Set 14, $s_t=2$	PSNR	30.23	31.34	31.99	**32.58**	32.45	32.54
	SSIM	0.8687	0.8928	0.8921	0.9056	0.9067	**0.9082**
Set 14, $s_t=3$	PSNR	27.54	28.31	28.26	29.13	**29.60**	29.49
	SSIM	0.7736	0.7954	0.8043	0.8188	0.8215	**0.8242**

solved, it also makes a better parameter estimate for solving the other. JSR is not a simple static weighted average of external SR (CSC) and internal SR (EPI). When optimized jointly, the external and internal subproblems can "boost" each other (through auxiliary variables), and each performs better than being applied independently. That is why JSR gets details that exist in neither internal or external SR result.

To further verify the superiority of JSR numerically, we compare the average PSNR and SSIM results of a few recently-proposed, state-of-the-art single image SR methods, including CSC, LSE, the Adjusted Anchored Neighborhood Regression (A+) [Timofte et al. (2014)], and the latest Super-Resolution Convolutional Neural Network (SRCNN) [Dong et al. (2014)]. Table 3.6 reports the results on the widely-adopted Set 5 and Set 14 datasets, in terms of both PSNR and SSIM. First, it is not a surprise to us, that JSR does not always yield higher PSNR than SRCNN, et. al., as the epitomic matching component is not meant to be optimized under Mean-Square-Error (MSE) measure, in contrast to the end-to-end MSE-driven regression adopted in SRCNN. However, it is notable that JSR is particularly more favorable by SSIM than other methods, owing to the self-similar examples that convey input-specific structural details. Considering SSIM measures image quality more consistently with human perception, the observation is in accordance with our human subject evaluation results (see Section 3.3.8.5).

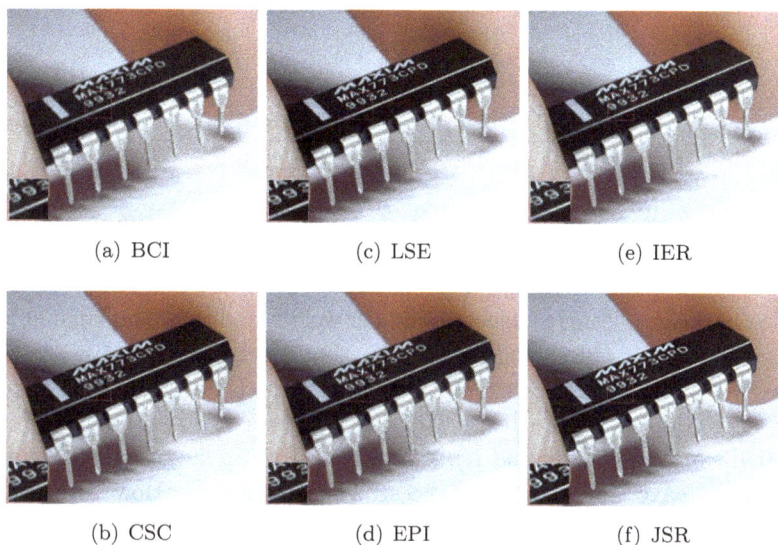

(a) BCI   (c) LSE   (e) IER

(b) CSC   (d) EPI   (f) JSR

Fig. 3.16   4× SR results of the *Chip* image.

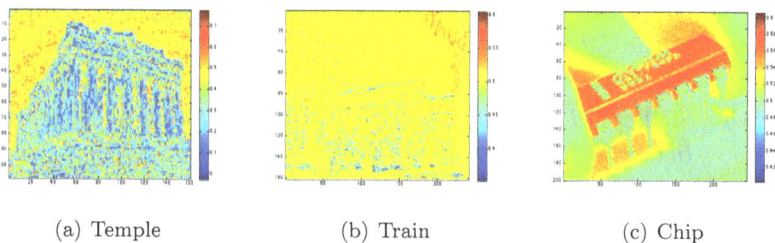

(a) Temple   (b) Train   (c) Chip

Fig. 3.17   The weight maps of (a) *Temple* image; (b) *Train* image; (c) *Chip* image.

3.3.8.3 *Effect of Adaptive Weight*

To demonstrate how the joint SR will benefit from the learned adaptive weight (3.29), we compare 4× SR results of *Kid* image, between joint SR solving (3.22), and its counterpart with fixed global weights, i.e. set the weight ω as constant for all patches. Table 3.7 shows that the joint SR with an adaptive weight gains a consistent PSNR advantage over the SR with a large range of fixed weights.

More interestingly, we visualize the patch-wise weight maps of joint SR results in Fig. 3.14-3.16, using heat maps, as in Fig. 3.17. The (i, j)-th pixel in the weight map denote the final weight of $\mathbf{X}_{ij}$ when the joint SR reaches

Table 3.7   The PSNR values (dB) of Joint SR
with various fixed global weights (PSNR =
24.1734 dB with an adaptive weight).

$\omega = 0.1$	$\omega = 1$	$\omega = 3$	$\omega = 5$	$\omega = 10$
23.13	23.23	23.32	22.66	21.22

a stable solution. All weights are normalized between [0,1], by the form of sigmoid function: $\frac{1}{1+\omega(\alpha_{ij},\mathbf{X}^E_{ij})}$, for visualization purpose. A larger pixel value in the weight maps denote a smaller weight and thus a higher emphasis on external examples, and vice versa. For *Temple* image, Fig. 3.17 (a) clearly manifests that self examples dominate the SR of the temple building that is full of texture patterns. The most regions of Fig. 3.17 (b) are close to 0.5, which means that $\omega(\alpha_{ij}, \mathbf{X}^E_{ij})$ is close to 1 and external and internal examples have similar performances on most patches. However, internal similar makes more significant contributions in reconstructing the brick regions, while external examples works remarkably better on the irregular contours of forests. Finally, the *Chip* image is an example where external examples have advantages on the majority of patches. Considering self examples prove to create artifacts here (see Fig. 3.16 (c) (d)), they are avoided in joint SR by the adaptive weights.

3.3.8.4   *SR Beyond Standard Definition: From HD Image to UHD Image*

In almost all SR literature, experiments are conducted with Standard-Definition (SD) images (720 × 480 or 720 × 576 pixels) or smaller. The High-Definition (HD) formats: 720p (1280 × 720 pixels) and 1080p (1920 × 1080 pixels) have become popular today. Moreover, Ultra High-Definition (UHD) TVs are hitting the consumer markets right now with the 3840 × 2160 resolution. It is thus quite interesting to explore whether SR algorithms established on SD images can be applied or adjusted for HD or UHD cases. In this section, we upscale HD images of 1280 × 720 pixels to UHD results of 3840 × 2160 pixels, using competitor methods and our joint SR algorithm.

Since most HD and UHD images typically contain much more diverse textures and a richer collection of fine structures than SD images, we enlarge the patch size from 5×5 to 25×25 (the dictionary pair is therefore re-trained as well) to capture more variations, meanwhile increasing the overlapping from one pixel to five pixels to ensure enough spatial consistency. Hereby

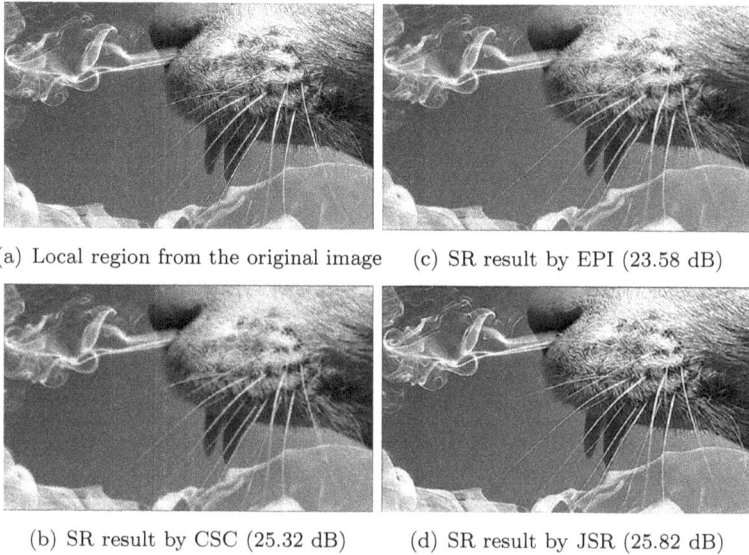

(a) Local region from the original image   (c) SR result by EPI (23.58 dB)

(b) SR result by CSC (25.32 dB)   (d) SR result by JSR (25.82 dB)

Fig. 3.18   3× SR results of the *Leopard* image (local region displayed) and their PSNRs.

JSR is compared with its two "component" algorithms, i.e., CSC and EPI. We choose several challenging SHD images (3840 × 2160 pixels) with very cluttered texture regions, downsampling them to HD size (1280 × 720 pixel) on which we apply the SR algorithm with a factor of 3. In all cases, our results are consistently sharper and clearer. The zoomed local regions of the *Leopard* image are displayed in Fig. 3.18, with the PSNR measurements of full-size results.

3.3.8.5   *Subjective Evaluation*

We conduct an online subjective evaluation on the quality of SR results produced by different methods in Section 3.3.8.2. Ground truth HR images are also included when they are available as references. Each participant of the survey is shown a set of HR image pairs obtained using two different methods for the same LR image. For each pair, the participant needs to decide which one is better than the other in terms of perceptual quality. The image pairs are drawn from all the competitive methods randomly, and the images winning the pairwise comparison will be compared again in the next round, until the best one is selected. We have a total of 101 participants giving 1,047 pairwise comparisons, over six images which are

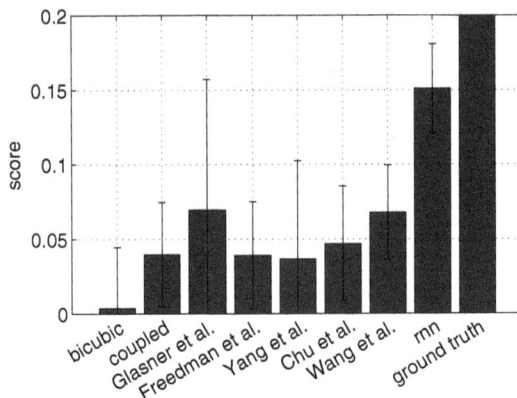

Fig. 3.19   Subjective SR quality scores for different methods. The ground truth has score 1.

commonly used as benchmark images in SR, with different scaling factors (*Kid*×4, *Chip*×4, *Statue*×4, *Leopard*×3, *Temple*×3 and *Train*×3). More details about the subjective test are included in A.1.2.

We fit a Bradley-Terry [Bradley and Terry (1952)] model to estimate the subjective scores for each method so that they can be ranked. Fig. 3.19 shows the estimated scores for the six SR methods in our evaluation. As expected, all SR methods receive much lower scores compared to ground truth (set as score 1), showing the huge challenge of the SR problem itself. Also, the bicubic interpolation is significantly worse than others. The RNN and JSR methods outperform all other state-of-the-art methods by a large margin, which proves that they can produce more visually favorable HR images by human perception.

Chapter 4

Image Deblurring

4.1 Definition of Deblurring

Image blur is a widely existing problem in image formation process due to the imperfection during the imaging process. Possible factors causing the blur are atmospheric turbulence (*e.g.*, in astronomy), defocusing, as well as the relative motion between camera and the scene.

Image deblurring is a well-known inverse problem which requires regularization to alleviate its ill-posedness and stabilize the solution [Fergus *et al.* (2006); Shan *et al.* (2008); Levin *et al.* (2009); Cho and Lee (2009)]. A lot of regularization methods have been proposed in the literature, using linear or non-linear regularization factors. Recently, the sparse property of natural images is explored extensively in many works [Fergus *et al.* (2006); Shan *et al.* (2008); Levin *et al.* (2007); Elad *et al.* (2010)] and has been proven to be an effective prior for natural image restoration. Levin *et al.* proposed a non-blind deblurring model using natural image statics to alleviating the ringing artifacts in the deblurred image [Levin *et al.* (2007)] and proposed an Iterative Reweighted Least Square (IRLS) method to solve the sparsity-constrained least square problem. This model is further generalized by Cho *et al.* [Cho *et al.* (2010)] by adapting the sparseness according to the image content using a learned regression model. Cai *et al.* proposed a blind motion deblurring method by exploiting the sparseness of natural images in over-complete frames, such as curvelet, to help with kernel estimation and sharp image estimation [Cai *et al.* (2009)].

If we assume that the blur is global and translation invariant, then the low quality image observation process can be modeled as:

$$\boldsymbol{y}_j = \mathbf{k}_j * \boldsymbol{x} + \varepsilon_j, \quad j = 1 \cdots J \tag{4.1}$$

where $\mathbf{k}$ is the Point Spread Function (PSF) or blur kernel and $*$ denotes the convolution operator. Note that while we use the convolutional blur model for easy of presentation, the approach introduced in this chapter can be naturally extended to handle non-uniform blur as well[Whyte *et al.* (2010); Harmeling *et al.* (2010); Zhang and Wipf (2013)]. The task of deblurring is to estimate the sharp image x given blurry and noisy observation(s) $\{y_i\}_{j=1}^{J}$. It is called a multi-frame deblurring problem [Sroubek and Milanfar (2012); Zhang *et al.* (2013b)] if $J > 1$ and a single image deblurring problem when $J = 1$.

We focus on sparse representation based *blind* single image deblurring method in this section by exploiting the sparsity property of natural images in terms of learned redundant and over-complete dictionary. In previous work, a sparse representation based method for *non-blind* image deblurring has been proposed in [Zhang and Zhang (2009)], which is shown to generate more desirable results than conventional deburring methods. This method utilizes the sparse representation of image patches as a prior to regularize the ill-posed inverse problem. In this section, we further present a blind image deblurring method based on sparse representation, which is based on the non-blind deblurring work [Zhang and Zhang (2009)] and the super resolution method recently proposed in [Yang *et al.* (2008)]. Based on compressive sensing theory, Yang *et al.* assumes that the same sparse representation coefficients are shared for the high resolution and low resolution patches with respect to a high-resolution dictionary and a corresponding low-resolution dictionary, respectively. This method has been shown to generate *state-of-the-art* results for image super resolution. For blind image deblurring, however, this method can not be applied directly, due the unknown blurring kernel (PSF), thus the construction of the coupled dictionary is not an easy task. Very recently, Hu *et al.* proposed to construct the blurry-sharp dictionary couple via the blurry image and deblurred image using the current estimation of the kernel [Hu *et al.* (2010)]. However, as the deblurring procedure will usually introduce severe artifacts, the dictionary pair constructed via this method is not desirable for deblurring. We present in this chapter another approach for blind image deblurring using sparse representation, which is a natural generalization of [Zhang and Zhang (2009)].

Apart from being a pure low-level vision problem, image deblurring also plays a key role in many real-world high-level recognition tasks. In many real world applications, such as video surveillance, the target of interest in the captured image usually suffers from low qualities, such as low resolution due to the long distance of the target, motion blur due to the relative

motion between the target and the camera, and out-of-focus blur if the
the target is not in the focus of the capture device, or even some complex
combinations of these factors. In such practical scenarios, it will present
a big challenge to perform many high-level vision tasks such as recognition. A natural solution to this problem would be to first perform image
restorations to obtain an image with better quality, and then feed the restored result into a recognition system. Such a straightforward approach
has the problem that many restoration algorithms are designed for improving human visual perception only, rather than machine perception, thus
there is no guarantee of recognition improvements. Even worse, when the
degradation model is unknown, general purpose restoration schemes, such
as deblurring, do not perform well on some realistic images that do not
exhibit strong edge structures, such as faces, and will typically introduce
severe artifacts that actually deteriorate the recognition performance. Instead of restoring the test image, another approach could be to estimate the
degradation model first, use it to transform the training images, and then
compare the input test image with the synthetically generated training set.
This method generally works better than the previous one. But for many
realistic data whose degradation model is very complex, it may easily fail.

In the following, we will first review briefly sparse image modeling and
then present the mathematical formulation, optimization and experimental results for sparse representation regularized blind deblurring technique.
In the second part of this chapter, we will show how to use domain knowledge via sparse representation to couple low-level restoration and high-level
recognition tasks for a joint solution.

4.2 Sparsity Regularized Blind Image Deblurring

4.2.1 *Sparse Modeling in Image Restoration*

In this section, we briefly summarize the basics of sparse representation and
its applications on low-level image restoration tasks. Sparse representation
modeling of data assumes an ability to describe signals as a linear combination of a few atoms from a pre-specified dictionary. Formally, given
a signal $x \in \mathbb{R}^n$ and a dictionary $D = [d_1, d_2, \cdots, d_k] \in \mathbb{R}^{n \times k}$, where
typically $n \leq k$, we can recover a sparse representation ($\epsilon = 0$) or sparse

approximation ($\epsilon > 0$) $\hat{\boldsymbol{\alpha}}$ for $\boldsymbol{x}$ by:

$$\min_{\boldsymbol{\alpha}} \|\boldsymbol{\alpha}\|_0$$
$$\text{s.t. } \|\boldsymbol{x} - \mathbf{D}\boldsymbol{\alpha}\|_2^2 \leq \epsilon. \tag{4.2}$$

The model tries to seek the most compact representation for the signal $\boldsymbol{x}$ given the dictionary $\mathbf{D}$, which can be orthogonal basis ($n = k$), over-complete basis ($n < k$) [Cai *et al.* (2009)] or dictionary learned from the training data [Yang *et al.* (2008)]. For orthonormal basis, solution to (4.2) is merely the inner products of the signal with the basis. However, for general dictionary (non-orthogonal and over-complete), the optimization for (4.2) is combinatorially NP-hard. Recent works show that, this NP-hard problem can be tackled by replacing the non-convex ℓ_0-norm with ℓ_1-norm under some mild conditions [Donoho (2006b)], which makes the objective function convex while exact solution can still be guaranteed.

Using the Lagrange multiplier, we can reformulate the relaxed ℓ_1-problem as

$$\hat{\boldsymbol{\alpha}} = \arg\min_{\boldsymbol{\alpha}} \|\mathbf{D}\boldsymbol{\alpha} - \boldsymbol{x}\|_2^2 + \lambda\|\boldsymbol{\alpha}\|_1. \tag{4.3}$$

Sparsity plays an important or even crucial role in many fields, such as image restoration [Elad *et al.* (2010); Cai *et al.* (2009); Yang *et al.* (2008)], compressive sensing, and recognition [Wright *et al.* (2010, 2009)]. In the following, we will make a brief discussion on the role of sparsity in both image restoration and pattern recognition.

A close inspection of the progress made in the field of image processing in the past decades reveals that much of it can be attributed to better modeling of the image content [Elad *et al.* (2010)]. Sparsity is arguably the most widely used prior for image restoration, such as image denoising, inpainting, super-resolution and deblurring [Elad *et al.* (2010)]. Among these, we specifically focus the discussion on image deblurring.

Image blurring is a widely existing degradation factor in the real life imaging process (*e.g.*, surveillance), possibly resulting from defocusing, relative motion between the object and the camera, to name a few [Fergus *et al.* (2006); Shan *et al.* (2008)], which may bring severe adverse impacts on both human perception and machine perception (*e.g.*, classification). Assuming convolutional blur model with additive white Gaussian noise as in (4.1), regularized blind deblurring problem can be formulated as follows:

$$\{\hat{\boldsymbol{x}}, \hat{\mathbf{k}}\} = \arg\min_{\boldsymbol{x},\mathbf{k}} \|\mathbf{k} * \boldsymbol{x} - \boldsymbol{y}\|_2^2 + \lambda\rho(\boldsymbol{x}) + \gamma\varrho(\mathbf{k}), \tag{4.4}$$

where $\rho(\boldsymbol{x})$ is a regularization term on the desired image, and $\varrho(\mathbf{k})$ regularizes the possible blur kernels, typically an ℓ_2-norm penalty [Cho and Lee

(2009)]. Most of the current restoration methods can be cast into such a regularization framework where the regularization terms based on image prior are crucial for obtaining better restoration results and are related somehow with the sparse property of natural images [Fergus *et al.* (2006); Shan *et al.* (2008); Krishnan and Fergus (2009); Yang *et al.* (2008); Cai *et al.* (2009); Elad *et al.* (2010)]. With the sparsity prior as regularization, we can arrive at the following formulation:

$$\{\hat{x}, \hat{k}\} = \arg\min_{x,k} \|k * x - y\|_2^2 + \lambda\|D^\top x\|_1 + \gamma\|k\|_2, \qquad (4.5)$$

where $D^\top$ is some sparse transformation (such as Wavelet, Curvelet, among others [Cai *et al.* (2009)]) or sparsity inducing operator (such as handcrafted derivative filters or filters learned from training images [Fergus *et al.* (2006); Shan *et al.* (2008); Krishnan and Fergus (2009); Roth and Black (2005)]). When D is orthonormal, we have $\alpha = D^\top x$ as the transform coefficients, and thus we can rewrite Eqn. (4.5) as:

$$\{\hat{\alpha}, \hat{k}\} = \arg\min_{\alpha,k} \|k * D\alpha - y\|_2^2 + \lambda\|\alpha\|_1 + \gamma\|k\|_2^2. \qquad (4.6)$$

To achieve better sparsity for the representation α, D can be generalized to be non-orthogonal and over-complete, by either combining different orthonormal basis or learning from the data [Yang *et al.* (2008)]. In this chapter, we learn D from training data, which leads to better representative ability.

4.2.2 *Sparse Representation Regularized Blind Deblurring*

In the Sparseland model [Bruckstein *et al.* (2009)], images are often decomposed into small patches to better fit the sparse representation assumption [Aharon *et al.* (2006)]. We also follow this convention in the method discussed here [Zhang *et al.* (2011c)]. The sparse representation regularized image deblurring method can be formulated as follows. Given the blurry observation y of size $\sqrt{N} \times \sqrt{N}$, and an over-complete dictionary $D \in \mathbb{R}^{n \times k}$, trained on $\sqrt{n} \times \sqrt{n}$ patches sampled from natural images[1], we want to estimate the latent sharp image x and the blur kernel k simultaneously by

$$\{\hat{x}, \hat{k}\} = \arg\min_{x,k} E(x, k), \qquad (4.7)$$

---

[1]These patches can either sampled from a separate training set or from the blurry image itself, as in [Zhang and Zhang (2009)] [Aharon *et al.* (2006)].

where

$$\mathbf{E}(\boldsymbol{x}, \mathbf{k}) = \|\mathbf{k} * \boldsymbol{x} - \boldsymbol{y}\|_2^2 + \sum_{i=1}^{I} \eta_i \|\boldsymbol{R}_i \boldsymbol{x} - \mathbf{D}\boldsymbol{\alpha}_i\|_2^2$$

$$+ \sum_{i=1}^{I} \lambda_i \|\boldsymbol{\alpha}_i\|_1 + \gamma \|\mathbf{k}\|_2^2. \tag{4.8}$$

$\boldsymbol{R}_i$ is an $n \times N$ matrix that extracts the i-th block from the image and I is the total number of patches in the image. In (4.8), the first term is the reconstruction constraint, *i.e.*, the restored image should be consistent with the observation with respect to the estimated degradation model; the second and third terms together enforce that the representation of the patches from the recovered image should be sparse with respect to a proper overcomplete dictionary; the last term is a ℓ_2-norm based regularization to stabilize the blur kernel estimation.

4.2.3   *Optimization Procedure*

We can optimize the model efficiently with the recent progress of sparse optimization techniques. We employ the Alternating Minimization scheme, which is widely adopted when dealing with multiple optimization variables. Following this scheme, we address each of the optimization variable separately and present an overall efficient optimization algorithm. We first initialize the sparse representation $\{\hat{\boldsymbol{\alpha}}_i\}_{i=1}^{I}$ as that recovered from $\boldsymbol{y}$ with respect to $\mathbf{D}$, and the latent sharp image $\hat{\boldsymbol{x}} = \left(\sum_{i=1}^{I} \boldsymbol{R}_i^\top \boldsymbol{R}_i\right)^{-1} \sum_{i=1}^{I} \boldsymbol{R}_i^\top \mathbf{D}\boldsymbol{\alpha}_i$.

4.2.3.1   *Blur Kernel Estimation:* **k**-*Subproblem*

In this subproblem, we fix all other variables and and optimize the image blurring kernel **k**. The model (4.8) reduces to the following form:

$$\hat{\mathbf{k}} = \arg\min_{\mathbf{k}} \|\mathbf{k} * \hat{\boldsymbol{x}} - \boldsymbol{y}\|_2^2 + \gamma \|\mathbf{k}\|_2^2. \tag{4.9}$$

This is a least square problem with Tikhonov regularization, which leads to a close-form solution for **k**:

$$\hat{\mathbf{k}} = \mathcal{F}^{-1}\left(\frac{\overline{\mathcal{F}(\hat{\boldsymbol{x}})} \circ \mathcal{F}(\boldsymbol{y})}{\overline{\mathcal{F}(\hat{\boldsymbol{x}})} \circ \mathcal{F}(\hat{\boldsymbol{x}}) + \gamma \mathbf{I}}\right),$$

where $\mathcal{F}(\cdot)$ denotes Fast Fourier Transform (FFT), $\mathcal{F}^{-1}(\cdot)$ denotes inverse FFT, $\overline{\mathcal{F}(\cdot)}$ denotes the complex conjugate of $\mathcal{F}(\cdot)$, and "$\circ$" denotes element-wise multiplication.

4.2.3.2 *Latent Image Updating:* x-*Subproblem*

Given the current kernel estimation $\hat{\mathbf{k}}$ and sparse representation $\{\hat{\boldsymbol{\alpha}}\}_{i=1}^{I}$, we want to update the estimation for the latent sharp image $\boldsymbol{x}$. The optimization problem (4.16) becomes

$$\hat{\boldsymbol{x}} = \arg\min_{\boldsymbol{x}} \|\boldsymbol{x} * \hat{\mathbf{k}} - \boldsymbol{y}\|_2^2 + \sum_{i=1}^{I} \eta_i \|\boldsymbol{R}_i \boldsymbol{x} - \mathbf{D}\boldsymbol{\alpha}_i\|_2^2. \tag{4.10}$$

This optimization problem can be solved efficiently with Fast Fourier Transform (FFT) as [Shan *et al.* (2008); Cho and Lee (2009)]:

$$\hat{\boldsymbol{x}} = \mathcal{F}^{-1}\left(\frac{\overline{\mathcal{F}(\hat{\mathbf{k}})} \circ \mathcal{F}(\boldsymbol{y}) + \mathcal{F}(\sum_{i=1}^{I} \eta_i \boldsymbol{R}_i^\top \mathbf{D}\hat{\boldsymbol{\alpha}})}{\overline{\mathcal{F}(\hat{\mathbf{k}})} \circ \mathcal{F}(\hat{\mathbf{k}}) + \mathcal{F}(\sum_{i=1}^{I} \eta_i \boldsymbol{R}_i^\top \boldsymbol{R}_i \mathbf{I})} \right).$$

In practice, we follow the multi-scale estimation scheme for stable estimations of the blurring kernel $\mathbf{k}$ and latent sharp image $\boldsymbol{x}$ [Fergus *et al.* (2006); Shan *et al.* (2008); Cho and Lee (2009)]. Conventional schemes such as structure prediction can also be incorporated into optimization [Cho and Lee (2009)].

4.2.3.3 *Sparse Representation:* $\{\boldsymbol{\alpha}_i\}_{i=1}^{I}$-*Subproblem*

Given current estimation $\hat{\boldsymbol{x}}$ for the image, minimization of model (4.8) reduces to the following problem:

$$\{\boldsymbol{\alpha}_i\} = \arg\min_{\{\boldsymbol{\alpha}_i\}} \sum_{i=1}^{I} \eta_i \|\boldsymbol{R}_i \hat{\boldsymbol{x}} - \mathbf{D}\boldsymbol{\alpha}_i\|_2^2 + \sum_{i=1}^{I} \lambda_i \|\boldsymbol{\alpha}_i\|_1. \tag{4.11}$$

It is easy to see that (4.11) is decomposable over each patch $\boldsymbol{R}_i \boldsymbol{x}$, thus (4.11) can be solved by solving the problem of sparse recovery for each image patch separately:

$$\hat{\boldsymbol{\alpha}}_i = \arg\min_{\boldsymbol{\alpha}_i} \eta_i \|\mathbf{D}\boldsymbol{\alpha}_i - \boldsymbol{R}_i \hat{\boldsymbol{x}}\|_2^2 + \lambda_i \|\boldsymbol{\alpha}_i\|_1. \tag{4.12}$$

The deblurred patch after sparse projection on to the learned over-completed dictionary $\mathbf{D}$ can be computed as $\mathbf{D}\hat{\boldsymbol{\alpha}}_i$. The overall algorithm optimizes over blurring kernel $\mathbf{k}$, latent sharp image $\boldsymbol{x}$ and sparse representation set $\{\boldsymbol{\alpha}_i\}_{i=1}^{I}$ alternatively. Although we do not offer convergence

Table 4.1 Deblurring result comparison on estimation quality under different blur kernels (no noise).

Methods		fast deblur [Cho and Lee (2009)]	presented method [Zhang *et al.* (2011c)]
Motion	cameraman	30.03	18.22
	babara	15.74	9.71
	boat	18.38	12.58
	house	16.34	9.14
Gaussian	cameraman	30.29	17.88
	babara	16.57	12.92
	boat	17.21	12.44
	house	17.59	10.22
CamShake	cameraman	32.14	21.54
	babara	22.36	12.91
	boat	27.25	19.83
	house	20.92	13.76

analysis of the method discussed here, we empirically observe that this iterative procedure usually converges fast, typically within in 10 iterations. In the following experiment, we set the number of iterations as 10.

4.2.3.4 *Dictionary Learning*

In our algorithm, we use a redundant and over-complete dictionary $\mathbf{D}$ trained on image patches to help exploit the sparsity prior of natural images. In this subsection, we mention briefly the learning process for obtaining such a dictionary. Given the patch set $\{\mathbf{p}_j\}_{j=1}^{J}$, we can train a dictionary adapted to natural images via [Aharon *et al.* (2006)]:

$$\mathbf{D} = \arg\min_{\mathbf{D},\mathbf{Z}} \|\mathbf{P} - \mathbf{D}\mathbf{Z}\|_F^2 + \hat{\lambda}\|\mathbf{Z}\|_1 \qquad (4.13)$$

where $\mathbf{P} = [\mathbf{p}_1, \mathbf{p}_2, \cdots, \mathbf{p}_J]$ is the matrix of all the training patches. $\mathbf{Z}$ are the matrix of sparse codes for all the patches where each column corresponding to one patch.

4.2.4 *Blind Image Deblurring Results*

We conduct several experiments to verify the effectiveness of the presented method. We set $\eta_i = 0.05$, $\lambda_i = 0.1\eta_i$ and $\gamma = 5$ in all our experiments. In the following, we first conduct experiments under noise-free condition and then test the robustness of the method under noisy setting.

We first examine the performance of the presented method under noise-free observation condition. In this experiment, we first generate blurry observations using different test images. Several different blur kernels are used in experimentations, including motion blur (direction 45° with motion length 5 pixels), Gaussian blur (standard derivation $\sigma = 2$ pixels) and a general camera shake blur as shown in Figure 4.1. We run the method with 10 iterations and compared our delburring result with that of the fast deblurring method from [Cho and Lee (2009)], which is one of the *state-of-the-art* blind deblurring method. The experimental results in terms of Root Mean Square Error (RMSE) under this setting are presented in Table 4.1. As can be seen from Table 4.1, the method presented here performs better than the fast deblurring method in terms of RMSE under different kinds of blur kernels. The deblurring results for 'cameraman' test image as well as the estimated blurring kernel are shown in Figure 4.1 (top). As we can see Figure 4.1 (top), the deblurred image using the fast deblurring method has severe 'ghost' effet. The deblurring result using the presented method has less artifacts due to the incorporation of the sparse representation, which is visually more appealing and agrees with the objective results in Table 4.1.

To further evaluate the performance of the presented method, we carry out experiments on blurry and noisy images in the following. In this experiment, we test the algorithms using blurry and noisy images generated with different blur kernel and additive Gaussian noise with standard deviation of 0.01.[2] The RMSE results under this noisy setting are summarized in Table 4.2. As can be seen from Table 4.2, the presented method again outperforms the fast deblurring method on different test images. The noisy and blurry observation used in this experiment under different blur kernels are shown in Figure 4.1 (2nd row to bottom). As can be seen, the deblurring results from the fast deblurring method suffered from amplified noise, implying its non-robustness to noise, which is an inevitable factor in real-world imaging process. The presented method, on the other hand, is robust to noise due to the sparse representation regularization, therefore, the deblurring results from this method can recover details without noise amplification. The RMSE plots for estimated blurring kernel and the deblurred image for the blurry 'barbara' image under motion blur and Gaussian noise are shown in Figure 4.2. As can be seen from Figure 4.2, the estimation errors for both the blurring kernel and the deblurred image are decreasing with increasing iterations, which empirically justifies the effectiveness of the aforementioned minimization scheme.

---

[2]The range of pixel value is $[0, 1]$.

Table 4.2   Deblurring result comparison on estimation quality under different blur kernels (additive Gaussian noise).

Methods		fast deblur [Cho and Lee (2009)]	presented method [Zhang *et al.* (2011c)]
Motion	cameraman	33.08	18.41
	barbara	22.34	11.05
	boat	24.73	12.06
	house	23.40	9.68
Gaussian	cameraman	31.85	21.41
	barbara	21.60	13.08
	boat	21.28	13.91
	house	21.57	10.44
CamShake	cameraman	33.68	18.10
	barbara	22.36	15.35
	boat	30.94	11.47
	house	26.00	15.04

4.3   Blind Deblurring with Domain Knowledge

As discussed above, recent works have shown that it is possible to estimate both the blur kernel and the latent sharp image with high quality from a single blurry observation [Fergus *et al.* (2006); Shan *et al.* (2008); Levin *et al.* (2009); Cai *et al.* (2009); Cho and Lee (2009)]. However, one significant limitation of these methods is that they rely on the existence of strong edge structures in the latent image, which facilitates the algorithms to find a meaningful local minimum [Levin *et al.* (2009)]. In situations of few strong edge structures, *e.g.*, face images, these methods may fail. Another point is that previous image restoration methods are mainly designed for improving human visual perception only and few works have studied the impacts of restoration on recognition, or vice versa, the effects of recognition on restoration. The method in [Das Gupta *et al.* (2005)] alternated between recognition and restoration to change the patch sampling prior using nonparametric belief propagation for digit recognition, with the assumption of a known image blur model. Hennings-Yeomans *et al.* [Hennings-Yeomans *et al.* (2008)] proposed a method to extract features from both the low-resolution faces and their super-resolved ones within a single energy minimization framework. Nishiyama *et al.* [Nishiyama *et al.* (2009)] proposed to improve the recognition of blurry faces with a pre-defined finite set of Point Spread Function (PSF) kernels. However, these methods only deal with some simple image degradations.

We present a Joint image Restoration and Recognition (JRR) approach

Fig. 4.1 Deblurring results with additive Gaussian noise. (a) ground truth image and kernel, (b) blurry (and noisy) image, (c) deblurring results from [Cho and Lee (2009)], and (d) deblurring results from the presented method [Zhang *et al.* (2011c)].

based on the sparse representation prior for face images [Zhang *et al.* (2011d)], to handle the challenging task of face recognition from low-quality images in a blind setting, *i.e.*, with no *a priori* knowledge on the blur kernels, which can be non-parametric and very complex. We assume that we have sharp and clean training face images for all the test subjects, and the degraded test image, if correctly restored, can be well represented as a linear combination of the training faces from the same subject up to some sparse errors, thus leading to a sparse representation in terms of all the

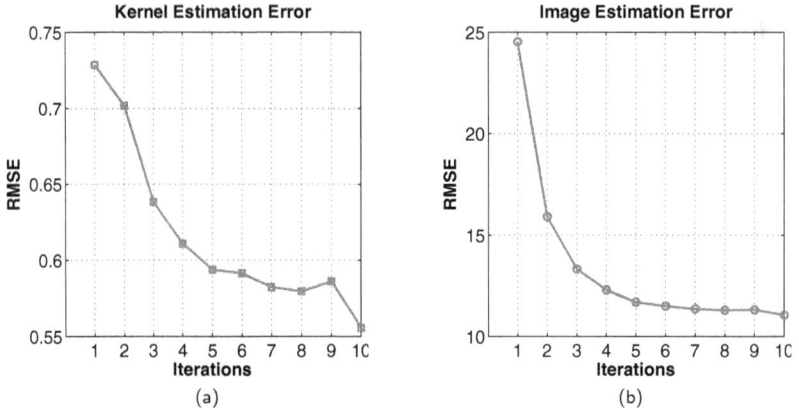

Fig. 4.2   RMSE plots from the presented algorithm [Zhang *et al.* (2011c)]: (a) Kernel estimation error plot. (b) Image estimation error plot.

training faces. When the test subject is not present in the gallery, it will violate our sparse representation assumption, and in principle the test subject can be rejected via a similar approach as in [Wright *et al.* (2009)], which is not considered here. With such a sparse representation prior, the presented method connects restoration and recognition in a unified framework by seeking sparse representations over the training faces via ℓ_1-norm minimization. On one hand, a better restored image can be better represented by the images from the same class, leading to a sparser representation in terms of the training set, thus facilitating recognition; on the other hand, a better resolved sparse representation, which implies better recognition ability, can give a more meaningful regularization in the solution space for blind restoration. Our approach iteratively restores the input image by searching for the sparsest representation, which can correct the initial possibly erroneous recognition decision and recognize the person's identity with increasing confidence.

4.3.1   *Domain Knowledge Learning via Sparse Representation*

The application of sparse representation for classification is based on the assumption that data samples belonging to the same class live in the same subspace of a much lower dimension, thus a new test sample can be well represented by the training samples of the same class, which leads to a natural sparse representation over the whole training set. Casting the recognition

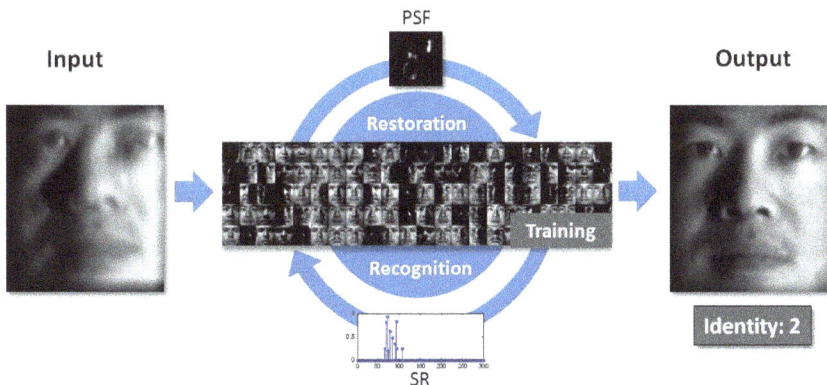

Fig. 4.3 Sparse Representation based Joint Blind Restoration and Recognition (JRR) framework. Given a blurry observation, JRR iteratively estimates the PSF and the underlying identity based on the sparse representation prior. The algorithm will output the estimated PSF, a deblurred image, and the identity of the observation.

problem as one of finding a sparse representation of the test image in terms of the training set as a whole up to some sparse errors due to occlusion, Wright *et al.* [Wright *et al.* (2009)] showed that such a simple sparse representation based approach is robust to partial occlusions and can achieve promising recognition accuracy on public face datasets. This idea is further extended in their later work [Wagner *et al.* (2009)] to handle face misalignment. Formally, given a set of training samples for the c-th class $\mathbf{D}_c = [\mathbf{d}_{c,1}, \mathbf{d}_{c,2}, \cdots]$, a test sample $\boldsymbol{x}$ from class c can be well represented by $\mathbf{D}_c$ with coefficients $\boldsymbol{\alpha}_c$. As the label for $\boldsymbol{x}$ is unknown, it is assumed that $\boldsymbol{\alpha}_c$ can be recovered from the sparse representation of $\boldsymbol{x}$ in terms of the dictionary constructed from training samples of all C classes by

$$\hat{\boldsymbol{\alpha}} = \arg\min_{\boldsymbol{\alpha}} \|\boldsymbol{\alpha}\|_1$$
$$\text{s.t.} \ \|\mathbf{D}\boldsymbol{\alpha} - \boldsymbol{x}\|_2^2 \leq \epsilon, \tag{4.14}$$

where $\mathbf{D} = [\mathbf{D}_1, \mathbf{D}_2, \cdots, \mathbf{D}_C], \boldsymbol{\alpha} = [\boldsymbol{\alpha}_1^\top, \boldsymbol{\alpha}_2^\top, \cdots, \boldsymbol{\alpha}_C^\top]^\top$. Then the label for the test sample $\boldsymbol{x}$ is determined as the class which gives the minimum reconstruction error:

$$\hat{c} = \arg\min_c \|\mathbf{D}\delta_c(\hat{\boldsymbol{\alpha}}) - \boldsymbol{x}\|_2^2 = \arg\min_c \|\mathbf{D}_c\hat{\boldsymbol{\alpha}}_c - \boldsymbol{x}\|_2^2.$$

$\delta_c(\cdot)$ is an indicator function keeping the elements corresponding to the c-th class while setting the rest to be zero.

4.3.2 Joint Blind Restoration and Recognition with Sparse Representation Prior

In this section, we present our joint restoration and recognition framework in the blind situation, *i.e.*, no *a priori* information on the image degradation process about the blurry query image is available, and develop an efficient minimization algorithm to solve the problem.

In conventional recognition works, the test image y is often assumed to be captured under ideal condition without any degradation, *i.e.* $y = x$. Some simple environmental variations, such as illumination and mild misalignment, can be fairly well handled given enough training samples [Wagner *et al.* (2009)]. In reality, however, we may only get observation y for x with degradations, *e.g.*, blur as in (4.1), which are hard to model beforehand and can bring serious problems to the recognition task. Therefore, recognition from a single blurry observation is a very challenging task, especially in the case of blind situation (dubbed as *blind recognition*), *i.e.*, no *a priori* information is available for the observation process. As far as we know, few works have been done on this challenging blind recognition problem. In this work, we aim to address the task of blind recognition by exploiting the interactions between restoration and recognition with the sparse representation prior. Formally, given the blurry observation y, and the sharp training image set $\mathbf{D}$, we want to estimate the latent sharp image x, blur kernel $\mathbf{k}$, as well as the class label c simultaneously by

$$\{\hat{x}, \hat{\mathbf{k}}, \hat{c}\} = \arg \min_{x,\mathbf{k},c} \mathbf{E}(x, \mathbf{k}, c), \qquad (4.15)$$

where

$$\mathbf{E}(x, \mathbf{k}, c) = \|\mathbf{k} * x - y\|_2^2 + \eta \|x - \mathbf{D}\alpha\|_2^2 + \lambda \|\alpha\|_1$$
$$+ \tau \sum_{l=1}^{L} |\mathbf{e}_l * x|^s + \gamma \|\mathbf{k}\|_2^2. \qquad (4.16)$$

We explain each term of the model in detail as follows.

(1) The first term is the conventional reconstruction constraint, *i.e.*, the restored image should be consistent with the observation with respect to the estimated degradation model.
(2) The second term means the recovered sharp image can be well represented by the clean training set.
(3) The third term enforces that the representation of the recovered image in terms of the training set should be sparse. In other words, the algorithm favors a solution x that can be sparsely represented by the

training set. Meanwhile, this sparse representation also recognizes the identity of the observation.

(4) The fourth term is a general sparse prior for natural images using sparse exponential of the responses of derivative filters to further stabilize the solution, where typically $0.5 \le s \le 0.8$.

(5) The last term is merely a ℓ_2-norm stable regularization for the blur kernel.

The basic idea of the model is that the restored image should have a sparse representation in terms of the training images if the blur kernel is correctly estimated, and meanwhile the sparse representation itself identifies the observed target. On one hand, the sparse representation prior effectively regularizes the solution space of the possible latent images and blur kernels; on the other hand, better estimated blur kernel will promote better sparse representations for recognition. As shown by Eqn. (4.16), our model unifies the restoration (4.6) and recognition (4.14) in a unified framework based on the sparse representation prior. Note that the presented model is a general framework which can handle different kinds of image degradations, *e.g.*, out-of-focus blur, various motion blurs, translation misalignment, and etc., which can be modeled by a linear operator.

4.3.3 *Optimization Procedure*

The model in (4.16) involves multiple variables and is hard to minimize directly. We adopt the alternating minimization scheme advocated by recent sparse optimization and image deblurring works [Wang *et al.* (2008); Shan *et al.* (2008); Krishnan and Fergus (2009); Cho and Lee (2009)], which reduces the original problem into several simpler subproblems. Following this scheme, we address the subproblems for each of the optimization variables in an alternating fashion and present an overall efficient optimization algorithm. In each step, our algorithm reduces the objective function value, and thus will converge to a local minima. To start, we initialize the sparse representation $\hat{\alpha}$ as that recovered from y with respect to $\mathbf{D}$, and the latent sharp image $\hat{x}$ as $\mathbf{D}\hat{\alpha}$.

4.3.3.1   *Blur Kernel Estimation: Optimizing for* **k**

In this subproblem, we fix all other variables and and optimize the image blur kernel **k** by

$$\hat{\mathbf{k}} = \arg\min_{\mathbf{k}} \|\hat{\boldsymbol{x}} * \mathbf{k} - \boldsymbol{y}\|_2^2 + \gamma\|\mathbf{k}\|_2^2. \tag{4.17}$$

This is a least square problem with Tikhonov regularization, which leads to a close-form solution for **k**:

$$\hat{\mathbf{k}} = \mathcal{F}^{-1}\left(\frac{\overline{\mathcal{F}(\hat{\boldsymbol{x}})} \circ \mathcal{F}(\boldsymbol{y})}{\overline{\mathcal{F}(\hat{\boldsymbol{x}})} \circ \mathcal{F}(\hat{\boldsymbol{x}}) + \gamma \mathbf{I}} \right),$$

where $\mathcal{F}(\cdot)$ denotes Fast Fourier Transform (FFT), $\mathcal{F}^{-1}(\cdot)$ denotes inverse FFT, $\overline{\mathcal{F}(\cdot)}$ denotes the complex conjugate of $\mathcal{F}(\cdot)$, and "$\circ$" denotes element-wise multiplication.

4.3.3.2   *Latent Image Recovery: Optimizing for* $\boldsymbol{x}$

Given the current kernel estimation $\hat{\mathbf{k}}$ and sparse representation $\hat{\boldsymbol{\alpha}}$, we want to update the estimation for the latent sharp image $\boldsymbol{x}$. The optimization problem (4.16) becomes

$$\hat{\boldsymbol{x}} = \arg\min_{\boldsymbol{x}} \|\boldsymbol{x} * \hat{\mathbf{k}} - \boldsymbol{y}\|_2^2 + \eta\|\boldsymbol{x} - \mathbf{D}\hat{\boldsymbol{\alpha}}\|_2^2 + \tau \sum_{l=1}^{L} |\mathbf{e}_l * \boldsymbol{x}|^s. \tag{4.18}$$

This optimization problem can be solved efficiently with variable substitution and FFT [Wang *et al.* (2008); Shan *et al.* (2008); Krishnan and Fergus (2009); Cho and Lee (2009)]. Introducing new auxiliary variables $\mathbf{u}_l (l \in 1, 2, \cdots, L)$, we can rewrite the energy function in (4.18) as:

$$\mathbf{E}(\boldsymbol{x}, \mathbf{u}) = \|\boldsymbol{x} * \hat{\mathbf{k}} - \boldsymbol{y}\|_2^2 + \eta\|\boldsymbol{x} - \mathbf{D}\hat{\boldsymbol{\alpha}}\|_2^2$$
$$+ \tau \sum_{l=1}^{L} |\mathbf{u}_l|^s + \beta \sum_{l=1}^{L} \|\mathbf{u}_l - \mathbf{e}_l * \boldsymbol{x}\|_2^2, \tag{4.19}$$

which can be divided into two sub-problems: $\boldsymbol{x}$-subproblem and **u**-subproblem. In the $\boldsymbol{x}$-subproblem, the energy function to be minimized becomes

$$\mathbf{E}(\boldsymbol{x}) = \|\boldsymbol{x} * \hat{\mathbf{k}} - \boldsymbol{y}\|_2^2 + \eta\|\boldsymbol{x} - \mathbf{D}\hat{\boldsymbol{\alpha}}\|_2^2 + \beta \sum_{l=1}^{L} \|\mathbf{e}_l * \boldsymbol{x} - \mathbf{u}_l\|_2^2$$

which can be solved efficiently using FFT as:

$$\hat{\boldsymbol{x}} = \mathcal{F}^{-1}\left(\frac{\overline{\mathcal{F}(\hat{\mathbf{k}})} \circ \mathcal{F}(\boldsymbol{y}) + \eta\mathcal{F}(\mathbf{D}\hat{\boldsymbol{\alpha}}) + \beta\sum_{l=1}^{L} \overline{\mathcal{F}(\mathbf{e}_l)} \circ \mathcal{F}(\mathbf{u}_l)}{\overline{\mathcal{F}(\hat{\mathbf{k}})} \circ \mathcal{F}(\hat{\mathbf{k}}) + \eta\mathbf{I} + \beta\sum_{l=1}^{L} \overline{\mathcal{F}(\mathbf{e}_l)} \circ \mathcal{F}(\mathbf{e}_l)} \right).$$

In the **u**-subproblem, $\mathbf{u}_l$ can be estimated by solving the following problem given fixed $\boldsymbol{x}$:

$$\hat{\mathbf{u}}_l = \arg\min_{\mathbf{u}_l} \tau |\mathbf{u}_l|^s + \beta \|\mathbf{u}_l - \mathbf{e}_l * \boldsymbol{x}\|_2^2, \qquad (4.20)$$

which can be solved efficiently over each dimension separately [Krishnan and Fergus (2009)]. In practice, we use first-order derivative filters $\{\mathbf{e}_1 = [1, -1], \mathbf{e}_2 = [1, -1]^\top\}$ and set $s = 0.5$ as [Krishnan and Fergus (2009)]. We follow the multi-scale estimation scheme for stable estimations of the blur kernel **k** and latent sharp image $\boldsymbol{x}$ as in [Fergus *et al.* (2006); Shan *et al.* (2008); Cho and Lee (2009)]. Conventional schemes such as structure prediction have also been incorporated into optimization [Cho and Lee (2009)].

4.3.3.3 *Sparse Projection: Optimizing for* $\boldsymbol{\alpha}$

With the recovered kernel $\hat{\mathbf{k}}$ and sharp training set **D**, we can generate the corresponding blurry dictionary $\mathbf{D}_b$ via

$$\mathbf{D}_b = \mathbf{D} * \hat{\mathbf{k}}, \qquad (4.21)$$

where the convolution $*$ is performed on each column of **D** with $\hat{\mathbf{k}}$. Then the sparse representation vector $\boldsymbol{\alpha}$ can be updated by

$$\hat{\boldsymbol{\alpha}} = \arg\min_{\boldsymbol{\alpha}} \|\mathbf{D}_b \boldsymbol{\alpha} - \boldsymbol{y}\|_2^2 + \lambda \|\boldsymbol{\alpha}\|_1, \qquad (4.22)$$

from which the classification decision is made using

$$\hat{c} = \arg\min_c \|\mathbf{D}_b \delta_c(\hat{\boldsymbol{\alpha}}) - \boldsymbol{y}\|_2^2. \qquad (4.23)$$

We do not use the deblurred image and the sharp training set to compute the sparse representation $\boldsymbol{\alpha}$ because the deblurring process may introduce artifacts which is disadvantageous for recovery and recognition. Based on compressive sensing theory, we can recover the sparse representation using the blurry observation $\boldsymbol{y}$ and the blurry dictionary $\mathbf{D}_b$ and thus circumvent the above problem. The overall algorithm optimizes over blur kernel **k**, latent sharp image $\boldsymbol{x}$, sparse representation $\boldsymbol{\alpha}$ and class label c alternatively. Algorithm 4.1 describes the procedures of our joint blind restoration and recognition algorithm.

4.3.4 *Experiments and Results*

In this section, we present several experiments to demonstrate the effectiveness of the JRR method in terms of both restoration accuracy and recognition accuracy. The Extended Yale B [Georghiades *et al.* (2001)] (48×42)

Algorithm 4.1 Joint Blind Image Restoration and Recognition with Sparse Representation Prior.

Require: blurry image y, training image set $\mathbf{D}$, number of iterations T

  1: FOR t=1 to T DO

  2: **Kernel Estimation:** update kernel $\mathbf{k}$ by minimizing Eqn.(4.17);

  3: **Image Estimation:** update the latent image X estimation via minimizing Eqn.(4.18);

  4: **Sparse Representation:** recovering the sparse coefficients by minimizing Eqn.(4.22);

  5: **Classification:** estimate the class label c from Eqn.(4.23).

  6: END FOR

Ensure: estimated blurring kernel $\hat{\mathbf{k}}$, restored image $\hat{x}$, and the class label $\hat{c}$.

---

and CMU Multi-PIE [Gross *et al.* (2008)](80×60) datasets are used for evaluation in this work. The Extended Yale B dataset contains 38 individuals, each with 64 near frontal view images under different illuminations. For CMU Multi-PIE dataset, We use the frontal images with neutral expression under varying illuminations from session 1 for computational considerations.

For restoration, we compare our algorithm with the fast deblurring method in [Cho and Lee (2009)], one of the *state-of-the-art* blind deblurring algorithms. Root Mean Square Error (RMSE) is employed to compare the estimation accuracy for both the blur kernel and the restored image. For classification, we compare our JRR algorithm with the following methods: (1) SVM: classification with linear SVM trained on the sharp training set; (2) SRC: directly feed the blurry observation into the sparse representation based classification algorithm [Wright *et al.* (2009)]; and (3) SRC-B: first estimate the kernel and then generate a blurred training set for SRC.[3]

4.3.4.1 *An Illustrative Example*

We illustrate the JRR method with a simple example in Figure 4.4. Given a blurry observation, we jointly recover the blur kernel, the latent sharp image, and the class label in an iterative way. Figure 4.4 shows that, as

---

[3]Another approach is first to deblur the test image and then use the deblurred image for recognition. Empirically, we observe that this method may perform even worse than using the original blurry image directly, mainly due to the artifacts induced by the deblurring step (Figure 4.6), and thus we do not compare with this method in the sequel.

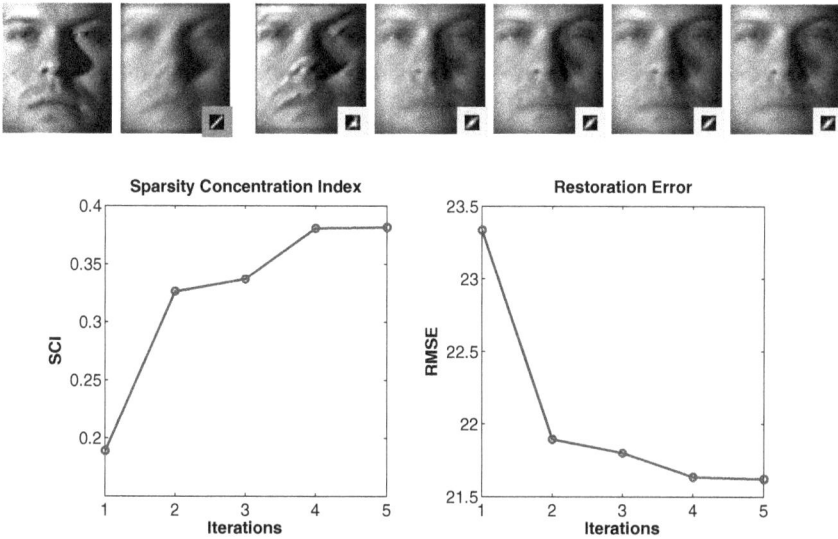

Fig. 4.4 The joint blind restoration and recognition optimization process for 5 iterations. Top row, left to right: ground-truth sharp image, blurry test image, and the restored images from iteration 1 to 5. The ground truth and estimated PSFs are framed in red and green borders respectively. Bottom row, left: sparsity of the recovered sparse coefficients in terms of SCI; right: restoration errors in terms of RMSE.

the optimization iteration increases, the latent representation becomes sparser and sparser as indicated by the increase of Sparsity Concentration Index (SCI) measure[4], which implies that the underlying class label of the test image can be determined with increasing confidence. At the same time, the restored image resembles more and more to the ground truth as indicated by the decrease of the restoration error, which means that the estimated blur kernel gets more and more accurate. Actually, in the first iteration, the blurry input is wrongly assigned with class label of subject 4, while the ground truth label is subject 1. After the second iteration, with better restored image and kernel, the algorithm can correctly finds the true class label. This illustrates that our approach can effectively regularize the ill-posed blind image restoration in pursuit of the sparsest representation for recognition. On one hand, a better recovered image will have a more meaningful sparse representation for recognition; on the other hand, the updated sparse representation, tightly connected with recogni-

---

[4]SCI is defined as $\mathrm{SCI}(\boldsymbol{x}) = \frac{C \cdot \max_i \|\delta_i(\boldsymbol{x})\|_1 / \|\boldsymbol{x}\|_1 - 1}{C-1}$, where C is the total number of classes [Wright *et al.* (2009)].

tion, will provides a powerful regularization for the followed blind image restoration. In practice, we notice that the joint optimization proces converges very quickly, typically in no more than 4 iterations. Therefore, we fix the iteration number as 4 in all the following experiments.

4.3.4.2 *Joint Blind Image Restoration and Recognition*

In this subsection, we conduct experiments on joint image restoration and recognition for face images under various blind degradation settings. In our JRR algorithm, the tasks of image restoration and recognition are tightly coupled. However, to facilitate the comparisons with conventional restoration and recognition approaches respectively, we will present the results for restoration and recognition separately in the sequel.

Blind Image Restoration. We first quantitatively evaluate the kernel estimation and image restoration accuracy on Extended Yale B face dataset. To be consistent with the recognition evaluation, we randomly select half of the images for each subject as the training set. We then randomly choose 10 images from the rest as our testing examples for restoration. For each test image, we generate its blurry images using the 8 realistic nonparametric complex blur kernels proposed by Levin *et al.* in [Levin *et al.* (2009)], shown in the first row of Table 4.4. Given a blurry input, our JRR algorithm estimates the unknown blur kernel without any prior knowledge and recovers the underlying sharp latent image, which are then evaluated in terms of RMSE with respect to the ground truth. We compare our JRR algorithm with the fast deblurring method in [Cho and Lee (2009)].

Figure 4.5 (a) shows the average RMSEs for each estimated kernels given the blurry inputs, where our JRR method improves the kernel estimation accuracy substantially compared with the fast deblurring algorithm. This can be explained by the fact that face images are lack of strong edge structures, especially in the case of blurry observation, which presents a great challenge to the existing blind deblurring methods. With the sparse representation prior, however, our method demonstrates much more robustness in estimating the complex blur kernels. Figure 4.5 (b) shows the comparisons of average restoration RMSEs for the 10 images under the 8 complex kernels. Due to the incorporation of the sparse representation prior, our algorithm improves the restoration accuracy significantly over the fast deblurring method for all the test images. By exploiting the sparse representation prior, the restored image has more details and less artifacts

(Figure 4.6), implying a more accurate sparse representation, thus facilitating recognition, as shown in the following.

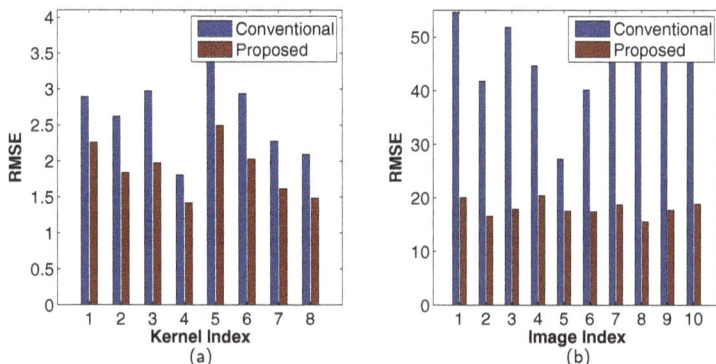

Fig. 4.5 Restoration results comparison in terms of RMSE. (a) kernel estimation; (b) image estimation.

Blind Image Recognition. For recognition, we first evaluate the recognition performance of the presented method on Extended Yale B dataset. We randomly select half of the images for each subject for training, and use the rest for testing. To generate the blurry inputs, we also add two more simple parametric blur kernels, *i.e.*, linear motion kernel and Gaussian blur kernel, in addition to the eight complex blur kernels [Levin *et al.* (2009)]. For each blur kernel, we generate a set of blurred testing images, leading to in total 10 testing sets. Table 4.3 summarizes the recognition results for a simple motion blur (10 pixel-length with 45 degree) and a Gaussian kernel (with standard deviation 3), where the kernel size is 9×9. Our JRR algorithm outperforms SRC remarkably, while slightly better than SRC-B. This is because the conventional blind deblurring method can estimate the blur kernel reasonably well in simple blur model case. Table 4.4 presents the recognition results under the complex non-parametric blur kernels. In this case, conventional blur kernel estimation methods fail easily due to the complexity of the kernels and lack of strong structures in the face images, and as a result, the recognition results of our JRR algorithm outperform those of SRC-B and SRC by a large margin in most cases.

We then evaluate our algorithm on Multi-PIE [Gross *et al.* (2008)] dataset, with 15 images from each subject of Session 1 for training and the rest of Session 1 for testing. The results are summarized in Table 4.5. Again, our algorithm performs much better than other methods. Note

Table 4.3   Recognition rate (%) on Extend Yale
B under simple parametric blur kernels.

Kernel Type	SVM	SRC	SRC-B	JRR
Motion	40.0	68.7	85.3	**86.0**
Gaussian	29.9	57.7	**84.8**	**84.8**

Table 4.4   Recognition accuracy (%) on Extend Yale B set under complex
non-parametric blur kernels.

Kernels								
Sizes	19	17	15	27	13	21	23	23
SVM	45.9	27.2	45.8	11.2	43.5	48.4	20.9	16.9
SRC	79.8	54.1	74.9	21.3	65.5	83.5	36.6	30.3
SRC-B	80.6	**79.3**	73.4	33.0	70.1	76.8	51.9	51.9
JRR	**86.2**	**79.3**	**85.7**	**43.1**	**81.9**	**86.4**	**64.7**	**54.8**

that as the conventional kernel estimation method is not robust enough in
this case, SRC-B performs even worse than SRC. We further evaluate our
algorithm in a more realistic scenario, where the blur kernel for generating a blurry image is not fixed but randomly chosen from {*Linear Motion
kernel, Gaussian kernel, Nonparametric Complex kernel, Delta (no blur)*}.
The recognition results for this case are shown in Table 4.6, and the JRR
method outperforms all the other methods with large margins on both
datasets.

Finally, to visually demonstrate the effectiveness of our JRR algorithm,
we compare the estimated kernels, deblurred images, and the top-10 selected atoms with the largest absolute coefficients from sparse representations under two different kernels, shown in Figure 4.6. Top row shows
the results of SRC; middle row shows the results of conventional blind deblur followed by SRC; and bottom row shows our results. The blur kernels
framed in red denote the ground truth kernels, and those framed in green
are the estimated kernels. In both cases, our algorithm can accurately
estimate the unknown blur kernels and can output sharp images close to
the ground truth, while the fast deblurring method is not robust and fails
drastically for the complex kernel. To the right of each restored image,
top-10 atoms from the sharp training set are selected by the largest absolute sparse representation coefficients, where red numbers denote atoms
chosen from the same class (correct) and blue numbers denote otherwise
(wrong). It is clear that our JRR algorithm can select more atoms from

Table 4.5 Recognition rate (%) on Multi-PIE with the third complex blur kernel.

Algorithm	SVM	SRC	SRC-B	JRR
Accuracy	84.8	85.2	79.1	**91.4**

Table 4.6 Recognition rate (%) with randomly blur kernels on both Extended Yale B and Multi-PIE.

Algorithm	SVM	SRC	SRC-B	JRR
Extended Yale B	57.0	68.8	66.3	**73.7**
Multi-PIE	49.4	53.6	54.9	**61.3**

the same class with more concentrated large coefficients, indicating better recognition ability.

However, a challenging situation is when the blurry test image suffers from extreme illuminations, as in Figure 4.7, where little information about the facial structures is kept for deblurring. In this case, the deblurring task becomes extremely challenging and the blur kernel may not be correctly estimated even with our algorithm, which will lead to incorrect classification decisions. In both datasets we use, there are in fact a notable amount of such kind of images, which pose great challenges to the task of blind recognition on these datasets. Yet, with the sparse representation prior, the deblurring result of our algorithm looks much more reasonable than that of the fast deblurring method.

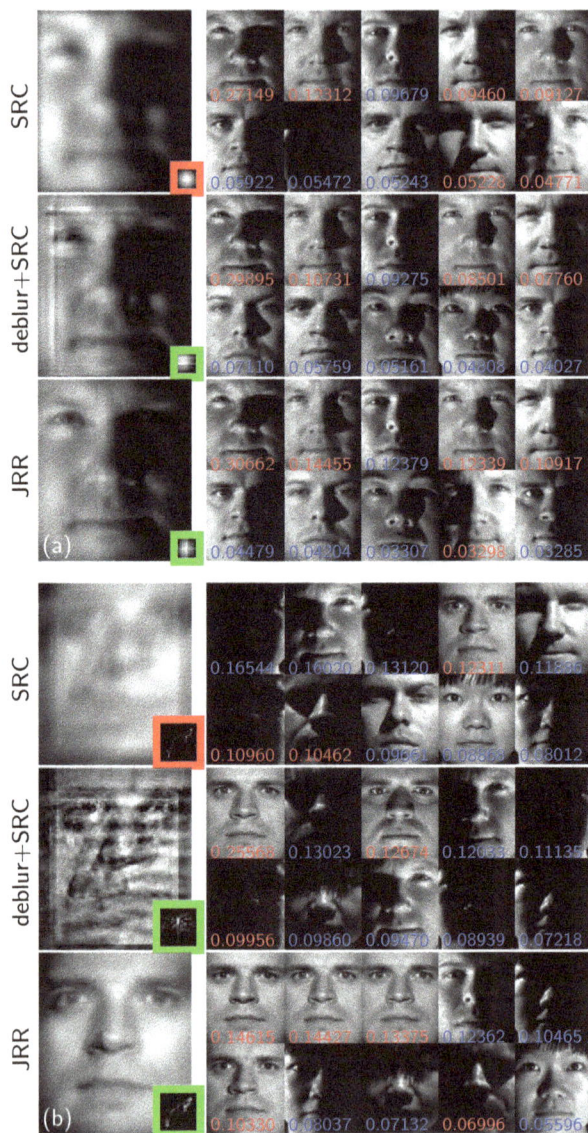

Fig. 4.6   Image restoration results under (a) parametric PSF (Gaussian blur) and (b) realistic non-parametric PSF (27×27 non-parametric motion blur). Top: SRC; Middle: conventional deblur + SRC; Bottom: JRR. The PSF kernels framed in red denote the ground-truth kernels while those in green are estimated kernels. Atoms corresponding to the top-10 largest absolute coefficient values are shown together with the absolute values for each method, with red indicating atoms selected from the same class as the test image.

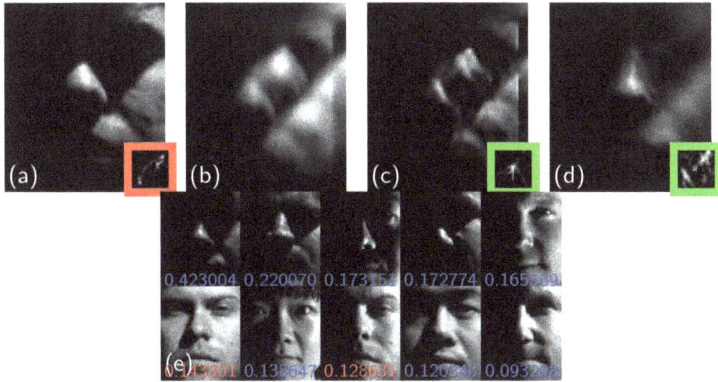

Fig. 4.7 Failure case analysis. (a) ground truth image and kernel; (b) blurry input; estimated image and kernel using (c) conventional deblurring method [Cho and Lee (2009)] and (d) the JRR method; (e) top-10 selected atoms with the JRR method. Kernel estimation is very challenging due to the extreme illumination.

Chapter 5

Sensor Fusion

5.1 Sparsity in Multiple Sensors

Recent dramatic increase in different kinds of visual data has created a surge in demand for effective processing and analysis algorithms. For instance, a video camera can generate multiple observations of the same object at different time instances; a camera network can capture the same subject from different viewpoints; systems with heterogeneous sensors (*e.g.*, visible light cameras, infrared cameras and laser range finders) can generate heterogeneous visual data for the same physical object. All these scenarios pose great challenges to the existing data processing techniques and require new schemes for effective data processing. In particular, object recognition and classification from multiple observations are interesting and are of great use for numerous applications (*e.g.*, surveillance, law enforcement). However, most existing techniques are designed for single observation based classification, which are clearly not optimal due to the failure of exploiting the correlations among the multiple observations of the same physical object.

Sparsity has been playing an important role in many fields such as signal processing [Huang and Aviyente (2006)], image processing [Elad *et al.* (2010)] and recognition [Wright *et al.* (2010)], and is the key factor of recent active research topics such as sparse coding [Grosse *et al.* (2007); Lee *et al.* (2006)] and compressive sensing [Candes *et al.* (2006); Donoho (2006a)]. Traditionally, sparsity acts as a strong prior for alleviating the ill-posedness of inverse problems [Elad *et al.* (2010)], but recent work shows that the sparse coefficients are also discriminative [Huang and Aviyente (2006); Grosse *et al.* (2007); Wright *et al.* (2010, 2009)]. Recently, a Sparse Representation based Classification (SRC) method for face images was proposed by Wright *et al.* in [Wright *et al.* (2009)]. This method is based on

75

the observation that the sparse representation (non-zero coefficients) of a test sample with respect to all the training training can reveal its identity. It has been shown that this method is robust to sparse corruption and partial outliers. This method has also been extended to other applications such as hyperspectral target detection [Chen *et al.* (2010)], IRIS recognition [K.Pillai *et al.* (2009)], speech recognition [Gemmeke and Cranen (2008)] and classification on several other classical databases as reported in [Majumdar and Ward (2010)].

Use of structured sparsity prior, such as incorporating additional structures other than pure coefficient-level sparsity, have been popular recently in signal processing, machine learning and statistics community to help with challenges such as the ill-posedness of inverse problems, curse of dimensionality, as well as feature and variable selection. This is due to the fact that many real world problems have intrinsic low degrees of freedom with structures. By exploiting the structural prior on non-zero sparse coefficients, we can greatly reduce the degrees of freedom of the problem, thus we may potentially avoid the risk of over-fitting and reduce the number of observations/measurements required for a proper model estimation. The structural sparsity priors that have been previously investigated are clustering prior sparsity [Tibshirani *et al.* (2005); Huang *et al.* (2009); Liu and Ye (2010); Baraniuk *et al.* (2010); Faktor *et al.* (2012)], group/block sparsity [Yuan and Lin (2006); Eldar and Mishali (2009)] and joint sparsity [van den Berg and Friedlander (2009); Cotter *et al.* (2005); Duarte *et al.* (2005); Mishali and Eldar (2008, 2009)]. In many situations the sparse coefficients tend to cluster and a clustering prior exploiting correlations between neighboring coefficients is enforced in the optimization algorithms in order to obtain a better representation. In group sparsity, the data is inherently represented by a small number of pre-defined groups of data samples, thus a sparsifying term over the groups is used to promote this property. In the case of multiple measurements, a specific group sparsity called joint structured sparsity is explored for joint sparse representation, where not only the sparsity property for each measurement is utilized, but the structural information across the multiple sparse representation vectors for the multiple measurements is exploited as well.

In this chapter, we generalize SRC to handle classification problem with multiple measurements with joint structured sparsity priors [Zhang *et al.* (2012c)]. The problem of recovering the sparse linear representation of a single query datum with respect to a set of reference datum (dictionary) has received wide interest recently in image processing, computer vision and pattern recognition communities [Elad *et al.* (2010); Wright *et al.* (2010)]. Recently, extensions on recovering the sparse representations of multiple query data samples jointly have been investigated and applied to multi-task visual recognition problem in [Yuan and Yan (2010)], where the multiple tasks (features) are assumed to have the same sparsity pattern in their sparse representation vectors. The presented Joint Dynamic Sparse Representation based Classification (JDSRC) method exploits the correlations among the multiple observations using a novel joint dynamic sparsity prior to improve the performance of a recognition system, with the assumption that the sparse representation vectors of multiple observations have the same sparsity pattern at class level, but not necessarily at atom level, thus the algorithm can not only exploit the correlations among the observations but is also more flexible than the same atom-level sparisty pattern assumption. Moreover, the JDSRC method is very general, and can handle both homogenous and heterogeneous data within the same framework.

The problem considered here is a common scenario in many applications where we have multiple observations or measurements about the same physical event. One typical example is the application that will be shown in the experimental section of this chapter. In this application, we use acoustic data collected from multi-channel acoustic sensor array to locate sources of hostile artillery (*i.e.*, Mortar/Rocket launch and impact) and improvised explosive devices. A sensor array consists of 4 microphone sensors (channels), as shown in Fig. 5.1, measuring simultaneously the same physical event, thus inherently capturing multiple measurements from different channels. We will use this as a driving example throughout this chapter. Another application we will show in the experimental section is multi-view face recognition, as shown in Figure 5.2.

To fuse multi-observation information from multiple sensors, a direct generalization of SRC is to apply it onto each observation separately. This simple generalization however, does not exploit the correlations among the multiple measurements during the sparse representation process. To handle this, we can use a Joint Sparse Representation based Classification (J-SRC) method for joint classification from multiple measurements. The J-SRC method first recovers the sparse representations for the multiple measurements simultaneously based on the assumption of a joint structured sparsity prior, and then makes a decision based on the total reconstruction error from all the measurements for each class. In this section, we discuss several different variations of the J-SRC algorithm for achieving joint classification. This is accomplished by exploiting the correlations

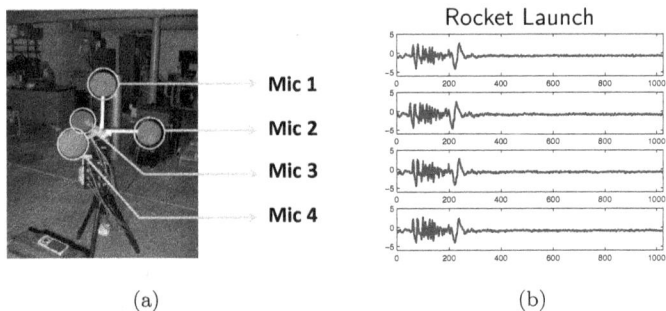

(a)   (b)

Fig. 5.1   (a) An acoustic sensor array. Each array has 4 microphones, collecting the multiple-measurement acoustic signals of the same physical event. (b) acoustic signal (4 channels) for a Rocket Launch event collected by the sensor array.

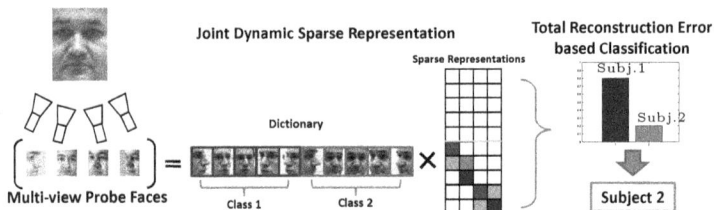

Fig. 5.2   Multi-view face recognition framework. Each subject is imaged from different viewpoints, generating multi-view probe faces, which is the input to our face recognition system. This multi-view probe face set is then used for joint dynamic sparse representation. Finally, the class-wise reconstruction errors are calculated, and the class with the minimum reconstruction error is regarded as the label for the probe subject.

among the multiple measurements and imposing different constraints on the joint structured sparsity. Specifically, we investigate the following joint structured sparse priors: (i) same sparse codes model, (ii) common sparse pattern model and (iii) joint dynamic sparse model.

The rest of this chapter is organized as follows. Starting with a short discussion on multiple measurements based classification, we present several different models of joint structured sparsity prior for multi-sensor fusion in Section 5.2. Then applications on acoustic sensor fusion based event classification and multi-camera view based visual recognition are shown in Section 5.3.

5.2 Multiple-Measurement Classification with Joint Structured Sparsity

In many practical applications, we have access to multiple measurements of the same physical event [Malioutov *et al.* (2005); Wipf *et al.* (2010); Yang *et al.* (2009a)]. By making a joint classification decision using multiple measurements, we can potentially improve the classification accuracy. To handle multiple measurements in classification, the simplest idea would be to perform SRC method for each measurement separately and then make a final decision. Formally, given J measurements of the same physical event $\mathbf{Y} = [\mathbf{y}_1, \mathbf{y}_2, \cdots, \mathbf{y}_J] \in \mathbb{R}^{M \times J}$, we first make a classification decision for each measurement separately and then make a final decision based on the fusion of all the individual classification decisions:

$$\hat{i} = f\left(\left[\mathrm{SRC}(\mathbf{y}_1), \mathrm{SRC}(\mathbf{y}_2), \cdots, \mathrm{SRC}(\mathbf{y}_J) \right]^\top \right), \qquad (5.1)$$

where $f(\cdot)$ is a pooling function which takes a decision vector $\mathbf{d} = \left[\mathrm{SRC}(\mathbf{y}_1), \mathrm{SRC}(\mathbf{y}_2), \cdots, \mathrm{SRC}(\mathbf{y}_J) \right]^\top$ as input and outputs a single decision. One of the most widely used methods is majority voting: $f(\mathbf{d}) = \arg\max_i \sum_{j=1}^{J} \delta\big(\mathbf{d}(j), i\big)$, $i = 1, \cdots, C$, where $\delta(a, b) = 1$ if and only if $a = b$. $\mathbf{d}(j)$ denotes the j-th element of vector $\mathbf{d}$. However, in this method, the correlations among multiple measurements (joint structured sparsity prior) are not exploited until the postprocessing which is during the decision fusion process. By performing sparse representation separately for each measurement, the recovered sparse representation vectors may be quite different, as shown by a graphical illustration in Fig. 5.3 (a). Rather than doing post-processing during the decision fusion, it is more robust to recover the sparse representation vectors for the J measurements simultaneously by exploiting the correlations among the multiple measurements during the sparse representation process and then make a single decision based on the J sparse representation vectors jointly to reinforce their joint classification labels. We argue that the correlations among the multiple measurements can help with classification by imposing proper structural sparsity priors during the reconstruction.

In the following subsections, we exploit the correlations among the multiple measurements by imposing different joint structured sparsity constraints on their sparse coefficient vectors (as shown in Fig. 5.3 (b)–(d)), *i.e.*, using different joint structured sparsity priors for recovering their sparse representation vectors simultaneously. For classification, each model provides a decision based on a specific joint structured sparsity prior.

Joint sparsity is an effective prior for multiple-measurement signal recovery, sensor network perception and image restoration, as have been shown in [Mishali and Eldar (2008); Yang *et al.* (2009a); Mairal *et al.* (2009b)]. Here, we explore more advanced sparsity – joint structured sparsity, for classification. More detailed descriptions of our joint structured sparsity priors will be given in the following sections.

For ease of presentation, we first introduce some notations. Let $\mathbf{X} = [\mathbf{x}_1, \mathbf{x}_2, \cdots, \mathbf{x}_J] \in \mathbb{R}^{N \times J}$ be a coefficient matrix consisting of the J sparse representation vectors for the J measurements $\mathbf{Y} = \mathbf{AX}$ with respect to a common structured dictionary $\mathbf{A} = [\mathbf{A}^1, \mathbf{A}^2, \cdots, \mathbf{A}^C] \in \mathbb{R}^{M \times N}$. $\mathbf{X}(i,:)$ denotes the i-th row of matrix $\mathbf{X}$ and $\mathbf{X}(:,j)$ denotes its j-th column. Given a row-index vector $\mathbf{i}$, $\mathbf{X}(\mathbf{i},:)$ refers to the sub-matrix consisting of all the rows indexed by $\mathbf{i}$, while $\mathbf{X}(\mathbf{i}, j)$ denotes the column-vector formed by selecting the elements according to $\mathbf{i}$ from column vector $\mathbf{X}(:,j)$. Similarly, given a column-index vector $\mathbf{j}$, $\mathbf{X}(:,\mathbf{j})$ refers to the sub-matrix consisting of all the columns indexed by $\mathbf{j}$, while $\mathbf{X}(i,\mathbf{j})$ denotes the row-vector formed by selecting the elements according to $\mathbf{j}$ from the row-vector $\mathbf{X}(i,:)$. Given an index matrix $\mathbf{I} = [\mathbf{i}_1, \mathbf{i}_2, \cdots, \mathbf{i}_J] \in \mathbb{R}^{K \times J}$ as a collection of row-index vectors for all the J measurements, we denote $\mathbf{X}(\mathbf{I})$ as a short hand for the sub-matrix of $\mathbf{X}$ indexed by the index matrix $\mathbf{I}$: $\mathbf{X}(\mathbf{I}) = [\mathbf{X}(\mathbf{I}(:,1),1), \mathbf{X}(\mathbf{I}(:,2),2), \cdots, \mathbf{X}(\mathbf{I}(:,J),J)] = [\mathbf{X}(\mathbf{i}_1,1), \mathbf{X}(\mathbf{i}_2,2), \cdots, \mathbf{X}(\mathbf{i}_J,J)] \in \mathbb{R}^{K \times J}$. The j-th column of this sub-matrix is comprised of the sub-vector of the j-th column of $\mathbf{X}$ indexed by the j-th column of $\mathbf{I}$. $Z = \{1, \cdots, N\}$ denotes an index set referring to the rows of coefficient matrix $\mathbf{X}$ (equivalently, referring to the columns/atoms of structured dictionary $\mathbf{A}$), and $\mathbf{z} = [1, \cdots, N]^\top$ is an index vector referring to all the rows of $\mathbf{X}$. Given the class label vector $\mathbf{L}$ corresponding to $\mathbf{A}$, we define a class-index extraction operator as $\mathbf{z}_i = \text{find}(\mathbf{L}, i)$, returning the indices of $\mathbf{L}$ where its elements equal to i. We denote the complement of an index vector $\mathbf{z}_i$ as $\mathbf{z}_i^c$, *i.e.*, the sub-vector of $\mathbf{z}$ formed by removing all the elements in $\mathbf{z}_i$ from $\mathbf{z}$. Note that for ease of presentation, we have used a single common dictionary $\mathbf{A}$ here for sensor fusion. The extension to using multiple dictionaries for heterogeneous sensor fusion can be achieved straightforwardly in a fashion similar to [Zhang *et al.* (2011b,a)].

5.2.1 *Joint Structured Sparsity with Same Sparse Codes*

The most direct method to enforce joint structures on the multiple sparse representation vectors would be making the assumption that all the

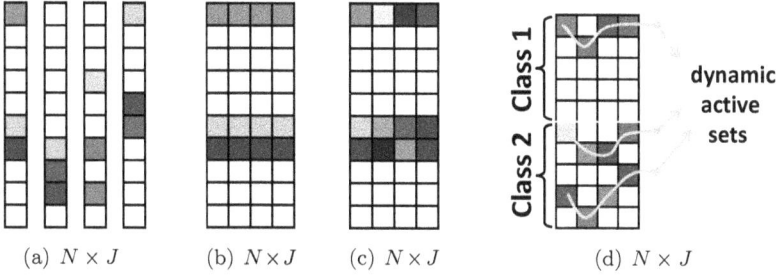

(a) $N \times J$ (b) $N \times J$ (c) $N \times J$ (d) $N \times J$

Fig. 5.3   Pictorial illustration of different sparsity models for coefficient matrix $\mathbf{X}$. Each column denotes a sparse representation vector and each squared block a coefficient value in the corresponding representation vector. A white block denotes zero entry value. Colored blocks denote entries with different non-zeros values. (a) separate sparse representation: the sparse representation vectors are not explicitly correlated and their sparse patterns may be quite different. (b) joint structured sparse representation with same sparse codes: all the representation vectors have equal values. (c) joint structured sparse representation with common sparse pattern: sparse coefficient vectors share similar patterns (selecting the same set of atoms), but with different coefficient values. (d) joint structured sparse representation with joint dynamic sparsity: the sparse coefficient vectors are only allowed to select different atoms within each sub-dictionary (class) referred to as *dynamic active sets* to represent each of the measurements.

measurements would have the same sparse representation vector with respect to a dictionary. To model this family of signals better, we can define a Same Sparse Codes (SSC) model to capture the above assumption formally as:

Definition 5.1. (Same Sparse Codes (SSC) model) Let $\mathbf{X} = [\mathbf{x}_1, \mathbf{x}_2, \cdots, \mathbf{x}_J]$ be the collection of the sparse representation vectors for the J-measurements, define the set of K-sparse signal ensemble with the same sparse codes as:

$$S_{SSC}^K = \left\{ \mathbf{X} = [\mathbf{x}_1, \mathbf{x}_2, \cdots, \mathbf{x}_J] \in \mathbb{R}^{N \times J}, \right.$$
$$\text{s.t.} \quad \mathbf{X}(r,:) = v_r \mathbf{1}^\top, \forall r \in \Omega, \quad \mathbf{X}(r,:) = \mathbf{0}^\top, \forall r \in \Omega^c,$$
$$\left. \Omega \subset Z, \quad |\Omega| = K \right\},$$

where Ω is the set of indices corresponding to the non-zero rows in $\mathbf{X}$ (*i.e.*, $\Omega = \{r | \mathbf{X}(r,:) = v_r \mathbf{1}^\top\}$) while Ω^c denotes the complementary set of Ω in Z (*i.e.*, $\Omega^c = \{r | \mathbf{X}(r,:) = \mathbf{0}^\top\}$). Furthermore, all the J elements in each non-zero row r of $\mathbf{X}$ (*i.e.*, $r \in \Omega$) are constrained to have exactly the same value v_r, thus all the columns of $\mathbf{X}$ are exactly the same: $\mathbf{x}_1 = \mathbf{x}_2 = \cdots = \mathbf{x}_J = \mathbf{x}$, as graphically illustrated in Fig. 5.3 (b).

Given multiple measurements $\mathbf{Y}$ which are assumed to be generated from SSC model, now the task is to recover their sparse representation coefficient matrix $\mathbf{X}$ with respect to $\mathbf{A}$. As shown below, this is equivalent to concatenating all the measurements for sparse representation, which is a conventional scheme to fuse multiple features and is extensively used in the classification literature [Yang *et al.* (2009c)]. By concatenating all the measurements to form a single large vector, we get a new form of test sample as $\bar{\mathbf{y}} = [\mathbf{y}_1^\top, \mathbf{y}_2^\top, \cdots, \mathbf{y}_J^\top]^\top \in \mathbb{R}^{JM}$. Correspondingly, we form a large concatenated dictionary as $\bar{\mathbf{A}} = [\mathbf{A}_1^\top, \mathbf{A}_2^\top, \cdots, \mathbf{A}_J^\top]^\top \in \mathbb{R}^{JM \times N}$, where each $\mathbf{A}_j$ can be constructed by the training samples from all the channels or constructed by the training samples from the corresponding j-th channel. By concatenating the multiple measurements, we in fact enforce all the measurements to have exactly the same sparse codes, *i.e.*, $\mathbf{x}_1 = \mathbf{x}_2 = \cdots = \mathbf{x}_J = \mathbf{x} \in \mathbb{R}^N$. This shared sparse representation vector $\mathbf{x}$ can then be recovered by solving the following single sparse representation problem using the concatenated test signal $\bar{\mathbf{y}}$ and the concatenated dictionary $\bar{\mathbf{A}}$ as:

$$\hat{\mathbf{x}} = \arg \min_{\mathbf{x}} \| \bar{\mathbf{y}} - \bar{\mathbf{A}}\mathbf{x} \|_{\ell_2}^2$$
$$\text{s.t.} \quad \| \mathbf{x} \|_{\ell_0} \leq K, \tag{5.2}$$

which has the same functional form as SRC and can be solved using CoSaMP algorithm [Needell and Tropp (2009)]. In each iteration, a K-sparse approximation is made based on the current residue, which is the key step and can be implemented via a simple sorting and hard thresholding operation with $\mathcal{O}(N \log(N))$ complexity, where N is the dimensionality of the sparse vector $\mathbf{x}$ [Needell and Tropp (2009)]. All the J measurements are assumed to follow the SSC model, therefore, the recovered sparse representation coefficient matrix is $\hat{\mathbf{X}} = [\hat{\mathbf{x}}_1, \hat{\mathbf{x}}_2, \cdots, \hat{\mathbf{x}}_J] = [\hat{\mathbf{x}}, \hat{\mathbf{x}}, \cdots, \hat{\mathbf{x}}]$.

Similar models have been previously used in the field of image restoration [Mairal *et al.* (2008c); Li and Fang (2010)], where the basic assumption is that the multiple observations of the same signal share the same sparse codes under their corresponding dictionaries. Although, it can reduce the degrees of freedom greatly, constraining all the observations/measurements to share the same sparse codes is a very strong requirement, which is often violated in typical classification problems. In the following, we will further discuss other models for exploiting the joint structured sparsity property among the multiple measurements. The J-SRC classifier using the same sparse codes model is denoted as J-SRC$_{\text{SSC}}$ in the sequel.

5.2.2   *Joint Structured Sparsity with Common Sparse Pattern*

The constraint that all the signals from the multiple measurements have exactly the same sparse codes is restrictive. Therefore, we can relax the same sparse codes assumption by assuming the multiple measurements share a common sparse pattern (*i.e.*, selecting the same set of atoms) in their sparse codes, but the values of the coefficients corresponding to the same atom may be different for different measurements. Specifically, this assumption allows all the J measurements to be represented by the same set of atoms selected from the dictionary, but weighed with different coefficient values. For the classification task, this is more practical than the same sparse codes assumption in the sense that: although highly correlated, different measurements are not likely to be exactly the same, thus the coefficient values of the sparse representation vector of one measurement can be different from that of another measurement, although a common sparsity pattern is shared by them. Formally, we have the following definition of the Common Sparse Pattern (CSP) model:

Definition 5.2. (Common Sparse Pattern (CSP) model) Let $\mathbf{X} = [\mathbf{x}_1, \mathbf{x}_2, \cdots, \mathbf{x}_J]$ be the collection of the sparse representation vectors for the J-measurements, define the set of K-sparse signal ensemble with common sparse pattern as:

$$S_{\text{CSP}}^K = \Big\{ \quad \mathbf{X} = [\mathbf{x}_1, \mathbf{x}_2, \cdots, \mathbf{x}_J] \in \mathbb{R}^{N \times J},$$
$$\text{s.t.} \quad \mathbf{X}(r,:) = \mathbf{v}_r^\top, \forall r \in \Omega, \quad \mathbf{X}(r,:) = \mathbf{0}^\top, \forall r \in \Omega^c,$$
$$\Omega \subset Z, \quad |\Omega| = K \quad \Big\},$$

where vector $\mathbf{v}_r \in \mathbb{R}^J$ represents the collection of coefficients for each of the J measurements associated with the r-th atom in the dictionary, which is active for representing all the J measurements.

Compared with the SSC model in Definition 5.1, the CSP model does not have the constraint on the coefficient values of the r-th row of coefficient matrix $\mathbf{X}$ (*i.e.*, $\mathbf{v}_r$) to be the same across all the measurements ($\mathbf{v}_r = v_r \mathbf{1}$), but keeps the constraint on the row-wise sparsity. A pictorial illustration of a typical sparsity pattern for coefficient matrix $\mathbf{X}$ using CSP model is given in Fig.5.3 (c). The sparse representation coefficient matrix $\mathbf{X}$ of the multiple measurements $\mathbf{Y}$ belonging to CSP model can be recovered by solving the following optimization problem with $\ell_0 \backslash \ell_2$ mixed-norm regularization [Tropp *et al.* (2006)] as:

$$\hat{\mathbf{X}} = \arg\min_{\mathbf{X}} \|\mathbf{Y} - \mathbf{A}\mathbf{X}\|_{\mathcal{F}}^2$$
$$\text{s.t.} \quad \|\mathbf{X}\|_{\ell_0\backslash\ell_2} \leq K,$$

(5.3)

where $\|\cdot\|_{\mathcal{F}}$ represents the Frobenius norm of a matrix. $\|\mathbf{X}\|_{\ell_0\backslash\ell_2}$ is called the $\ell_0\backslash\ell_2$-mixed-norm of matrix $\mathbf{X}$ which is obtained by first applying ℓ_2-norm on each row of $\mathbf{X}$ and then apply ℓ_0-norm on the resulting vector:

$$\|\mathbf{X}\|_{\ell_0\backslash\ell_2} = \left\| \left[\|\mathbf{X}(1,:)\|_{\ell_2}, \|\mathbf{X}(2,:)\|_{\ell_2}, \cdots \right] \right\|_{\ell_0}.$$

(5.4)

When used in multivariate regression as in (5.3), this norm promotes sparsity of the coefficient matrix $\mathbf{X}$ at row-level, thus all the J measurements are represented by the same set of atoms.

The rationale behind this method is that the multiple measurements are highly correlated, thus they tend to be represented by the same set of atoms, *i.e.*, sharing the same sparsity patterns. However, as mentioned above, due to the variation of environment and imperfection of the measurement process, all the J measurements are not exactly the same. Therefore, it is more reasonable to represent them with respect to the same set of atoms but weigh them with different coefficient values. Similar models have been previously used in Multiple-Measurement Vectors (MMV) for signal processing [Cotter *et al.* (2005); Duarte *et al.* (2005); Mishali and Eldar (2008, 2009)], addressing the problem of recovery of a set of sparse signal vectors that share a common non-zero support. The problem (5.3) involves $\ell_0\backslash\ell_2$ mixed-norm constrained minimization, which is NP-hard and is more challenging than the single sparse representation problem (1.4) due to the existence of multiple measurements. A few greedy algorithms have been proposed in the past to solve this problem, such as Simultaneous Orthogonal Matching Pursuit (SOMP) [Tropp *et al.* (2006)] and CoSOMP method [Duarte *et al.* (2009)], which is a multi-measurement generalization of CoSaMP [Needell and Tropp (2009)]. In these greedy algorithms, the basic idea is that at each iteration, a common candidate set for all the J measurements is chosen according to the sum of the total correlation values of all measurements with respect to each atom in the dictionary, and this procedure is iterated on the residual until certain conditions are satisfied. This atom selection step in each iteration can be implemented by sorting the rows of the coefficient matrix by their ℓ_2-norms and then selecting the rows with largest norm, which has the computational complexity of $\mathcal{O}(N\log(N) + JN)$ [Duarte *et al.* (2009)]. Note that the joint sparse representation problem can also be cast as a group lasso problem, with ℓ_1-relaxation [Yuan and Lin (2006); Rakotomamonjy (2010); Berg and Friedlander (2010)]. Here, we have chosen the CoSOMP [Duarte *et al.* (2009); Rakotomamonjy (2010)] greedy algorithm to solve (5.3) due to its efficiency as well as accuracy. We denote the joint sparse representation classifier using CSP model as J-SRC$_{\text{CSP}}$.

5.2.3 *Joint Dynamic Sparsity Prior*

Although the CSP model is more flexible than the SSC model, it still has some limitations. Since the dictionary is constructed from the training samples, the correlations between some of the atoms are very high, thus it is possible that each of the J measurements can be better represented by selecting different sets of atoms, but with the constraint that they belong to the same sub-dictionary (*i.e.*, the non-zero supports of the J sparse representation vectors for the J measurements are not exactly the same, but still belong to the same class). In other words, the J sparse representation vectors have the same sparsity pattern at class-level, but not necessarily at atom-level. Therefore, the restriction for all measurements to select the same set of atoms within a sub-dictionary as in CSP model is removed and now at each iteration each of the J measurements may select a different atom but the selected atoms are constrained to be from the same sub-dictionary. This will further reduce the reconstruction error and still enforce sparsity. We have named this model as the Joint Dynamic Sparsity (JDS) model for reasons that will be stated below. A graphical illustration of the JDS pattern is shown in Fig. 5.3 (d).

One of the key ingredients in the JDS model is the *dynamic active set*. A dynamic active set $\mathbf{g}_k \in \mathbb{R}^J$ refers to the indices of a set of coefficients associated with the same class in the coefficient matrix $\mathbf{X}$, which are activated jointly during sparse representation of multiple measurements. Each dynamic active set $\mathbf{g}_k$ contains one and only one index for each column of $\mathbf{X}$, where $\mathbf{g}_k(j)$ indexes the selected coefficient for the j-th column of $\mathbf{X}$, as shown in Fig. 5.3 (d). Assume there are K dynamic active sets involved in sparse representation, then there are K non-zero elements in the sparse representation vector for each measurement. We can collect all the dynamic active sets for $\mathbf{X}$ into an index matrix $\mathbf{I} \in \mathbb{R}^{K \times J}$ as:

$$\mathbf{I} = [\mathbf{g}_1, \mathbf{g}_2, \cdots, \mathbf{g}_k, \cdots, \mathbf{g}_K]^\top = [\mathbf{i}_1, \mathbf{i}_2, \cdots, \mathbf{i}_j, \cdots, \mathbf{i}_J], \tag{5.5}$$

where $\mathbf{i}_j \in \mathbb{R}^K$ is the index vector containing the indices through $\mathbf{g}_1 \sim \mathbf{g}_K$

for the j-th measurement, corresponding to the non-zero elements of the sparse representation vector $\mathbf{x}_j$. Using this notation, we can restate the SSC model and CSP model as follows. For SSC model, we enforce the constraint that $\mathbf{I}(k,:) = r\mathbf{1}^\top$ and $\mathbf{X}(r,:) = v_r\mathbf{1}^\top$, which means we not only require all the sparse representation vector to have the same non-zero patterns, but also require the non-zero values of $\mathbf{X}$ within the same row to be the same. The CSP model relaxes the above restriction by allowing the coefficient values in each row of $\mathbf{X}$ to be different, *i.e.*, $\mathbf{X}(r,:) = \mathbf{v}_r^\top$ and keeping only the constraint condition on the index set $\mathbf{I}(k,:) = r\mathbf{1}^\top$, *i.e.*, the elements in the same row of $\mathbf{I}$ are the same, indexing the same atom. In the JDS model, we have further relaxed the constraints in the CSP model to increase its representative power by allowing the elements of each row in $\mathbf{I}$ to be different but with the constraint that it is indexing the atoms belonging to the same class. The formal definition of JDS model is given in the following.

Definition 5.3. (Joint Dynamic Sparsity (JDS) model) Let $\mathbf{X} = [\mathbf{x}_1, \mathbf{x}_2, \cdots, \mathbf{x}_J]$ be the collection of the sparse representation vectors for the J-measurements, define the set of K-sparse signal ensemble with joint dynamic sparsity as:

$$S_{\text{JDS}}^K = \Big\{ \mathbf{X} = [\mathbf{x}_1, \mathbf{x}_2, \cdots, \mathbf{x}_J] \in \mathbb{R}^{N \times J},$$
$$\text{s.t.}\quad \mathbf{X}(\mathbf{I}(k,:)) = \mathbf{v}_k^\top, \mathbf{I}(k,:) = \mathbf{g}_k^\top, \forall k = 1, \cdots, K,$$
$$\mathbf{L}(\mathbf{g}_k(j_1)) = \mathbf{L}(\mathbf{g}_k(j_2)), \forall 1 \leq j_1, j_2 \leq J$$
$$\mathbf{X}(\mathbf{I}^c(\tilde{k},:)) = \mathbf{0}^\top, \quad \forall \tilde{k} = 1, \cdots, N - K \Big\}.$$

Recall that $\mathbf{L} \in \mathbb{R}^N$ is the label vector for the atoms in the structured dictionary $\mathbf{A}$. $\mathbf{I}^c = [\mathbf{i}_1^c, \mathbf{i}_2^c, \cdots, \mathbf{i}_J^c] \in \mathbb{R}^{(N-K) \times J}$ is an index matrix of the zero elements in $\mathbf{X}$, and $\mathbf{i}_j^c$ is a vector consisting of the indices of the zero elements for the jth column of matrix $\mathbf{X}$. Up to now, it is easy to see that for both SSC and CSP models they will have a fixed active set of selected atoms defined by a single row of coefficient matrix $\mathbf{X}$ (*i.e.*, $\mathbf{I}(k,:) = r\mathbf{1}^\top$); while for the JDS model, the active set is not restricted to the same row of $\mathbf{X}$ but is relaxed to the same class, *i.e.*, $\mathbf{I}(k,:) = \mathbf{g}_k^\top$, $\mathbf{L}(\mathbf{g}_k(j_1)) = \mathbf{L}(\mathbf{g}_k(j_2))$, $\forall 1 \leq j_1, j_2 \leq J$, thus JDS model is dynamic and more flexible than SSC and CSP models.

To combine the strength of all the atoms within a dynamic active set (thus across all the measurements), we apply ℓ_2-norm over each dynamic active set, and to promote sparsity, *i.e.*, to allow a small number of dynamic active sets to be involved in joint sparse representation, we apply ℓ_0-norm across the ℓ_2-norm of the dynamic active sets. Therefore, we define the following joint dynamic sparsity matrix regularization term:

$$\|\mathbf{X}\|_G = \left\| \left[\|\mathbf{x}_{\mathbf{g}_1}\|_{\ell_2}, \|\mathbf{x}_{\mathbf{g}_2}\|_{\ell_2}, \cdots \right] \right\|_{\ell_0}, \tag{5.6}$$

where $\mathbf{x}_{\mathbf{g}_k}$ denotes the vector formed by collecting the coefficients associated with the k-th dynamic active set $\mathbf{g}_k$: $\mathbf{x}_{\mathbf{g}_k} = \mathbf{X}(\mathbf{I}(k,:))^\top = \left[\mathbf{X}(\mathbf{g}_k(1),1), \mathbf{X}(\mathbf{g}_k(2),2), \cdots, \mathbf{X}(\mathbf{g}_k(J),J) \right]^\top \in \mathbb{R}^J$.

To recover the sparse representation coefficient matrix $\mathbf{X}$ with the joint dynamic sparsity constraint for the multiple measurement matrix $\mathbf{Y}$, we can use the following formulation:

$$\hat{\mathbf{X}} = \arg\min_{\mathbf{X}} \|\mathbf{Y} - \mathbf{AX}\|_{\mathcal{F}}^2$$
$$\text{s.t.} \quad \|\mathbf{X}\|_G \leq K. \tag{5.7}$$

Algorithm 5.1 Joint Dynamic Sparse Representation (JDSR).

Require: multi-measurement matrix $\mathbf{Y}$, structured dictionary $\mathbf{A}$, sparsity level K, number of measurements J

1: **Initialize: $\mathbf{R} \leftarrow \mathbf{Y}$, $\mathbf{I} \leftarrow \emptyset$**
2: WHILE stopping criteria false DO
3:      $\mathbf{E} = \mathbf{A}^\top \mathbf{R}$ % compute correlation matrix
4:      $\mathbf{I}_{\text{new}} \leftarrow \mathbb{P}_{\text{JDS}}(\mathbf{E}, 2K)$ % **(i)** select atoms via joint dynamic sparse mapping
5:      $\mathbf{I} \leftarrow [\mathbf{I}^\top, \mathbf{I}_{\text{new}}^\top]^\top$ % **(ii)** update index matrix
6:      $\mathbf{B} \leftarrow \mathbf{0}$
7:      For $j = 1, 2, \cdots, J$ % **(iii)** update representation coefficients
8:          $\mathbf{i} \leftarrow \mathbf{I}(:,j)$
9:          $\mathbf{B}(\mathbf{i},j) \leftarrow (\mathbf{A}(:,\mathbf{i})^\top \mathbf{A}(:,\mathbf{i}))^{-1} \mathbf{A}(:,\mathbf{i})^\top \mathbf{Y}(:,j)$
10:      $\mathbf{I} \leftarrow \mathbb{P}_{\text{JDS}}(\mathbf{B}, K)$ % **(iv)** prune atoms via joint dynamic sparse mapping

11:      $\mathbf{X} \leftarrow \mathbf{0}$
12:      For $j = 1, 2, \cdots, J$
13:          $\mathbf{i} \leftarrow \mathbf{I}(:,j), \quad \mathbf{X}(\mathbf{i},j) \leftarrow \mathbf{B}(\mathbf{i},j)$
14:      $\mathbf{R} = \mathbf{Y} - \mathbf{AX}$ % **(v)** update residue
15: END WHILE

Ensure: Sparse coefficients matrix $\mathbf{X}$.

Algorithm 5.2 Joint Dynamic Sparsity Mapping $\mathbb{P}_{\mathrm{JDS}}(\mathbf{Z}, L)$.

Require: coefficient matrix $\mathbf{Z}$, desired number of dynamic active sets L, label vector $\mathbf{L}$ for atoms in the dictionary, number of classes C, number of measurements J

1: **Initialize:** $\mathbf{I}_L \leftarrow \emptyset$ % initialize the index matrix as empty

2: **For** $j = 1, 2, \cdots, L$

3:      $\mathbf{c} \leftarrow \mathrm{find}(\mathbf{L}, i)$ % get the index vector for the i-th class

4:      **For** $j = 1, 2, \cdots, J$ % **(i)** find the maximum absolute value v and its index t for the i-th class, j-th measurement

5:          $[v, t] \leftarrow \max(|\mathbf{Z}(\mathbf{c}, j)|)$

6:          $\mathbf{V}(i, j) \leftarrow v, \quad \tilde{\mathbf{I}}(i, j) \leftarrow \mathbf{c}(t)$

7:      $\mathbf{s}(i) \leftarrow \sqrt{\sum_{j=1}^{J} \mathbf{V}(i, j)^2}$ % **(ii)** combine the max-coefficients for each class

8:      $[\hat{v}, \hat{t}] = \max(\mathbf{s})$ % **(iii)** find the best cluster of atoms belonging to the same class across all the classes

9:      $\mathbf{I}_L(l, :) = \tilde{\mathbf{I}}(\hat{t}, :), \quad \mathbf{Z}(\tilde{\mathbf{I}}(\hat{t}, :)) \leftarrow \mathbf{0}^{\top}$.

Ensure: index matrix $\mathbf{I}_L$ for the top-L dynamic active sets

---

Problem (5.7) is even more challenging to solve than (5.3) due to the co-existence of ℓ_0-norm and the joint dynamic property induced by $\mathbf{I}$. We can solve the problem (5.7) by a greedy algorithm referred to as Joint Dynamic Sparse Representation (JDSR), which is described in detail in the Algorithm 5.1. The algorithm has a similar algorithmic structure as SOMP [Tropp *et al.* (2006)] and CoSOMP [Duarte *et al.* (2009)], which includes the following general steps: (i) select new candidates based on the current residue; (ii) merge the newly selected candidate set with previous selected atom set; (iii) estimate the representation coefficients based on the merged atom set; (iv) prune the merged atom set to a specified sparsity level based on the newly estimated representation coefficients; (v) update the residue. This procedure is iterated until certain conditions are satisfied. The major difference of our algorithm with CoSOMP [Duarte *et al.* (2009)] lies in the atom selection criteria as outlined in steps (i) and (iv) of Algorithm 5.1, which is detailed in the sequel.

At each iteration of JDSR (Algorithm 5.1), given a coefficient matrix $\mathbf{Z} \in \mathbb{R}^{N \times J}$, we need to select L most representative dynamic active sets from $\mathbf{Z}$ (this is done in steps (i) and (iv) of Algorithm 5.1), *i.e.*, constructing the best approximation $\hat{\mathbf{Z}}_L$ to $\mathbf{Z}$ with L dynamic active sets (*i.e.*, $\|\hat{\mathbf{Z}}_L\|_G = L$). This approximation can be obtained as the solution to the following problem:

$$\hat{\mathbf{Z}}_L = \arg \min_{\mathbf{Z} \in \mathbb{R}^{N \times J}} \|\mathbf{Z} - \mathbf{Z}_L\|_{\mathcal{F}}$$

$$\text{s.t} \quad \|\mathbf{Z}_L\|_G \leq L.$$

(5.8)

The dynamic active sets corresponding to the solution to (5.8) can be obtained by a procedure called the Joint Dynamic Sparsity mapping (JDS mapping):

$$\mathbf{I}_L = \mathbb{P}_{\text{JDS}}(\mathbf{Z}, L), \tag{5.9}$$

which provides an index matrix $\mathbf{I}_L \in \mathbb{R}^{L \times J}$ for all the J measurements corresponding to the top-L dynamic active sets. The implementation of this mapping is detailed in Algorithm 5.2. In each iteration of JDS mapping, it will select a new dynamic active set. This is achieved via three steps: (i) for each measurement, find the maximum absolute coefficient for each class; (ii) combine the maximum absolute coefficients across the measurements for each class as the total response; (iii) select the dynamic active set as the one which gives the maximum total response. After a dynamic active set is determined, we keep a record of the selected indices as a row of $\mathbf{I}_L$ and set their associated coefficients in the coefficient matrix to be zero in order to ensure that none of the coefficients will be selected again. This procedure is iterated until the specified number (L) of dynamic active sets are determined. After that, $\hat{\mathbf{Z}}_L$ can be obtained as $\hat{\mathbf{Z}}_L(\mathbf{I}_L(l,:)) = \mathbf{Z}(\mathbf{I}_L(l,:))$, $\forall 1 \leq l \leq L$, *i.e.*, keeping the values of the selected entries and setting the remaining entries to be zero. As mentioned above, Algorithm 5.2 is used as a sub-routine in Algorithm 5.1 for selection of active sets at each iteration of Algorithm 5.1 and this active set selection process is repeated on the residue until certain conditions are satisfied [Needell and Tropp (2009)].

The joint structured sparse classifier with joint dynamic sparsity model is denoted as J-SRC$_{\text{JDS}}$ in the sequel. Note that in ideal case, if the J measurements share the same sparse pattern, which is valid for both SSC and CSP models, then only K atoms are selected which are shared by all the measurements and the total number of non-zeros values in the recovered coefficient matrix $\mathbf{X}$ is JK; however, in the case where multiple measurements do not share the same atom-level sparsity patterns (may be partially similar), the total number of non-zeros values in the recovered coefficient matrix $\mathbf{X}$ will still be JK but the number of selected atoms $\hat{K}$ overall may be larger than K. The actual number of distinct atoms satisfy $K \leq \hat{K} \leq JK$. However, we still refer to K as the sparsity level of the JDS model.

Essentially, the JDS model implies that for J measurements, rather than restricting the dynamic active set to a single row of the coefficient matrix $\mathbf{X}$, we can relax this to allow the dynamic active set to belong to J-different row-indices of $\mathbf{X}$ (which corresponds to selecting different atoms from $\mathbf{A}$ for each measurement), as long as these selected atoms belong to the same class. By using dynamic active set idea in the JDSR algorithm, the recovered sparse representation vectors will share the same sparsity pattern at class-level but do not necessarily have the same sparsity pattern at atom-level, as shown in Fig. 5.3 (d).

5.2.4   *Classification with Joint Structured Sparse Representation*

After recovering the sparse representation coefficient matrix $\hat{\mathbf{X}}$ using any of the joint structured sparsity models for the multi-measurement data matrix $\mathbf{Y}$, we can estimate the class label based on $\hat{\mathbf{X}}$. Similar to the single measurement case, where minimal reconstruction residual vector criteria is used, we can use the minimum reconstruction residual matrix criteria for final class label estimation as:

$$\hat{i} = \arg\min_{i} \| \mathbf{Y} - \mathbf{A}\delta^{i}(\hat{\mathbf{X}}) \|_{\mathcal{F}}^{2}. \tag{5.10}$$

The usage of Frobenius norm $\|\cdot\|_{\mathcal{F}}$ allows us to make a decision based on the total reconstruction error from all the measurements. Here we overload $\delta^{i}(\cdot)$ to denote the operation of preserving the rows of matrix $\hat{\mathbf{X}}$ corresponding to class i and setting all others to be zero. The overall procedure of joint structured sparsity based classification method is summarized in Algorithm 5.3.

Algorithm 5.3 Joint Structured Sparse Representation based Classification.

Require: observation set $\mathbf{Y}$, dictionary $\mathbf{A}$, sparsity level K

1: **Perform** Joint Structured Sparse Representation : $\hat{\mathbf{X}} = \mathrm{JSR}(\mathbf{A}, \mathbf{Y}, K)$

2: **Perform** reconstruction: $\hat{\mathbf{Y}}_{i} = \mathbf{A}\delta^{i}(\hat{\mathbf{X}})$

3: **Calculate** residue matrix: $\mathbf{E}_{i} = \mathbf{Y} - \hat{\mathbf{Y}}_{i}$;

4: **Infer** class label: $\hat{i} = \arg\min_{i} \|\mathbf{E}_{i}\|_{\mathcal{F}}^{2}$

Ensure: class label $\hat{i}$

5.3 Application: Multi-Channel Acoustic Sensor Fusion based Classification

In this section, we show the application of the joint structured sparse model for acoustic sensor fusion based event classification.

5.3.1 *Experiment Setups*

5.3.1.1 *Data Description*

The transient acoustic data is collected for launch and impact of different weapons (mortar and rocket) using the acoustic sensor array (see Fig. 5.1). For each event, the sensor array records the signal from a launch/impact event using 4 acoustic sensors simultaneously, where the sampling rate is 1001.6 Hz. Overall, we have 4 data sets: CRAM04, CRAM05, CRAM06 which were collected on different years, and another data set called Foreign containing acoustic signals of foreign weapons [Mirelli *et al.* (2009)].

5.3.1.2 *Segmentation*

The event can occur at arbitrary location of the raw acoustic signal. To extract salient information for classification, we first segment the raw signal with spectral maximum detection [Engelberg and Tadmor (2008)] and then extract appropriate features from those segmented signals. In our experiments, we take a segment with 1024 sampling points, which corresponds to roughly 1 seconds of transient acoustic signal.

5.3.1.3 *Feature Extraction*

We use Cepstral features [Childers *et al.* (1977)] for classification, which have been proven to be effective in speech recognition and acoustic signal classification. We discard the first Cepstral coefficient and keep the following 50 Cepstral coefficients, thus the feature dimension $M = 50$. To evaluate the effectiveness of the presented method, we compare the results with several classical algorithms, such as NN, Nearest Subspace method (NS) [Lee *et al.* (2005)], linear multinomial Logistic Regression [Bishop *et al.* (2006)], Linear SVM and Kernel SVM [Cristianini and Shawe-Taylor (2004)]. One-vs-all scheme is used for SVM in the case of multi-class classification. As for Kernel SVM, we use RBF kernel with band width selected via cross validation, which has been reported to generate *state-of-the-art* results for acoustic signal based weapon classification task [Mirelli *et al.*

Table 5.1   Multi-channels signal classification results.

Method	04	05	06	Foreign	Avg.
NN	0.7115	0.6131	0.6477	0.6909	0.6658
NS	0.7216	0.7403	0.6200	0.7199	0.7004
Logistic	0.7420	0.7437	0.6928	0.7495	0.7320
SVM	0.7314	0.7264	0.6968	0.7629	0.7294
Kernel SVM	0.7669	0.7648	0.7437	0.8036	0.7698
SRC	0.7847	0.7671	0.7423	0.7831	0.7693
J-SRC$_{\text{SSC}}$	0.8032	0.7778	0.7474	0.7812	0.7774
J-SRC$_{\text{CSP}}$	0.8036	0.7847	0.7431	0.7960	0.7818
J-SRC$_{\text{JDS}}$	**0.8092**	**0.7935**	**0.7704**	**0.8047**	**0.7944**

(2009)]. Results for SVM and SRC are obtained as the average performances from all the channels when operating independently. We set the maximum number of iterations to 10 as the stopping criteria for the sparse representation algorithms for all the sparsity based classification methods (SRC, J-SRC$_{\text{Prox}}$, J-SRC$_{\text{SSC}}$, J-SRC$_{\text{CSP}}$ and J-SRC$_{\text{JDS}}$) and set the sparsity level $K = 15$, which gives good results while maintaining computational efficiency.

5.3.2   *Results*

We test the algorithms on a 4-class classification problem, where we want to make inference on whether the event is launch or impact and what kind of weapon it is (mortar or rocket). This is a much more challenging problem. Similarly, we perform 5 rounds of $\lceil \frac{1}{r} \rceil$-fold cross validation with training ratio $r = 0.5$ and report the average performance for each data set, respectively, as well as the overall average classification accuracy and computational time for each test sample in Table 5.1. Here we have similar observations: both SRC and J-SRC outperform Logistic Regression and linear SVM by a notable margin, and generally, the J-SRC methods outperform other methods. Overall, the J-SRC$_{\text{JDS}}$ method performs the best on this data set.

5.4   Application: Multi-View Face Recognition

In this section, we will apply joint structured sparse models for multi-view face recognition. In reality, it is often the case that due to the variation of observation conditions (*e.g.*, viewpoint, illumination), each view can be better represented by a *different* set of samples but from the *same* classsubdictionary, *i.e.*, sharing the same sparsity pattern at class-level, but not necessarily at atom-level. Therefore, the desired sparse representation vectors for the multiple observations should share the same class-level sparsity pattern while their atom-level sparsity patterns may be distinct, *i.e.*, following joint dynamic sparsity. In the following, we will use the Joint Dynamic Sparse Representation base Classification (JDSRC) method as introduced earlier for face recognition, and compare it with several state-of-the-art methods.

Experiments are conducted on the CMU Multi-PIE database [Gross *et al.* (2008)], which contains a large number of face images under different illuminations, view points and expressions, up to 4 sessions over the span of several months. Subjects were imaged under 20 different illumination conditions, using 13 cameras at head height, spaced at 15° intervals. Illustrations for the multiple camera configurations as well as the captured multi-view images are shown in Figure 5.4. We use the multi-view face images with neutral expression under varying illuminations for 129 subjects for experiment, which are present in all the 4 sessions. The face regions for all the poses are extracted manually and are resized to 30×23. The images captured from all the 13 different poses with the view angles $\Theta = \{0°, \pm15°, \pm30°, \pm45°, \pm60°, \pm75°, \pm90°\}$ are used for experiment. We compare the presented method with classical Mutual Subspace Method (MSM) [Fukui and Yamaguchi (2005)], *state-of-the-art* Graph-based image set recognition method [Kokiopoulou and Frossard (2010)] as well as SRC [Wright *et al.* (2009)] method with majority voting. Method using joint sparsity prior as shown in Figure 5.3 (b) is not used for comparison in our experiments, as assuming that the multiple testing views can be represented by the same set of atoms is very restrictive and not appropriate for multi-view face recognition where large pose variation may exist between different views. We set the sparsity level $K = 11$ for SRC and $K = 15$ for JDSRC in all our experiments, and these sparsity levels were empirically found to provide best results generally. Random projection is used for dimensionality reduction [Wright *et al.* (2009)] in our experiments.

5.4.1 *Face Recognition with Increasing Number of Views*

In this subsection, we examine the effectiveness of using multiple views for face recognition. We first examine the face recognition performance using a single face image captured from different viewpoints. In this experiment, training images are from Session 1 using view-subset $\Theta_{\text{train}} = \{0°, \pm30°, \pm60°, \pm90°\}$, while testing images are generated from Session 2

(a) Multi-view Camera Configuration

(b) Example Multi-view Face Images

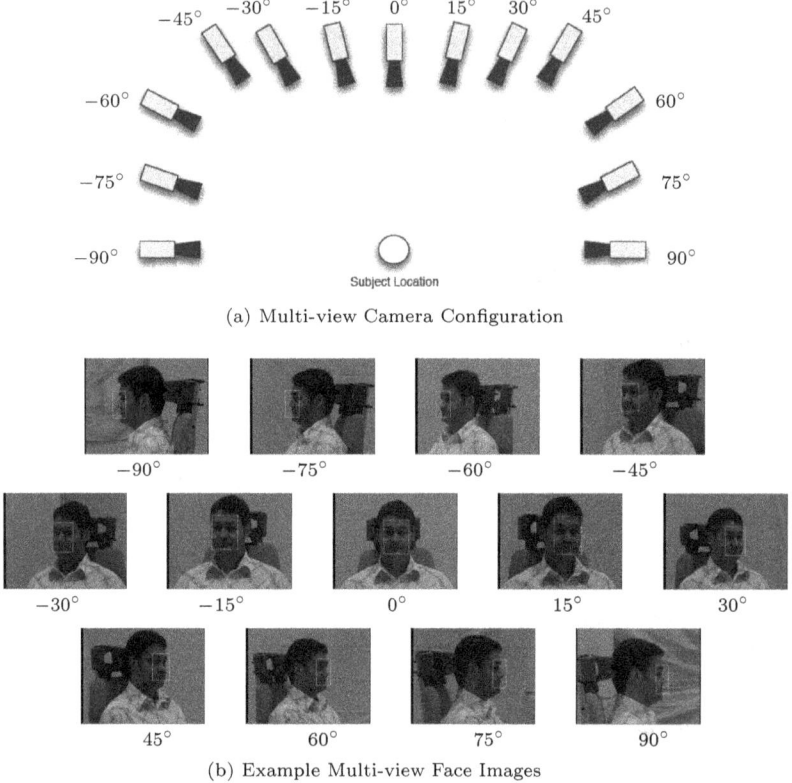

Fig. 5.4 Illustration of the multi-view face images. (a) The configurations of the 13 head-height cameras in Multi-PIE and (b) example multi-view face images captured using the multi-camera configuration shown in (a).

from all the views $\Theta_{test} = \Theta$. This is a more realistic and challenging setting in the sense that the data sets used for training and testing are collected separately and even not all the poses in the testing sets are available for training. To generate a test sample with M views, we first randomly select a subject $i \in \{1, 2, \cdots, 129\}$ from the test set and then select $M \in \{1, 2, 3, 4, 5, 6, 7\}$ different views randomly from Θ_{test} captured at the same time instance for subject i. 2000 test samples are generated with this scheme for testing. The recognition results on Session 2 of Multi-PIE database with $d = 64$ are summarized in Table 5.2 and the corresponding plots are shown in Figure 5.5 (a). It is demonstrated that the multi-view based methods ($M > 1$) outperform their single-view counterparts ($M = 1$) by a large margin, indicating the advantage of using multiple views in face

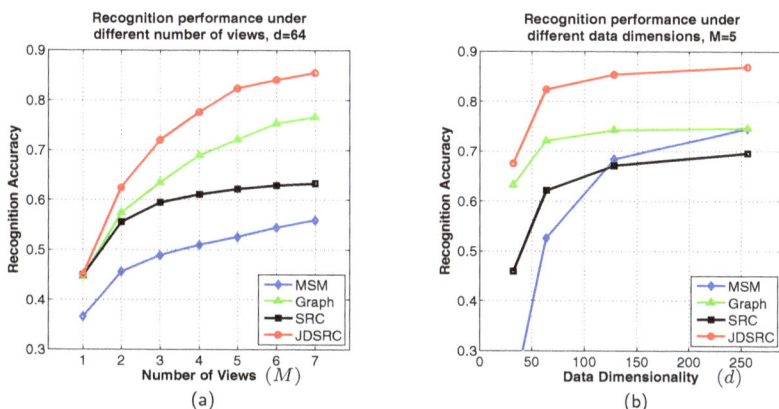

Fig. 5.5 Recognition rate under (a) different number of views with $d = 64$ and (b) different feature dimensions with $M = 5$.

recognition task. This is natural to expect as face images from different views offer complementary information for recognition. Therefore, by combining the face images from different views properly, we can potentially achieve better recognition performance than that of just using a single view face image. Also, it is noted that the performance of all the algorithms improves as the number of views is increased. Furthermore, the presented method outperforms all the other methods under all the different number of views when $M > 1$, which indicates that it is more effective in exploiting the inter-correlation between the multiple views for achieving a joint classification.

Table 5.2 Recognition rate (%) under different number of views ($C = 129, d = 64$).

View (M)	MSM	Graph	SRC	JDSRC
1	36.5	44.5	**45.0**	**45.0**
3	48.9	63.4	59.5	**72.0**
5	52.5	72.0	62.2	**82.3**
7	55.9	76.5	63.3	**84.5**

5.4.2 Face Recognition under Different Feature Dimensions

In this subsection, we further examine the effects of data (feature) dimensionality d on the recognition rate using Multi-PIE. The test samples are generated using $\Theta_{\text{train}} = \Theta$ with $M = 5$. Random projection is used for dimensionality reduction, which has been shown to be effective for face recognition in [Wright *et al.* (2009)]. We vary the data dimensionality in the range of $d \in \{32, 64, 128, 256\}$ and the plots in Figure 5.5 (b) give the performance of all the algorithms on Session 2 of Multi-PIE dataset. It is shown that MSM does not perform well when the dimensionality of feature is low. However, as the dimensionality of feature increases, its performance increases quickly. Graph based recognition method [Kokiopoulou and Frossard (2010)] performs relatively well under low dimensionality. However, its performance becomes saturated after $d > 64$. Similar saturation phenomenon can be observed for SRC. The presented method outperforms all the compared methods by a large margin and performs the best under all the examined dimensionality of features, which implies its effectiveness for multi-view face recognition task.

Table 5.3   Multi-view recognition rate (%) under different view-differences ($C = 129, d = 64, M = 5$).

View Subset	MSM	Graph	SRC	JDSRC
Same views	63.5	80.7	71.1	**87.5**
Mixed views	52.5	72.0	62.2	**82.3**
Different views	35.8	46.2	47.3	**66.5**

5.4.3   *Face Recognition in the Presence of View Difference between Training and Testing*

In the above experiments, we have used an experiment setup such that *not all* the testing viewpoints were used in the training process, *i.e.*, recognition performance was evaluated in the presence of view differences between training and testing. In this subsection, we further examine the effects of the view differences on the face recognition performance. Specifically, we examine the recognition performance of having images from a different set of viewpoints in testing where no gallery images are available from those views in the dictionary. We set $M = 5, d = 64$ and use images from Session 1 with the following view angles for training: $\Theta_{\text{train}} = \{0°, \pm30°, \pm60°, \pm90°\}$. 2000 test samples are generated following the same scheme as described in Section 5.4.1 but using the following three different view subset selection schemes in order to choose the test subsets: (1) same views as the training: $\Theta_{\text{s}} = \Theta_{\text{train}}$, (2) completely different views from the training: $\Theta_{\text{d}} = \Theta - \Theta_{\text{train}}$ and (3) mixed view sampling: $\Theta_{\text{m}} = \Theta$ (which is the setup used in Section 5.4.1). The recognition results of all the algorithms on Session 2 are presented in Table 5.3. As can be seen from Table 5.3, the presented method performs better under different range of view differences. The Graph based method [Kokiopoulou and Frossard (2010)] performs relatively well under the 'Same views' setting, which is much better than MSM and SRC. However, as the view difference between training and testing increases (from 'Same views' setting to 'Mixed views' setting and further to 'Different views' setting), Graph-based method [Kokiopoulou and Frossard (2010)] degenerates quickly, which implies its sensitivity to the view-differences between training and testing, thus it does not generalize well. The presented method, on the other hand, is much more robust to the view-differences and outperforms all the other methods significantly, thus is more suitable for real-world applications.

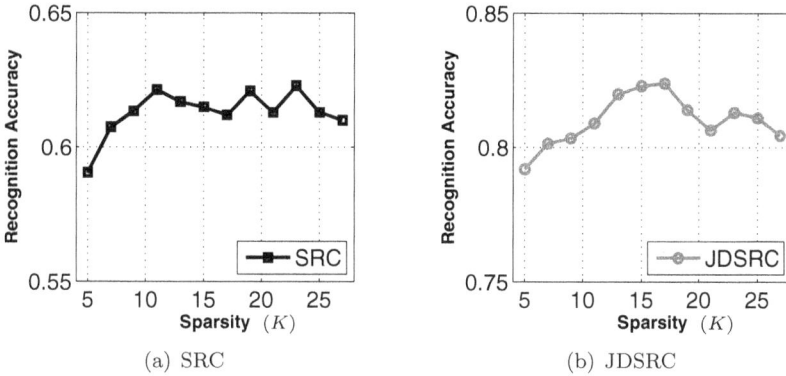

Fig. 5.6   Recognition rate with increasing sparsity level for (a) SRC and (b) JDSRC with $d = 64$ and $M = 5$.

5.4.4   *The Effects of Sparsity Level*

In the sparsity based recognition method, the sparsity level is an important factor on the recognition performance. In this subsection, we examine the effects of the sparsity level on the recognition performance of the sparsity based methods. $\Theta_{\text{train}} = \{0°, \pm30°, \pm60°, \pm90°\}$ is used as the training view subset and $\Theta_{\text{test}} = \Theta_{\text{m}}$ is the test view subset. We vary the sparsity level within the range $K \in \{5, 7, 9, \cdots, 25, 27\}$ and examine the recognition rate under each sparsity level for SRC and JDSRC. The recognition results with $d = 64$ and $M = 5$ on Session 2 are shown in Figure 5.6. It is noted that for both recognition methods, the recognition performance first increases with increasing level of sparsity K; when the sparsity level surpasses certain threshold, the recognition performance will decrease. The possible reason is that when the sparsity is larger than a certain level, more atoms from the incorrect classes are likely to be selected, thus deteriorating the classification performance. In our experiment, for a specific training view, there are 20 training images per-subject. Therefore, it is reasonable to expect the sparsity level of a test view be below this level, which is in accordance with the plots in Figure 5.6. This is the reason we set the sparsity level $K = 11$ for SRC and $K = 15$ for JDSRC respectively in all the experiments reported here, which give good performances.

5.4.5 *Face Recognition Across Different Sessions*

In the above experiments, we used the multi-view face images from Session 1 for training and the images from Session 2 for testing. To further evaluate the robustness of the presented method, we present the recognition results using multi-view face images from Session 1 for training and test on the images captured during several different sessions with the span of several months. Recognition results on Session 2 ∼ 4 data set with $M = 5$ and $d = 64$ are summarized in Table 5.4. It is demonstrated that this method outperforms all the other algorithms under different test sessions. Note that the time interval between Session 1 and other sessions increases with increasing session number, thus increasing the difficulties for face recognition. This explains the gap between the recognition performances of each algorithm on different test sessions.

Table 5.4   Multi-view face recognition rate (%) on different test sessions ($C = 129, d = 64, M = 5$).

Session	MSM	Graph	SRC	JDSRC
2	52.5	72.0	62.2	**82.3**
3	49.5	65.1	56.5	**77.1**
4	45.9	62.5	52.7	**73.1**

Chapter 6

Clustering

Clustering [Yang *et al.* (2014b)] plays an important role in many real world data mining applications. To learn the hidden patterns of the dataset in an unsupervised way, existing clustering algorithms can be described as either generative or discriminative in nature. Generative clustering algorithms model categories in terms of their geometric properties in feature spaces, or as statistical processes of data. Examples include K-means and Gaussian mixture model (GMM) clustering [Biernacki *et al.* (2000)], which assume a parametric form of the underlying category distributions. Discriminative clustering techniques search for the boundaries or distinctions between categories. With fewer assumptions being made, these methods are powerful and flexible in practice. For example, maximum-margin clustering [Xu *et al.* (2004)], [Xu and Schuurmans (2005)], [Zhao *et al.* (2008)] aims to find the hyperplane, that can separate the data from different classes with maximum margins. Information theoretic clustering [Li *et al.* (2004)], [Barber and Agakov (2005)] minimize the conditional entropy of all samples. Many recent discriminative clustering methods have achieved satisfactory performances [Zhao *et al.* (2008)].

Moreover, many clustering methods extract discriminative features from data prior to clustering. The Principal Component Analysis (PCA) feature is a common choice but not necessarily discriminative [Zheng *et al.* (2011)]. In [Roth and Lange (2003)], the features are selected for optimizing the discriminativity by Linear Discriminant Analysis (LDA). More recently, sparse codes prove to be both robust to noise and scalable to high dimensional data [Wright *et al.* (2009)]. Furthermore, ℓ^1-graph [Cheng *et al.* (2010)] builds the graph by reconstructing each data point sparsely and locally with other data. A spectral clustering [Ng *et al.* (2002)] is followed based on the constructed graph matrix. In [Sprechmann and Sapiro (2010)], dictionary learning is combined with the clustering process, which makes the use of Lloyd's algorithms that iteratively re-assign data to clusters and then optimize the dictionary associated with each cluster. In [Zheng *et al.* (2011)], the authors learned the sparse codes that explicitly consider the local data manifold structures. Their results indicate that encoding geometrical information will significantly enhance the learning performance. However, their clustering step is neither discriminative nor jointly optimized.

In the following, we will see how sparse coding can be used to find clusters with compact and descriptive latent structures.

6.1   Learning with ℓ^1-Graph for High Dimensional Data Analysis

An informative graph essentially determines the potentials of the vast graph-oriented learning algorithms in machine learning for high-dimensional data analysis. In this Chapter, we present a novel procedure to build the so called directed ℓ^1-graph, where the ingoing edge weights for each vertex is determined by its nonzero sparse reconstruction coefficients driven by ℓ^1-norm minimization with respect to the remaining data samples. Subsequently, a series of new algorithms for various machine learning applications, e.g., clustering, subspace learning, and semi-supervised learning, are developed based on this ℓ^1-graph. Compared with the conventional k-nn graph and ϵ-ball graph, our ℓ^1-graph possesses the following advantages: 1) not relying on the local neighborhood in high-dimensional spaces; 2) robustness to noise; and 3) adaptive sparsity. Extensive experiments on real-world datasets show the consistent superiority of ℓ^1-graph over those conventional graphs in high-dimensional data clustering, subspace learning, and semi-supervised learning tasks.

An informative graph, directed or undirected, is critical for those graph-orientated algorithms designed for data analysis, such as clustering, subspace learning, and semi-supervised learning. Data clustering often starts with a pairwise similarity graph and then translates into a graph partition problem [Shi and Malik (2000)], and thus the quality of the graph essentially determines the clustering quality. The pioneering works on manifold learning, e.g., ISOMAP [Tenenbaum *et al.* (2000)], Locally Linear Embedding (LLE) [Roweis and Saul (2000)], and Laplacian Eigenmaps [Belkin and Niyogi (2002)], all rely on different graphs reflecting the data similarities. Most popular subspace learning algorithms, e.g., Principal Component

Analysis (PCA) [Joliffe (1986)], Linear Discriminant Analysis (LDA) [Belhumeur *et al.* (1997)], and Locality Preserving Projections (LPP) [He and Niyogi (2003)], can all be explained within the graph embedding framework in [Yan *et al.* (2007)]. Also, most semi-supervised learning algorithms are driven by certain graphs constructed over both labeled and unlabeled data. Zhu et al. [Zhu *et al.* (2003)] explored the harmonic property of Gaussian random field over the graph for semi-supervised learning. Belkin and Niyogi [Belkin *et al.* (2004)] instead learned a regression function that fits the labels on the labeled data while preserving the smoothness of data manifold modeled by a graph.

There exist two popular ways for graph construction: the k-nearest-neighbor (k-nn) method and the ϵ-ball method. In k-nn graph construction, for each datum, its k-nearest-neighbor samples are connected with it, while in ϵ-ball graph construction, data samples falling into its ϵ-ball neighborhood are connected with it. Then various approaches, e.g, binary, Gaussian kernel [Belkin and Niyogi (2002)], or ℓ^2-reconstruction [Roweis and Saul (2000)], are used to determine the graph edge weights. Since the ultimate goals of the constructed graphs are for data analysis, the following graph characteristics are desired:

(1) **Similarity fidelity**. The desired graph should reflect the underlying relationships between data samples, i.e., data samples from the same class or cluster should be connected and not be connected otherwise.
(2) **Robustness to noise**. Noise and outliers are inevitable in practical applications, especially for visual data, and therefore, the graph construction procedure should be robust to such corruptions. The graph constructed based on k-nn or ϵ-ball method is founded on the pair-wise Euclidean distance, which is very sensitive to noise, especially in high dimensional spaces. That is, the graph structure is not stable with the presence of noise.
(3) **Adaptive sparsity**. Studies on manifold learning [Belkin and Niyogi (2002)] show that sparse graph can convey valuable information for classification purposes. Also for large-scale applications, sparse graphs are required due to the storage limitation. In real world scenarios, it is likely that data samples are not evenly sampled from the space. Therefore, we want to adaptively select the most likely kindred neighbors for each datum.

In this section, we are particularly interested in building an informative graph for data analysis in high dimensional spaces, where the data samples

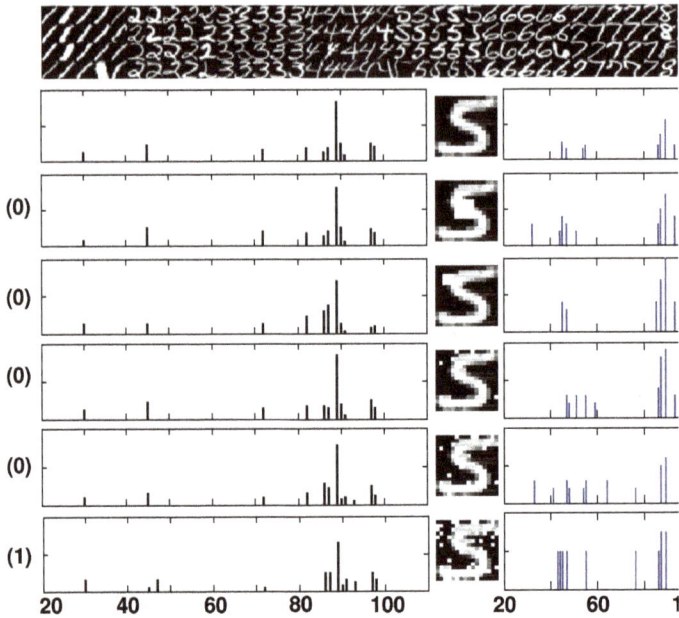

Fig. 6.1 Robustness comparison for neighbors selected by ℓ^1-graph and k-nn graph, where different levels of noise are added to the middle testing sample.

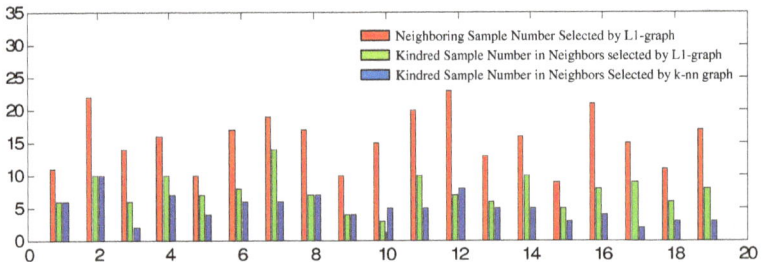

Fig. 6.2 The numbers of kindred neighbors selected by ℓ^1-graph and k-nn graph on 19 testing samples.

are sparsely distributed in the space and the local neighborhood becomes less and less useful for k-nn and ϵ-ball methods [Hastie *et al.* (2008)]. Empirically, many types of high dimensional data tend to lie in a union of low-dimensional linear subspaces [Wright *et al.* (2009)], where our ℓ^1-graph is of particular interest. In Section 6.1.1, we present the procedure to construct our robust ℓ^1-graph by taking advantage of the overall contextual information instead of only pairwise Euclidean distance as conventionally. The neighboring samples of a datum and their corresponding edges weights are simultaneously derived by solving an ℓ^1-norm minimization problem, where each datum is reconstructed by a sparse linear combination of the remaining samples and a noise term. Compared with graphs constructed by k-nn and ϵ-ball methods, the ℓ^1-graph can better recover the subspace structures in high dimensional spaces, is robust to noise, and can adaptively and sparsely choose the kindred neighbors. Figure 6.1 demonstrates the graph robustness comparison between our ℓ^1-graph and the k-nn graph. The first row illustrate some data samples from the USPS dataset [Hull (1994)]. The left column shows the edges weights in ℓ^1-graph; the middle row shows the current datum (noise added from the third row on); and the right column shows the edges wights in the k-nn graph. Here, the horizontal axes indicate the index number of the remaining data samples. The number in parenthesis of each row and column shows the number of neighbors changed compared with the noiseless results in the second row. As shown, our ℓ^1-graph shows much greater robustness to noise, compared with k-nn graph.[1] On the same dataset, figure 6.2 shows the kindred neighbor selection comparison between the ℓ^1-graph and k-nn graph on 19 testing samples. As shown, the ℓ^1-graph can adaptively and sparsely select the neighboring samples. The red bars indicate the numbers of the neighbors selected by ℓ^1-graph (weights are not considered here). The green bars indicates the numbers of kindred samples selected by ℓ^1-graph, while the blue bars indicate those selected by k-nn graph. Note that for the k-nn graph we adjust k based on the red bar number for each testing sample. Clearly, the ℓ^1-graph selects more kindred data samples than the k-nn graph, implying that our ℓ^1-graph better recovers the underlying data relationships.

This ℓ^1-graph is then utilized in Section 6.1.2 to instantiate a series of graph-oriented algorithms for various machine learning tasks, e.g., data clustering, subspace learning, and semi-supervised learning. Owing to the above advantages over classical graphs, the ℓ^1-graph brings consistent performance gain in all these tasks as detailed in Section 6.1.3.

6.1.1   *Rationales on ℓ^1-Graph*

We denote the training samples by a matrix $X = [x_1, x_2, \ldots, x_N], x_i \in \mathbb{R}^m$, where N is the sample number and m is the feature dimension. For

---

[1]We compare with k-nn graph only because ϵ-ball graph is generally inferior to k-nn graph in practice.

each x_i, we want to find its connections and weights with the remaining samples X/x_i, which will be represented as a graph. In this section, we discuss the motivation and construction procedure for our ℓ^1-graph. The graph construction includes both neighbor selection and graph edge weight assignment, which are assumed to be unsupervised in this work, without harnessing any data label information.

6.1.1.1 *Motivation*

The k-nn and ϵ-ball [Belkin and Niyogi (2002)] [Roweis and Saul (2000)] approaches are the two most popular ones for graph construction in the literature. Both of them determine the neighboring samples based on the *pairwise* Euclidean distance, which is, however, very sensitive to data noises, especially in high dimensional spaces, i.e, the graph structure may dramatically changes with the presence of noise. Also, both methods are based on the local neighborhood on the data manifold, which becomes less and less useful in high dimensional feature spaces due to the curse of dimensionality [Hastie *et al.* (2008)]. Moreover, both k-nn and ϵ-ball methods are prone to overfitting or underfitting when data samples are not evenly distributed, i.e., the global parameter k and ϵ may be too large for some data samples while too small for other samples. To avoid the above limitations of the conventional graph construction methods, we present a novel way of graph construction based on seeking the sparse representations of the data samples by ℓ^1-norm minimization, and thus the new graph is termed ℓ^1-graph.

Our ℓ^1-graph is motivated by the recent advances in sparse representation [Donoho (2006b); Meinshausen and Bühlmann (2006); Wright *et al.* (2009)] for high dimensional data analysis. The quest for sparse representation has a long history in signal processing [Rubinstein *et al.* (2010)]. Recent studies show that sparse representation [Olshausen and Field (1998)] appears to be biologically plausible as well as essential for high dimensional signal recovery [Candès (2006)] [Elad and Aharon (2006)] and effective for pattern recognition [Wright *et al.* (2009)]. In particular, Wright et al. [Wright *et al.* (2009)] proposed to perform face recognition by seeking a robust sparse representation of the test sample with respect to the training samples from all classes. Inspecting which classes those non-zero coefficients fall into reveals the identity of the test sample. The rationale behind this work is to assume that human faces lie in a union of low dimensional linear subspaces for different subjects, and the sparse representation through ℓ^1-

norm minimization can correctly identify which linear subspace a testing sample belongs to. In this work, we generalize this observation from faces [Wright *et al.* (2009)] to more general high dimensional data types, where the data approximately distributes as a union of low dimensional linear subspaces, and we show that building a graph based on such sparse representations is very effective for many graph-orientated machine learning algorithms.

6.1.1.2 *Robust Sparse Representation*

Much interest has been shown in seeking sparse representations with respect to an overcomplete dictionary of the basis elements in signal processing [Rubinstein *et al.* (2010)] [Candès (2006)] [Elad and Aharon (2006)] and pattern recognition [Wright *et al.* (2009)]. Suppose we have an underdetermined system of linear equations: $x = D\alpha$, where $x \in \mathbb{R}^m$ is the vector to be represented, $\alpha \in \mathbb{R}^n$ is the unknown reconstruction coefficients, and $D \in \mathbb{R}^{m \times n}(m < n)$ is the overcomplete dictionary with n bases. Among the infinite many solutions to the above underdetermined linear system, we are interested in the sparsest solution, i.e., the one with the fewest non-zero coefficients.

$$\min_{\alpha} \|\alpha\|_0, \quad s.t. \quad x = D\alpha. \tag{6.1}$$

where the ℓ^0-norm $\| \cdot \|_0$ counts the number of nonzero entries in a vector. It is well known that the above optimization is NP-hard in general case. However, recent results [Donoho (2006b)] show that if the solution is sparse enough, the sparse representation can be approximated by the following convex ℓ^1-norm relaxation,

$$\min_{\alpha} \|\alpha\|_1, \quad s.t. \quad x = D\alpha, \tag{6.2}$$

which can be solved efficiently by linear programming [Chen *et al.* (2001)]. In practice, there may exist noise on certain elements of x. In order to recover these elements and provide a robust estimation of α, we can reformulate

$$x = D\alpha + \zeta + \xi = \begin{bmatrix} D \ I \end{bmatrix} \begin{bmatrix} \alpha \\ \zeta \end{bmatrix} + \xi, \tag{6.3}$$

where $\zeta \in \mathbb{R}^m$ is a sparse error term and $\xi \in \mathbb{R}^m$ denotes a Gaussian noise term. Then by setting $B = \begin{bmatrix} D \ I \end{bmatrix} \in \mathbb{R}^{m \times (m+n)}$ and $\alpha' = \begin{bmatrix} \alpha \\ \zeta \end{bmatrix}$, we can solve the following ℓ^1-norm minimization to recover the sparse representation,

$$\min_{\alpha'} \|\alpha'\|_1, \quad s.t. \quad \|x - B\alpha'\|_2^2 \le \epsilon, \tag{6.4}$$

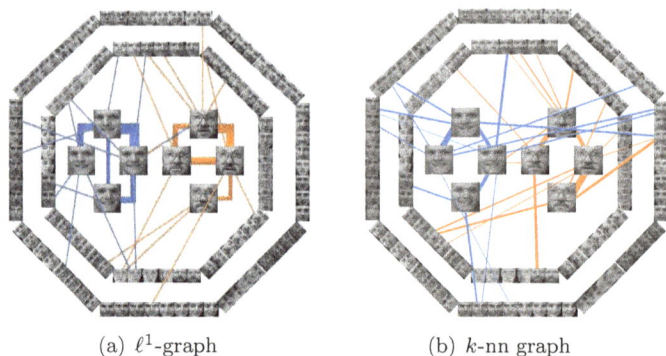

(a) ℓ^1-graph   (b) k-nn graph

Fig. 6.3   Visualization comparison of (a) the ℓ^1-graph and (b) the k-nn graph. The thickness of the edge lines indicates the edge weights. Gaussian kernel is used for the k-nn graph. For ease of display, we only show the graph edges related to the samples from two classes, where in total 30 classes from the YALE-B database are used for graph construction.

This optimization problem is convex can be readily solved by many optimization toolboxes [Donoho *et al.* (2007)]. It has been shown that even with the presence of noise on x, Eqn 6.4 can correctly recover the underlying sparse representation (and thus can denoise x).

6.1.1.3 ℓ^1-*graph Construction*

The ℓ^1-graph characterizes the overall behavior of the entire sample set by their sparse representations. The construction procedure is formally summarized in Algorithm 6.1. Figure 6.3 illustrates the ℓ^1-graph constructed on the data samples from YALE-B face database [Lee *et al.* (2005)]. As shown, the ℓ^1-graph indeed better connects those kindred samples for faces, and thus it conveys more discriminative information later processing, which aligns well with [Wright *et al.* (2009)]. Figure 6.4 depicts another example of ℓ^1-graph on the USPS digit database [Hull (1994)]. Top ten neighbors selected by ℓ^1-graph and k-nn graph are shown, respectively, for the same testing sample. It is clearly that the ℓ^1-graph can select many more kindred examples than the k-nn graph, again demonstrating that the ℓ^1-graph better discovers the underlying data relationships.

Discussions

(1) Our ℓ^1-graph constructed in Eqn. 6.4 is based on the assumption that the feature dimension, m, is high and the data distribution can be well

---

Algorithm 6.1 ℓ^1-graph construction.

Inputs: A sample data set denoted by the matrix $X = [x_1, x_2, ..., x_N]$, where $x_i \in \mathbb{R}^m$, and parameter ϵ based on the noise level.

for $i = 1 \to N$ **do**

compute the sparse representation for x_i by

$$\alpha_i = \arg\min_\alpha \|\alpha\|_1, \quad \text{s.t.} \quad \|x - B\alpha\|_2^2 \leq \epsilon,$$

where $B = [x_1, ..., x_{i-1}, 0, x_{i+1}, ..., x_N, I]$.

end for

Construct an affinity matrix for X by setting $W_{ij} = W_{ji} = \alpha_i(j)$.

Outputs: ℓ^1-graph $G = \{X, W\}$ with the samples set X as graph vertices and W the graph weight matrix.

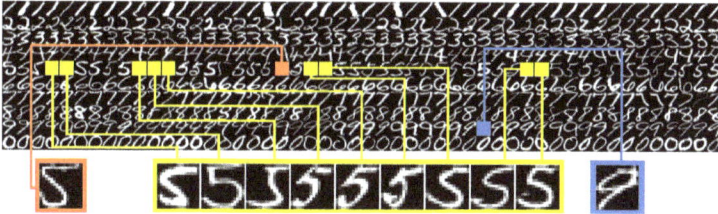

(i) Neighbors selected by L1-graph robustly and contextually

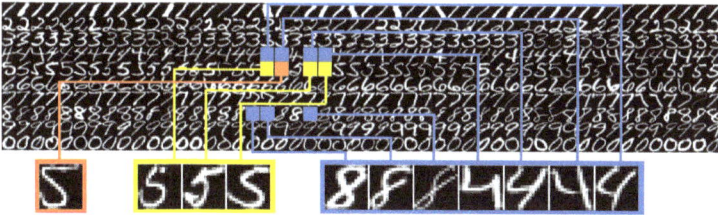

(ii) Pair-distance based k nearest neighbors with many outliers

Fig. 6.4 Illustration on the positions of a testing sample (red), its kindred neighbors (yellow), and its inhomogeneous neighbors (blue) selected by (i) ℓ^1-graph and (ii) k-nn graph on samples from the USPS digit database [Hull (1994)].

approximated as a union of low dimensional linear subspaces. Therefore, our ℓ^1-graph would not be applicable for low dimensional, say 2 or 3 dimensions, feature spaces.

(2) In our implementation, we found that data normalization, i.e., $\|x_i\|_2 =$

1, is needed for obtaining semantically reasonable coefficients.

(3) The k-nn graph is flexible in terms of the selection metric, whose optimality is heavily data dependent. In this work, we simply use the most common Euclidean distance for searching the k nearest neighbors.

(4) In many practical applications, it may happen that some data samples in X are highly correlated, which may cause unstable solution for Eqn. 6.4. In such cases, we could add a small ℓ^2 norm regularization on the solution as in elastic net [Zou and Hastie (2005)],

$$\min_{\alpha'} \|\alpha'\|_1 + \beta \|\alpha'\|_2^2, \quad s.t. \quad \|x - B\alpha'\|_2^2 \le \epsilon. \tag{6.5}$$

6.1.2 *Learning with ℓ^1-Graph*

An informative graph is critical for those graph-oriented learning algorithms. Similar to classical graphs constructed by k-nn or ϵ-ball method, ℓ^1-graph can be applied with different learning algorithms for various tasks, e.g., data clustering, subspace learning, and semi-supervised learning. In this section, we briefly introduce how to use ℓ^1-graph for these tasks.

6.1.2.1 *Spectral Clustering*

Data clustering is the unsupervised classification of samples into different groups, or more precisely, the partition of samples into subsets, such that the data within each subset are similar to each other. Spectral clustering [Shi and Malik (2000)] is among the most popular algorithms for this task, which is summarized as follows.

(1) Find the symmetrical similarity matrix by $W = (|W| + |W^T|)/2$.

(2) Compute the graph Laplacian matrix $L = D^{-1/2}WD^{-1/2}$, where D is a diagonal matrix with $D_{ii} = \sum_j w_{ij}$.

(3) Find eigenvectors $c_1, c_2, \cdots, c_K$ of L corresponding to the K largest eigenvalues, and form the matrix $C = [c_1, c_2, \cdots, c_K]$ by stacking the eigenvectors in columns.

(4) Treat each row of C as a point in $\mathbb{R}^K$, and cluster them into K clusters via K-means.

(5) Assign x_i to the cluster j if the i-th row of the matrix C is assigned to the cluster j.

6.1.2.2 *Subspace Learning*

In many computer vision and pattern recognition problems, the signal or feature involved is often in a very high dimensional space, and thus, it is necessary and beneficial to transform the data from the original high dimensional space to a low dimensional one for alleviating the curse of dimensionality. A popular dimensionality reduction and feature extraction technique is subspace learning, which has been successfully applied in various recognition applications. Representative subspace learning methods include principal component analysis (PCA) [Joliffe (1986)], fisher linear discriminant analysis (LDA) [Belhumeur *et al.* (1997)], locality preserving projection (LPP) [He and Niyogi (2003)], and neighborhood preserving embedding (NPE) [He *et al.* (2005)]. As shown by Yan et al. [Yan *et al.* (2007)], all these works can be formulated into a unified graph embedding framework based on an adjacency graph.

Similar to the graph construction process in Locally Linear Embedding (LLE), our ℓ^1-graph characterizes the neighborhood reconstruction relationships. In LLE, the graph is constructed by reconstructing each datum with its k-nearest neighbors or samples within the ϵ-ball neighborhood. However, both LLE and its linear extension, Neighborhood Preserving Embedding (NPE) [He *et al.* (2005)], rely on a global graph parameter (k or ϵ), which may lead to over-fitting or under-fitting for different data samples due to their uneven distribution in the signal space. In comparison, our ℓ^1-graph can adaptively select the the most relevant neighbors based on the trade-off between reconstruction quality and representation sparsity. Following the same idea of the NPE algorithm, we apply our ℓ^1-graph for subspace learning.

The purpose of subspace learning is to search for a transformation matrix $P \in \mathbb{R}^{m \times d}$ (usually $d \ll m$), where m is the dimension of the original high dimensional space and d is the dimension of the projected low dimensional space. The transformation matrix P is used to project the original high dimensional data in into a low dimensional space while preserving the original data relationships. The ℓ^1-graph discovers the underlying sparse reconstruction relationships among the data samples, and it is desirable to preserve these reconstruction relationships in the low dimensional feature space. The pursue of such a transformation matrix can be formulated as the following optimization problem

$$\min_{P^T X X^T P = I} \sum_{i=1}^{N} \| P^T x_i - \sum_{j=1}^{N} W_{ij} P^T x_j \|^2, \tag{6.6}$$

where W_{ij} is determined by our ℓ^1-graph, and the constraints $P^T X X^T P = I$ is to remove the arbitrary scaling factor in the projection. After several easy mathematical manipulations, the above optimization is reduces to finding

$$\min_{P^T X X^T P = I} trace(P^T X M X^T P), \qquad (6.7)$$

where $M = (I - W)^T (I - W)$. This minimization problem is readily to be solved with the generalized eigenvalue decomposition as

$$X M X^T p_{m+1-j} = \lambda_j X X^T p_{m+1-j}, \qquad (6.8)$$

where p_{m+1-j} is the $(m + 1 - j)$-th column vector of the matrix P as well as the eigenvector corresponding to the j-th largest eigenvalue λ_j. The derived transformation matrix is then used for dimensionality reduction, $y_i = P^T x_i$, where y_i is the corresponding low dimensional representation of the sample x_i.

6.1.2.3 *Semi-Supervised Learning*

As shown in Figure 6.1 and 6.2, our ℓ^1-graph is robust to data noise and better discovers the underlying data relationships compared with conventional graphs based on k-nearest neighbors. These properties recommend ℓ^1-graph as a good candidate for label propagation over the graph. Semi-supervised learning has attracted much attention recently, and has been widely used for both regression and classification tasks. The main idea of semi-supervised learning is to utilize unlabeled data for improving the classification and generalization capability on the testing data. Commonly, the unlabeled data is used as an extract regularization term in the traditional supervised learning objective function. In this work, we build our unsupervised ℓ^1-graph over both labeled and unlabeled data to better explore the data relationships in the entire data sampling space. Then this ℓ^1-graph can serve as a regularization for many supervised learning algorithms. In this work, we take Marginal Fisher Analysis (MFA) [Yan *et al.* (2007)] as an example for the supervised learning part. Similar to the philosophy in [Yang *et al.* (2009b)] and [Cai *et al.* (2008)], the objective for ℓ^1-graph based semi-supervised learning is defined as

$$\min_P \frac{\gamma S_c(P) + (1 - \gamma) \sum_{i=1}^{N} \| P^T x_i - \sum_{j=1}^{N} W_{ij} P^T x_j \|^2}{S_p(P)},$$

where $\gamma \in (0,1)$ is a threshold for balancing the supervised term and ℓ^1-graph regularization term, and the supervised part is defined as

$$S_c(P) = \sum_i \sum_{j \in N_{k_1}^+(i)} ||P^T x_i - P^T x_j||^2, \qquad (6.9)$$

$$S_p(P) = \sum_i \sum_{(i,j) \in P_{k_2}(l_i)} ||P^T x_i - P^T x_j||^2, \qquad (6.10)$$

where S_c indicates the intra-class compactness, which is represented as the sum of distances between each point and its neighbors of the same class and $N_{k_1}^+(i)$ is the index set of the k_1 nearest neighbors of the sample x_i in the same class, S_p indicates the separability of different classes, which is characterized as the sum of distances between the marginal points and their neighboring points of different classes and $P_{k_2}(l)$ is a set of data pairs that are the k_2 nearest pairs among the set $\{(i,j), l_i = l, l_j \neq l\}$, and W is the weight matrix of the ℓ^1-graph. Similar to (6.6), the optimum can be obtained via the generalized eigenvalue decomposition method, and the derived projection matrix P is then used for dimensionality reduction and consequent classification.

6.1.3   *Experiments*

In this section, we extensively evaluate the effectiveness of our ℓ^1-graph on three learning tasks, including data clustering, subspace learning, and semi-supervised learning. For comparison purpose, the classical k-nn graph and ϵ-ball graph with different edge weight assignment approaches are implemented as the baselines. For all algorithms based on k-nn and ϵ-ball graphs, the reported results are based on the best tuned parameters k and ϵ.

6.1.3.1   *Data Sets*

For all the experiments, we evaluate on three databases. The USPS handwritten digit database [Hull (1994)] includes 10 classes (0-9 digit characters) and 11000 samples in total. We randomly select 200 samples for each digit for the experiments, and all of these images are normalized to the size of 32×32 pixels. The forest covertype database [Blackard and Dean (1999)] was collected for predicting forest cover type from cartographic variables. It includes seven classes and 581012 samples in total. We randomly select 100 samples for each type in the following experiments for computational efficiency. The Extended YALE-B database [Lee *et al.* (2005)] contains 38 individuals and around 64 near frontal images under different illuminations per individual, where the face images are manually cropped and normalized to the size of 32×32 pixels. All the images were taken against a dark homogeneous background with the subjects in an upright and frontal position.

6.1.3.2 *Spectral Clustering*

For spectral clustering, we compare our ℓ^1-graph with Gaussian kernel graph [Shi and Malik (2000)], LE-graphs (used in Laplacian Eigenmaps [Belkin and Niyogi (2002)] algorithm), LLE-graphs (used in LLE [Roweis and Saul (2000)]), and also with the K-means clustering based on the low dimensional representations from Principal Component Analysis (PCA) [Joliffe (1986)]. Two evaluation metrics, accuracy (AC) and normalized mutual information (NMI) [Zheng *et al.* (2004)], are used for performance evaluations. Suppose L is the ground truth sample label vector and $\hat{L}$ is the label vector predicted from the clustering algorithms, AC is defined as

$$\text{AC} = \frac{1}{N} \sum_{i=1}^{N} \delta(L(i), M_{(L,\hat{L})}(i)) \tag{6.11}$$

where N denotes the total number of samples, $\delta(a, b)$ is the Kronecker delta function ($\delta(a, b)$ equals to 1 if $a = b$, and 0 otherwise), $M_{(L,\hat{L})}$ is the resulting vector by permuting $\hat{L}$ in order to best match L.[2] The Kuhn-Munkres algorithm can be used to obtain the best mapping [Chen *et al.* (2001)]. To avoid the clustering label permutation problem, we use normalized mutual information (NMI) as a second metric,

$$\text{NMI}(L, \hat{L}) = \frac{\text{MI}(L, \hat{L})}{max(H(L), H(\hat{L}))}, \tag{6.12}$$

where $\text{MI}(L, \hat{L})$ is the mutual information between L and $\hat{L}$,

$$\text{MI}(L, \hat{L}) = \sum_{l \in L} \sum_{\hat{l} \in \hat{L}} p(l, \hat{l}) \log(\frac{p(l, \hat{l})}{p(l)p(\hat{l})}), \tag{6.13}$$

and $H(L)$ and $h(\hat{L})$ denote the entropies of L and $\hat{L}$, respectively. It is obvious that NMI takes values in $[0, 1]$. Unlike AC, NMI is invariant with the permutation of labels, and therefore, is more efficient to compute.

---

[2]After clustering, the cluster i.d. assignment for the predicted clusters are arbitrary. In order to compare with the ground truth, we need to find the assignment vector that best matches the ground truth labels.

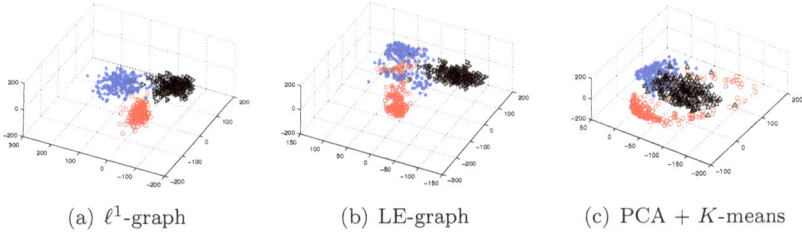

(a) ℓ^1-graph   (b) LE-graph   (c) PCA + K-means

Fig. 6.5   Visualization of the clustering results with (a) ℓ^1-graph, (b) LE-graph, and (c) PCA for three clusters (handwritten digits 1, 2 and 3 in the USPS database).

The visualization the clustering results (digit characters 1-3 from the USPS database) for spectral clustering based on ℓ^1-graph and LE-graph, and K-means are plotted in Figure 6.5, where different digits are denoted by different colors. The coordinates of the points in (a) and (b) are obtained from the eigenvalue decomposition in the third step of spectral clustering 6.1.2.1. It is clear that our ℓ^1-graph can better separate different classes. Quantitative comparison results on clustering are list in Table 6.1-6.3 for the three databases, respectively. The cluster number K indicates the number of classes used from the database as the data samples for clustering. From the listed results, three observations can be made: 1) the clustering results from ℓ^1-graph based spectral clustering algorithm are consistently much better than those baselines in terms of both metrics; 2) Spectral clustering based on k-nn based LLE-graph is relatively more stable compared with other baselines; and 3) ϵ-ball based algorithms show to be generally inferior, in both accuracy and robustness, than the corresponding k-nn based graphs, and thus for the subsequent experiments, we only report the results from k-nn based graphs. All the results listed in the tables are from the best tuned algorithmic parameters, e.g., kernel parameter for G-graph, the number of neighbors k and neighborhood diameter ϵ for LE-graphs and LLE-graphs, and the retained PCA feature dimension for K-means.

6.1.3.3   *Subspace Learning*

In this section, classification experiments based on subspace learning are conducted on the above three databases. To make the comparison fair, for all the evaluated algorithms we first apply PCA as a preprocessing step for denoising by retaining 98% of the energy. To extensively evaluate the classification performances, on the USPS database, we randomly sampled

Table 6.1   Clustering accuracies, measured by normalized mutual information (NMI) and accuracy (AC), for spectral clustering algorithms based on ℓ^1-graph, Gaussian kernel graph (G-graph), LE-graphs, and LLE-graphs, as well as PCA + K-means on the USPS digit database.

USPS	Metric	ℓ^1-graph	G-graph	LE-graph		LLE-graph		PCA+K-means
Cluster #				k-nn	ϵ-ball	k-nn	ϵ-ball	
$K=2$	NMI	**1.000**	0.672(110)	0.858(7)	0.627(3)	0.636(5)	0.717(4)	0.608(10)
	AC	**1.000**	0.922	0.943	0.918	0.917	0.932	0.905
$K=4$	NMI	**0.977**	0.498(155)	0.693(16)	0.540(6)	0.606(5)	0.465(7)	0.621(20)
	AC	**0.994**	0.663	0.853	0.735	0.777	0.668	0.825
$K=6$	NMI	**0.972**	0.370(120)	0.682(5)	0.456(6)	0.587(5)	0.427(9)	0.507(4)
	AC	**0.991**	0.471	0.739	0.594	0.670	0.556	0.626
$K=8$	NMI	**0.945**	0.358(150)	0.568(7)	0.371(4)	0.544(12)	0.404(7)	0.462(17)
	AC	**0.981**	0.423	0.673	0.453	0.598	0.499	0.552
$K=10$	NMI	**0.898**	0.346(80)	0.564(6)	0.424(5)	0.552(16)	0.391(4)	0.421(10)
	AC	**0.873**	0.386	0.578	0.478	0.537	0.439	0.433

Table 6.2   Spectral clustering results on the forest covertype database.

COV	Metric	ℓ^1-graph	G-graph	LE-graph		LLE-graph		PCA+K-means
Cluster #				k-nn	ϵ-ball	k-nn	ϵ-ball	
$K=3$	NMI	**0.792**	0.651(220)	0.554(16)	0.419(6)	0.642(20)	0.475(6)	0.555(5)
	AC	**0.903**	0.767	0.697	0.611	0.813	0.650	0.707
$K=4$	NMI	**0.706**	0.585(145)	0.533(13)	0.534(6)	0.622(20)	0.403(5)	0.522(13)
	AC	**0.813**	0.680	0.608	0.613	0.782	0.519	0.553
$K=5$	NMI	**0.623**	0.561(240)	0.515(12)	0.451(5)	0.556(10)	0.393(7)	0.454(15)
	AC	**0.662**	0.584	0.541	0.506	0.604	0.448	0.486
$K=6$	NMI	**0.664**	0.562(200)	0.545(6)	0.482(6)	0.602(20)	0.465(7)	0.528(8)
	AC	**0.693**	0.585	0.564	0.523	0.632	0.509	0.547
$K=7$	NMI	**0.763**	0.621(130)	0.593(9)	0.452(6)	0.603(11)	0.319(6)	0.602(17)
	AC	**0.795**	0.642	0.629	0.498	0.634	0.394	0.631

Table 6.3   Spectral clustering results on the Extended YALE-B database. Note that the G-graph performs extremely bad in this case, possibly due to dramatic illumination changes on this database.

YALE-B	Metric	ℓ^1-graph	G-graph	LE-graph		LLE-graph		PCA+K-means
Cluster #				k-nn	ϵ-ball	k-nn	ϵ-ball	
$K=10$	NMI	**0.738**	0.07(220)	0.420(4)	0.354(16)	0.404(3)	0.302(3)	0.255(180)
	AC	**0.758**	0.175	0.453	0.413	0.450	0.383	0.302
$K=15$	NMI	**0.759**	0.08(380)	0.494(4)	0.475(20)	0.438(5)	0.261(5)	0.205(110)
	AC	**0.762**	0.132	0.464	0.494	0.440	0.257	0.226
$K=20$	NMI	**0.786**	0.08(290)	0.492(2)	0.450(18)	0.454(4)	0.269(3)	0.243(110)
	AC	**0.793**	0.113	0.478	0.445	0.418	0.241	0.238
$K=30$	NMI	**0.803**	0.09(50)	0.507(2)	0.417(24)	0.459(7)	0.283(4)	0.194(170)
	AC	**0.821**	0.088	0.459	0.383	0.410	0.236	0.169
$K=38$	NMI	**0.776**	0.11(50)	0.497(2)	0.485(21)	0.473(8)	0.319(4)	0.165(190)
	AC	**0.785**	0.081	0.443	0.445	0.408	0.248	0.138

10, 20, 30 and 40 images from each digit for training. Similarly, on the forest covertype database, we randomly sampled 5, 10, 15 and 20 samples from each class for training, and on the Extended YALE-B database, we randomly sampled 10, 20, 30 , 40 and 50 training images for each individual for training. All the remaining data samples are used for testing. We use

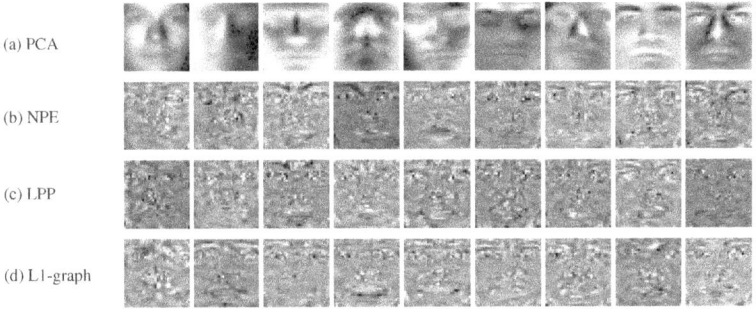

(a) PCA

(b) NPE

(c) LPP

(d) L1-graph

Fig. 6.6   Visualization of the learned subspaces. They are the first 10 basis vectors of (a) PCA, (b) NPE, (c) LPP, and (d) ℓ^1-graph calculated from the face images in YALE-B database.

the classification error rate to measure the performance,

$$\text{err} = 1 - \frac{\sum_{i=1}^{N_t} \delta(\hat{y}_i, y_i)}{N_t} \tag{6.14}$$

where $\hat{y}_i$ is the predicted data label and y_i is the ground truth label, N_t is the total number of testing samples, and $\delta(\hat{y}_i, y_i)$ is the Kronecker delta function. The best performances of each algorithm over the tuned graph parameters and feature dimensions are reported. The popular unsupervised subspace learning algorithms PCA, NPE and LPP[3], and the supervised algorithm Fisherfaces [Belhumeur *et al.* (1997)] are evaluated for comparison with our unsupervised subspace learning based on our ℓ^1-graph. For LPP, we use the cosine metric in graph construction for better performance. The detailed comparison results on classification are listed in Table 6.4-6.6 for the three databases. From these results, we observe that our ℓ^1-graph based subspace learning algorithm is much better than all the other evaluated unsupervised learning algorithms. On the forest covertype and Extended YALE-B databases, our unsupervised ℓ^1-graph even performs better than the supervised algorithm Fisherfaces. For all the classification experiments, we simply use the classical nearest neighbor classifier [Belhumeur *et al.* (1997)] [He *et al.* (2005)] [He and Niyogi (2003)] for fair comparisons with the literature algorithms. The visualization of learned subspaces based on ℓ^1-graph and those based on PCA, LPP and NPE are shown in Figure 6.6, from which we see that the PCA bases are most similar to real faces as PCA is motivated for data reconstruction.

---

[3]Here we use the unsupervised version of NPE and LPP for fair comparison.

Table 6.4   USPS digit recognition error rates (%) for different subspace learning algorithms. The numbers in the parentheses are the feature dimensions retained with the best accuracies.

USPS	Unsupervised				Supervised
Train #	PCA	NPE	LPP	ℓ^1-graph	Fisherfaces
10	37.21(17)	33.21(33)	30.54(19)	21.91(13)	**15.82**(9)
20	30.59(26)	27.97(22)	26.12(19)	18.11(13)	**13.60**(9)
30	26.67(29)	23.46(42)	23.19(26)	16.81(15)	**13.59**(7)
40	23.25(25)	20.86(18)	19.92(32)	14.35(19)	**12.29**(7)

Table 6.5   Forest cover recognition error rates (%) for different subspace learning algorithms.

COV	Unsupervised				Supervised
Train #	PCA	NPE	LPP	ℓ^1-graph	Fisherfaces
5	33.23(17)	28.80(6)	35.09(12)	**23.36**(6)	23.81(6)
10	27.29(18)	25.56(11)	27.30(16)	**19.76**(15)	21.17(4)
15	23.75(14)	22.69(16)	23.26(34)	**17.85**(7)	19.57(6)
20	21.03(29)	20.10(10)	20.75(34)	**16.44**(6)	18.09(6)

Table 6.6   Face recognition error rates (%) for different subspace learning algorithms on the Extended YALE-B database.

YALE-B	Unsupervised				Supervised
Train #	PCA	NPE	LPP	ℓ^1-graph	Fisherfaces
10	44.41(268)	23.41(419)	24.61(234)	**14.26**(112)	**13.92**(37)
20	27.17(263)	14.62(317)	14.76(281)	**5.30**(118)	9.46(37)
30	20.11(254)	9.40(485)	8.65(246)	**3.36**(254)	12.45(34)
40	16.98(200)	5.84(506)	5.30(263)	**1.93**(143)	3.79(37)
50	12.68(366)	3.78(488)	3.02(296)	**0.75**(275)	1.64(37)

6.1.3.4   *Semi-Supervised Learning*

We again use the above three databases for evaluating the effectiveness of the semi-supervised algorithm based on ℓ^1-graph by comparing with algorithms based on Gaussian-kernel graph, LE-graph and LLE-graph. For all the semi-supervised learning algorithms, the supervised part is based on the Marginal Fisher Analysis (MFA) [Yan *et al.* (2007)] algorithm. For fair comparisons, the parameters k_1 and k_2 in MFA, and γ are tuned for best performance. The detailed comparisons for different semi-supervised leaning algorithms, the original supervised MFA algorithm and the baseline PCA, are shown in Table 6.7-6.9. The semi-supervised learning based on our ℓ^1-graph generally achieves the highest classification accuracy compared with semi-supervised learning based on other graphs, and outperforms the

Table 6.7   USPS digit recognition error rates (%) for different semi-supervised, supervised and unsupervised learning algorithms. The numbers in the parentheses are the feature dimensions that give the best accuracies.

USPS	Semi-supervised			Supervised	Unsupervised
Train #	ℓ^1-graph	LLE-graph	LE-graph	MFA [Yan *et al.* (2007)]	PCA
10	**25.11**(33)	34.63(9)	30.74(33)	34.63(9)	37.21(17)
20	**26.94**(41)	41.38(39)	30.39(41)	41.38(39)	30.59(26)
30	**23.25**(49)	36.55(49)	27.50(49)	44.34(47)	26.67(29)
40	**19.17**(83)	30.28(83)	23.55(83)	35.95(83)	23.35(25)

supervised learning counterparts without considering the unlabeled data.

Table 6.8   Forest cover recognition error rates (%) for different semi-supervised, supervised and unsupervised learning algorithms.

COV	Semi-supervised			Supervised	Unsupervised
Train #	ℓ^1-graph	LLE-graph	LE-graph	MFA [Yan *et al.* (2007)]	PCA
5	**22.50**(9)	29.89(5)	25.81(7)	29.89(5)	33.23(17)
10	**17.45**(10)	24.93(10)	22.74(8)	24.93(10)	27.29(18)
20	**15.00**(8)	19.17(10)	17.38(9)	19.17(10)	23.75(14)
30	**12.26**(8)	15.32(8)	13.81(10)	16.40(8)	21.03(29)

Table 6.9   Face recognition error rates (%) for different semi-supervised, supervised and unsupervised learning algorithms on the Extended YALE-B database.

YALE-B	Semi-supervised			Supervised	Unsupervised
Train #	ℓ^1-graph	LLE-graph	LE-graph	MFA [Yan *et al.* (2007)]	PCA
5	**21.63**(51)	33.47(51)	33.47(51)	33.47(51)	61.34(176)
10	**9.56**(61)	18.39(33)	18.39(33)	18.39(33)	44.41(268)
20	**5.05**(57)	14.30(29)	11.26(53)	14.30(29)	27.17(263)
30	**2.92**(73)	9.15(70)	7.37(71)	11.06(70)	20.11(254)

6.2   A Joint Optimization Framework of Sparse Coding and Discriminative Clustering

In this section, we investigate jointly optimizing feature extraction and discriminative clustering, in which way they mutually reinforce each other. We focus on sparse codes as the extracted features, and develop our loss functions based on two representative discriminative clustering methods, the entropy-minimization [Li *et al.* (2004)] and maximum-margin [Xu *et al.* (2004)] clustering, respectively. A task-driven bi-level optimization model [Mairal *et al.* (2012)], [Wang *et al.* (2015a)] is then built upon the proposed framework. The sparse coding step is formulated as the lower-level constraint, where a graph regularization is enforced to preserve the local manifold structure [Zheng *et al.* (2011)]. The clustering-oriented cost functions are considered as the upper-level objectives to be minimized. Stochastic gradient descent algorithms are developed to solve both bi-level models. Experiments on several popular real datasets verify the noticeable performance improvement led by such a joint optimization framework.

6.2.1 *Model Formulation*

Sparse Coding with Graph Regularization Sparse codes prove to be an effective feature for clustering. In [Cheng *et al.* (2010)], the authors suggested that the contribution of one sample to the reconstruction of another sample was a good indicator of similarity between these two samples. Therefore, the reconstruction coefficients (sparse codes) can be used to constitute the similarity graph for spectral clustering. ℓ^1-graph performs sparse representation for each data point separately without considering the geometric information and manifold structure of the entire data. Further research shows that the graph regularized sparse representations produce superior results in various clustering and classification tasks [Zheng *et al.* (2011)], [Yang *et al.* (2014d)]. Here, we adopt the graph regularized sparse codes as the features for clustering.

We assume that all the data samples $\mathbf{X} = [\mathbf{x}_1, \mathbf{x}_2, \cdots, \mathbf{x}_n], \mathbf{x}_i \in R^{m \times 1}, i = 1, 2, \cdots, n$, are encoded into their corresponding sparse codes $\mathbf{A} = [\mathbf{a}_1, \mathbf{a}_2, \cdots, \mathbf{a}_n], \mathbf{a}_i \in R^{p \times 1}, i = 1, 2, \cdots, n$, using a learned dictionary $\mathbf{D} = [\mathbf{d}_1, \mathbf{d}_2, \cdots, \mathbf{d}_p]$, where $\mathbf{d}_i \in R^{m \times 1}, i = 1, 2, \cdots, p$ are the learned atoms. Moreover, given a pairwise similarity matrix $\mathbf{W}$, the sparse representations that capture the geometric structure of the data according to the manifold assumption should minimize the following objective: $\frac{1}{2} \sum_{i=1}^{n} \sum_{j=1}^{n} \mathbf{W}_{ij} \|\mathbf{a}_i - \mathbf{a}_j\|_2^2 = Tr(\mathbf{A}\mathbf{L}\mathbf{A}^{\mathbf{T}})$, where $\mathbf{L}$ is the graph Laplacian matrix constructed from $\mathbf{W}$. We set $\mathbf{W}$ as the Gaussian Kernel: $\mathbf{W}_{ij} = \exp(-\frac{\|\mathbf{x}_i - \mathbf{x}_j\|_2^2}{\delta^2})$, where δ is the controlling parameter selected by cross-validation.

The graph regularized sparse codes are obtained by solving the following convex optimization

$$\mathbf{A} = \arg\min_{\mathbf{A}} \frac{1}{2} \|\mathbf{X} - \mathbf{D}\mathbf{A}\|_F^2 + \lambda \sum_i \|\mathbf{a}_i\|_1$$

$$+ \alpha Tr(\mathbf{A}\mathbf{L}\mathbf{A}^{\mathbf{T}}) + \lambda_2 \|\mathbf{A}\|_F^2. \tag{6.15}$$

Note $\lambda_2 > 0$ is necessary for proving the differentiability of the objective function (see [A.2.1] in A.2.1). However, setting $\lambda_2 = 0$ proves to work well in practice, and thus the term $\lambda_2||\mathbf{A}||_F^2$ will be omitted by default hereinafter (except for the differentiability proof).

Obviously, the effect of sparse codes $\mathbf{A}$ largely depends on the quality of dictionary $\mathbf{D}$. Dictionary learning methods, such as K-SVD algorithm [Elad and Aharon (2006)], are widely used in sparse coding literature. In regard to clustering, the authors in [Cheng *et al.* (2010)], [Yang *et al.* (2014d)], [Yang *et al.* (2014c)] constructed the dictionary by directly selecting atoms from data samples. [Zheng *et al.* (2011)] learned the dictionary that can reconstruct input data well. However, it does not necessarily lead to discriminative features. In contrast, we will optimize $\mathbf{D}$ together with the clustering task.

Bi-level Optimization Formulation The objective cost function for the joint framework can be expressed by the following bi-level optimization:

$$\begin{aligned}
\min_{\mathbf{D},\mathbf{w}} \quad & C(\mathbf{A},\mathbf{w}) \\
s.t. \quad & \mathbf{A} = \arg\min_{\mathbf{A}} \tfrac{1}{2}||\mathbf{X} - \mathbf{DA}||_F^2 + \lambda\sum_i ||\mathbf{a}_i||_1 \\
& \quad + \alpha Tr(\mathbf{ALA}^{\mathbf{T}}).
\end{aligned} \tag{6.16}$$

where $C(\mathbf{A},\mathbf{w})$ is a cost function evaluating the loss of clustering, with $\mathbf{A}$ as its input and $\mathbf{w}$ as the parameter. It can be formulated differently based on various clustering principles, two of which will be discussed and solved in the next section.

Bilevel optimization [Yang *et al.* (2012b)] has been investigated in both theory and application sides. In [Yang *et al.* (2012b)], the authors proposed a general bilevel sparse coding model for learning dictionaries across coupled signal spaces. Another similar formulation has been studied in [Mairal *et al.* (2012)] for general regression tasks.

6.2.2 *Clustering-Oriented Cost Functions*

Assuming K clusters, and $\omega = [\omega_1, ..., \omega_K]$ as the set of parameters of the loss function, where ω_i corresponds to the i-th cluster, $i = 1, 2, ..., K$. We introduce two forms of loss functions, each of which is derived from a representative discriminative clustering method.

Entropy-Minimization Loss Maximization of the mutual information with respect to parameters of the encoder model effectively defines a discriminative unsupervised optimization framework. The model is parame-

terized similarly to a conditionally trained classifier, but the cluster alloca-
tions are unknown [Barber and Agakov (2005)]. In [Dai and Hu (2010)], [Li
et al. (2004)], the authors adopted an information-theoretic framework as
an implementation of the low-density separation assumption by minimizing
the conditional entropy. By substituting the logistic posterior probability
into the minimum conditional entropy principle, the authors got the logistics clustering algorithm, which is equivalent to find a labelling strategy so
that the total entropy of data clustering is minimized.

Since the true cluster label of each $\mathbf{x_i}$ is unknown, we introduce the
predicted confidence probability p_{ij} that sample $\mathbf{x_i}$ belongs to cluster j, $i =
1, 2, \cdots, N$, $j = 1, 2, \cdots, K$, which is set as the likelihood of multinomial
logistic (softmax) regression:

$$p_{ij} = p(j|\mathbf{w}, \mathbf{a}_i) = \frac{e^{-j\mathbf{w}_j^T \mathbf{a}_i}}{\sum_{l=1}^{K} e^{-l\mathbf{w}_l^T \mathbf{a}_i}}, \tag{6.17}$$

The loss function for all data could be defined accordingly in a entropy-like
form:

$$C(\mathbf{A}, \mathbf{w}) = -\sum_{i=1}^{n} \sum_{j=1}^{K} p_{ij} \log p_{ij}. \tag{6.18}$$

The predicted cluster label of $\mathbf{a}_i$ is the cluster j where it achieves the largest
likelihood probability p_{ij}. The logistics regression can deal with multi-class
problems more easily compared with the support vector machine (SVM).
The next important thing we need to study is the differentiability of (6.16).

Theorem 6.2.1. *The objective $C(\mathbf{A}, \mathbf{w})$ defined in (6.18) is differentiable
on $\mathbf{D} \times \mathbf{w}$.*

Proof: Denote $\mathbf{X} \in \mathcal{X}$, and $\mathbf{D} \in \mathcal{D}$. Also let the objective function
$C(\mathbf{A}, \mathbf{w})$ in (6.18) be denoted as C for short. The differentiability of C
with respect to $\mathbf{w}$ is easy to show, assuming the compactness of $\mathcal{X}$, as well
as the fact that C is twice differentiable.

We will therefore focus on showing that C is differentiable with respect
to $\mathbf{D}$, which is more difficult since $\mathbf{A}$, and thus $\mathbf{a}_i$, is not differentiable
everywhere. Without loss of generality, we use a vector $\mathbf{a}$ instead of $\mathbf{A}$ for
simplifying the derivations hereinafter. In some cases, we may equivalently
express $\mathbf{a}$ as $\mathbf{a}(\mathbf{D}, \mathbf{w})$ in order to emphasize the functional dependence.
Based on [A.2.1] in A.2.1, and given a small perturbation $\mathbf{E} \in R^{m \times p}$, it
follows that

$$\begin{aligned} C(\mathbf{a}(\mathbf{D} + \mathbf{E}), \mathbf{w}) &- C(\mathbf{a}(\mathbf{D}), \mathbf{w}) \\ &= \nabla_{\mathbf{z}} C_{\mathbf{w}}^T (\mathbf{a}(\mathbf{D} + \mathbf{E}) - \mathbf{a}(\mathbf{D})) + O(||\mathbf{E}||_F^2), \end{aligned} \tag{6.19}$$

where the term $O(||\mathbf{E}||_F^2)$ is based on the fact that $\mathbf{a}(\mathbf{D}, \mathbf{x})$ is uniformly Lipschitz and $\mathcal{X} \times \mathcal{D}$ is compact. It is then possible to show that

$$C(\mathbf{a}(\mathbf{D} + \mathbf{E}), \mathbf{w}) - C(\mathbf{a}(\mathbf{D}), \mathbf{w})$$
$$= Tr(\mathbf{E}^T g(\mathbf{a}(\mathbf{D} + \mathbf{E}), \mathbf{w})) + O(||\mathbf{E}||_F^2), \quad (6.20)$$

where g has the form given in Algorithm I. This shows that C is differentiable on $\mathcal{D}$. $\qquad \square$

Building on the differentiability proof, we are able to solve (6.15) using a projected first order stochastic gradient descent (SGD) algorithm, whose detailed steps are outlined in Algorithm 1. At a high level overview, it consists of an outer SGD loop that incrementally samples the training data. It uses each sample to approximate gradients with respect to $\mathbf{w}$ and $\mathbf{D}$, which are then used to update them.

Convergence and Complexity Analysis SGD converges to stationary points under a few stricter assumptions than the ones satisfied in this model. A non-convex convergence proof assumes three times differentiable cost functions [Mairal *et al.* (2012)]. As a typical case in machine learning, we use SGD in a setting where it is not guaranteed to converge in theory, but behaves well in practice.

Assuming n samples and dictionary size p, in each iteration of Algorithm 1, step 8 takes $O(n)$ time. Step 4 is solved by the feature-sign algorithm [Lee *et al.* (2006)], which is reduced to a series of quadratic programming (QP) problems. The computational bottleneck lies in solving the inverse of matrix $\mathbf{D}^T\mathbf{D}$ of size $p \times p$, where applying the Gauss-Jordan elimination method takes $O(p^3)$ time per sample. Thus, Algorithm 1 takes $O(np^3)$ time per iteration, and $O(Cnp^3)$ in total (C is a constant absorbing epoch numbers, etc.). Further, if p is a constant, Algorithm I reaches O(Cn) time complexity.

Maximum-Margin Loss Xu et al. [Xu *et al.* (2004)] proposed maximum margin clustering (MMC), which borrows the idea from the SVM theory. Their experimental results showed that the MMC technique could often obtain more accurate results than conventional clustering methods. Technically, what MMC does is just to find a way to label the samples by running an SVM implicitly, and the SVM margin obtained would be maximized over all possible labelings [Zhao *et al.* (2008)]. However, unlike supervised large margin methods which are usually formulated as convex optimization problems, maximum margin clustering is a non-convex integer optimization problem, which is much more difficult to solve. [Li *et al.*

Algorithm 6.2 Stochastic gradient descent algorithm for solving (6.16), with $C(\mathbf{A}, \mathbf{w})$ as defined in (6.18).

Require: $\mathbf{X}, \sigma; \lambda; \mathbf{D}_0$ and $\mathbf{w}_0$ (initial dictionary and classifier parameter); ITER (number of iterations); t_0, ρ (learning rate)

1: Construct the matrix $\mathbf{L}$ from $\mathbf{X}$ and σ.
2: FOR t=1 to ITER DO
3: Draw a subset $(\mathbf{X}_t, \mathbf{Y}_t)$ from $(\mathbf{X}, \mathbf{Y})$
4: Graph-regularized sparse coding: computer $\mathbf{A}^*$:
$\mathbf{A}^* = \arg\min_{\mathbf{A}} \frac{1}{2}\|\mathbf{X} - \mathbf{DA}\|_F^2 + \lambda \sum_i \|\mathbf{a}_i\|_1 + Tr(\mathbf{ALA^T})$.
5: Compute the active set S (the nonzero support of $\mathbf{A}^*$)
6: Compute β^*: Set $\beta^*_{S^C} = 0$ and $\beta^*_S = (\mathbf{D}_S^T\mathbf{D}_S + \lambda_2\mathbf{I})^{-1}\nabla_{\mathbf{A_s}}[C(\mathbf{A}, \mathbf{w})]$
7: Choose the learning rate $\rho_t = \min(\rho, \rho\frac{t_0}{t})$
8: Update $\mathbf{D}$ and $\mathbf{W}$ by a projected gradient step:
$\mathbf{w} = \prod_{\mathbf{w}}[\mathbf{w} - \rho_t \nabla_{\mathbf{w}} C(\mathbf{A}, \mathbf{w})]$
$\mathbf{D} = \prod_{\mathbf{D}}[\mathbf{D} - \rho_t(\nabla_{\mathbf{D}}(-\mathbf{D}\beta^*\mathbf{A}^T + (\mathbf{X}_t - \mathbf{DA})\beta^{*T})]$
where $\prod_{\mathbf{w}}$ and $\prod_{\mathbf{D}}$ are respectively orthogonal projections on the embedding spaces of $\mathbf{w}$ and $\mathbf{D}$.
9: END FOR

Ensure: $\mathbf{D}$ and $\mathbf{w}$

(2009)] made several relaxations to the original MMC problem and reformulated it as a semi-definite programming (SDP) problem. The cutting plane maximum margin clustering (CPMMC) algorithm was presented in [Zhao *et al.* (2008)] to solve MMC with a much improved efficiency.

To develop the multi-class max-margin loss of clustering, we referr to the multi-class SVM formulation [Crammer and Singer (2002)], and similarly formulate the multi-cluster model:

$$f(\mathbf{a}_i) = \arg\max_{j=1,\dots,K} f^j(\mathbf{a}_i) = \arg\max_{j=1,\dots,K}(\omega_j^T \mathbf{a}_i), \quad (6.21)$$

where f^j is the prototype for the j-th cluster. The predicted cluster label of $\mathbf{a}_i$ is the cluster of the weight vector that achieves the maximum value $\omega_j^T \mathbf{a}_i$. The multi-class max-margin loss for $\mathbf{a}_i$ could be defined as:

$$C(\mathbf{a}_i, \mathbf{w}) = \max(0, 1 + f^{r_i}(\mathbf{a}_i) - f^{y_i}(\mathbf{a}_i))$$
$$\text{where} \quad y_i = \arg\max_{j=1,\dots,K} f^j(\mathbf{a}_i)$$
$$r_i = \arg\max_{j=1,\dots,K, j\neq y_i} f^j(\mathbf{a}_i). \quad (6.22)$$

Note that different from training a multi-class SVM classier, where y_i is given as a training label, the clustering scenario requires us to jointly estimate y_i as a variable. The overall max-margin loss to be minimized is (λ as the coefficient):

$$C(\mathbf{A}, \mathbf{w}) = \tfrac{\lambda}{2}||\mathbf{w}||^2 + \sum_{i=1}^{n} C(\mathbf{a}_i, \mathbf{w}). \qquad (6.23)$$

But to solve (6.22) or (6.23) with respect to the same framework as logistic loss will involve two additional concerns, which needs to be handled specifically.

First, the hinge loss of the form (6.22) is non-differentiable, with only subgradients existing. That makes the objective function $C(\mathbf{A}, \mathbf{w})$ non-differentiable on $\mathbf{D} \times \mathbf{w}$, and further the analysis in Theorem [6.2.1] proof can not be applied. We could have used the squared hinge loss or modified Huber loss for a quadratically smoothed loss function [Lee and Lin (2013)]. However, as we checked in the experiments, the quadratically smoothed loss is not as good as hinge loss in training time and sparsity. Also, though not theoretically guaranteed, using the subgradient of $C(\mathbf{A}, \mathbf{w})$ works well in our case.

Second, given that $\mathbf{w}$ is fixed, it should be noted that y_i and r_i are both functions of $\mathbf{a}_i$. Therefore, calculating the derivative of (6.22) over $\mathbf{a}_i$ would involve expanding both r_i and y_i, and become quite complicated. Instead, we borrow ideas from the regularity of the elastic net solution [Mairal *et al.* (2012)], that the set of non-zero coefficients of the elastic net solution should not change for small perturbations. Similarly, due to the continuity of the objective, it is assumed that a sufficiently small perturbation over the current $\mathbf{a}_i$ will not change y_i and r_i. Therefore in each iteration, we could directly pre-calculate y_i and r_i using the current $\mathbf{w}$ and $\mathbf{a}_i$ and fix them for $\mathbf{a}_i$ updates [4].

Given the above two handling, for a single sample $\mathbf{a}_i$, if the hinge loss is above 0, the derivative of (6.22) over $\mathbf{w}$ is:

$$\Delta_i^j = \begin{cases} \lambda \mathbf{w}_i^j - \mathbf{a}_i & \text{if} \quad j = y_i \\ \lambda \mathbf{w}_i^j + \mathbf{a}_i & \text{if} \quad j = r_i \\ \lambda \mathbf{w}_i^j & \text{otherwise,} \end{cases} \qquad (6.24)$$

where Δ_i^j denote the j-th element of the derivative for the sample $\mathbf{a}_i$. If the hinge loss is less than 0, then $\Delta_i^j = \lambda \mathbf{w}_i^j$. The derivative of (6.22) over $\mathbf{a}_i$ is $\mathbf{w}^{r_i} - \mathbf{w}^{y_i}$ if the hinge loss is over 0, and 0 otherwise. Note the above deduction can be conducted in a batch mode. It is then similarly solved

---

[4]To avoid ambiguity, if y_i and r_i are the same, i.e., the max value is reached by two cluster prototypes simultaneously in current iteration, then we ignore the gradient update corresponding to $\mathbf{a}_i$.

using a projected SGD algorithm, whose steps are outlined in Algorithm 2. The convergence and complexity analysis is similar to Algorithm 1.

Algorithm 6.3 Stochastic gradient descent algorithm for solving (6.16), with $C(\mathbf{A}, \mathbf{w})$ as defined in (6.23).

Require: $\mathbf{X}, \sigma; \lambda; \mathbf{D}_0$ and $\mathbf{w}_0$ (initial dictionary and classifier parameter); ITER (number of iterations); t_0, ρ (learning rate)

  1: Construct the matrix $\mathbf{L}$ from $\mathbf{X}$ and σ.

  2: Estimate the initialization of y_i and r_i by pre-clustering, $i = 1, 2, ..., N$

  3: FOR t=1 to ITER DO

  4: Conduct the same step 4-7 in Algorithm 1.

  5: Update $\mathbf{D}$ and $\mathbf{W}$ by a projected gradient step, based on the derivates of (6.23) over $\mathbf{a}_i$ and $\mathbf{w}$ (6.24).

  6: Update y_i and r_i using the current $\mathbf{w}$ and $\mathbf{a_i}$, $i = 1, 2, ..., N$.

  7: END FOR

Ensure: $\mathbf{D}$ and $\mathbf{w}$

6.2.3   *Experiments*

Table 6.10   Comparison of all datasets.

Name	Number of Images	Class	Dimension
ORL	400	10	1,024
MNIST	70,000	10	784
COIL20	1,440	20	1,024
CMU-PIE	41,368	68	1,024

Dataset and Evaluation   We conduct our clustering experiments on four popular real datasets, which are summarized in Table 6.10. We apply two widely-used measures to evaluate the performance of the clustering methods: the accuracy and the Normalized Mutual Information(NMI) [Zheng *et al.* (2011)], [Cheng *et al.* (2010)]. Suppose the predicted label of the $\mathbf{x}_i$ is $\hat{y}_i$ which is produced by the clustering method, and y_i is the ground truth label. The accuracy is defined as:

$$Acc = \frac{\mathbb{1}_{\Phi(\hat{y}_i) \neq y_i}}{n}, \tag{6.25}$$

where $\mathbb{1}$ is the indicator function, and Φ is the best permutation mapping function [Lovász and Plummer (2009)]. On the other hand, suppose the clusters obtained from the predicted labels $\{\hat{y}_i\}_{i=1}^n$ and $\{y_i\}_{i=1}^n$ as $\hat{C}$ and

Table 6.11   Accuracy and NMI performance comparisons on all datasets.

		KM	KM + SC	EMC	EMC + SC	MMC	MMC + SC	joint EMC	joint MMC
ORL	Acc	0.5250	0.5887	0.6011	0.6404	0.6460	0.6968	0.7250	**0.7458**
	NMI	0.7182	0.7396	0.7502	0.7795	0.8050	0.8043	0.8125	**0.8728**
MNIST	Acc	0.6248	0.6407	0.6377	0.6493	0.6468	0.6581	0.6550	**0.6784**
	NMI	0.5142	0.5397	0.5274	0.5671	0.5934	0.6161	0.6150	**0.6451**
COIL20	Acc	0.6280	0.7880	0.7399	0.7633	0.8075	0.8493	0.8225	**0.8658**
	NMI	0.7621	0.9010	0.8621	0.8887	0.8922	0.8977	0.8850	**0.9127**
CMU-PIE	Acc	0.3176	0.8457	0.7627	0.7836	0.8482	0.8491	0.8250	**0.8783**
	NMI	0.6383	0.9557	0.8043	0.8410	0.9237	0.9489	0.9020	**0.9675**

C, respectively. The mutual information between $\hat{C}$ and C is defined as:

$$MI(\hat{C}, C) = \sum_{\hat{c} \in \hat{C}, c \in C} p(\hat{c}, c) \log \frac{p(\hat{c},c)}{p(\hat{c})p(c)}, \tag{6.26}$$

where $p(\hat{c})$ and $p(c)$ are the probabilities that a data point belongs to the clusters $\hat{C}$ and C, respectively, and $p(\hat{c}, c)$ is the probability that a data point jointly belongs to $\hat{C}$ and C. The normalized mutual information(NMI) is defined as:

$$NMI(\hat{C}, C) = \frac{MI(\hat{C},C)}{\max\{H(\hat{C}),H(C)\}}, \tag{6.27}$$

where $H(\hat{C})$ and $H(C)$ are the entropies of $\hat{C}$ and C, respectively. NMI takes values between [0,1].

Comparison Experiments   *Comparison Methods* We compare the following eight methods on all four datasets:

- **KM:** K-Means clustering on the input data.
- **KM + SC:** A dictionary **D** is first learned from the input data by K-SVD [Elad and Aharon (2006)]. Then KM is performed on the graph-regularized sparse code features (6.15) over **D**
- **EMC:** Entropy-minimization clustering, by minimizing (6.18) on the input data.
- **EMC + SC:** EMC performed on the graph-regularized sparse codes over the pre-learned K-SVD dictionary **D**.
- **MMC:** Maximum-margin clustering [Xu and Schuurmans (2005)].
- **MMC + SC:** MMC performed on the graph-regularized sparse codes over the pre-learned K-SVD dictionary **D**.
- **Joint EMC:** The joint optimization (6.16), with $C(\mathbf{A}, \mathbf{w})$ as defined in (6.18).
- **Joint MMC:** The joint optimization (6.16), with $C(\mathbf{A}, \mathbf{w})$ as defined in (6.23).

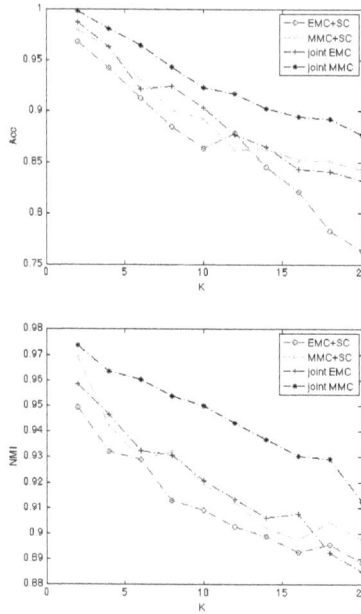

Fig. 6.7   The clustering accuracy and NMI measurements versus the number of clusters K.

All images are first reshaped into vectors, and PCA is then applied to reducing the data dimensionality by keeping 98% information, which is also used in [Zheng *et al.* (2011)] to improving efficiency. The multi-class MMC algorithm is implemented based on the publicly available CPMMC code for two-class clustering [Zhao *et al.* (2008)], following the multi-class case descriptions in the original paper. For all algorithms that involve graph-regularized sparse coding, the graph regularization parameter α is fixed to be 1, and the dictionary size p is 128 by default. For joint EMC and joint MMC, we set ITER as 30, ρ as 0.9, and t_0 as 5. Other parameters in competing methods are tuned in cross-validation experiments.

Comparison Analysis All the comparison results (accuracy and NMI) are listed in Table. 6.11, from which we could conclude the following:

- **1:** The joint EMC and joint MMC methods each outperform their "non-joint" counterparts, e.g., EMC + SC and MMC + SC, respectively. For example, on the *ORL* dataset, joint MMC surpasses MMC + SC by around 5% in accuracy and 7% in NMI. Those demonstrate that the

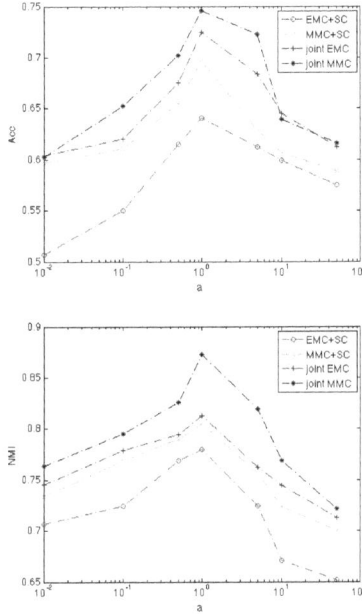

Fig. 6.8 The clustering accuracy and NMI measurements versus the parameter choices of α.

key contribution of this model, i.e., jointly optimizing the sparse coding and clustering steps, indeed leads to improved performances.

- **2:** KM + SC, EMC + SC, and MMC + SC all outperform their counterparts using raw input data, which verifies that sparse codes are effective features that help improve the clustering discriminability.
- **3:** The joint MMC obtains the best performances in all cases, outperforming the others, including joint EMC, with significant margins. The MMC + SC obtains the second best performance for the last three datasets (for ORL, it is joint EMC that ranks the second). The above facts reveal the power of the max-margin loss (6.23).

Varying the number of clusters On the COIL20 dataset, We re-conduct the clustering experiments with the cluster number K ranging from 2 to 20, using EMC + SC, MMC + SC, joint EMC, and joint MMC. For each K except for 20, 10 test runs are conducted on different randomly chosen clusters, and the final scores are obtained by averaging over the 10 tests. Fig. 6.7 shows the clustering accuracy and NMI measurements versus the

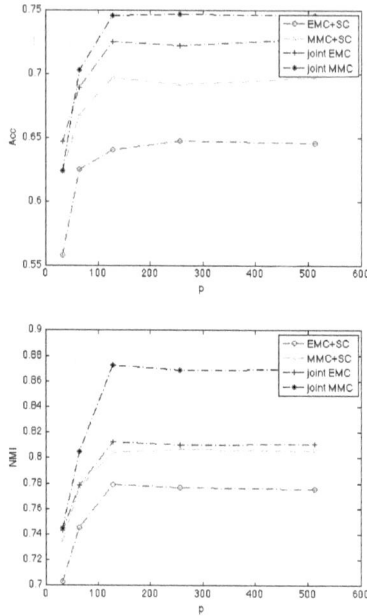

Fig. 6.9   The clustering accuracy and NMI measurements versus the parameter choices of p.

number of clusters. It is revealed that the two joint methods consistently outperforms their non-joint counterparts. When K goes up, the performances of joint methods seem to degrade less slowly.

Initialization and Parameters

As observed in our experiments, a good initialization of $\mathbf{D}$ and $\mathbf{w}$ can affect the final results notably. We initialize Joint EMC by the $\mathbf{D}$ and $\mathbf{w}$ solved from EMC + SC, and Joint MMC by the solutions from MMC + SC, respectively.

There are two parameters that we need to set empirically: the graph regularization parameter α, and the dictionary size p. The regularization term imposes stronger smoothness constraints on the sparse codes when α grows larger. Also, while a compact dictionary is more desirable computationally, more redundant dictionaries may lead to less cluttered features that can be better discriminated. We investigate how the clustering performances EMC + SC, MMC + SC, joint EMC, and joint MMC change on the ORL dataset, with various α and p values. As depicted in Fig. 6.8 and 6.9, we observe that:

- **1:** While α goes up, the accuracy result will first grow up then go down (the peak is around $\alpha =1$). That could be interpreted as when α is too small, the local manifold information is not sufficiently encoded. On the other hand, when α turns overly large, the sparse codes are "over-smoothened" with a reduced discriminability.
- **2:** Increasing dictionary size p will first improve the accuracy sharply, which however soon reaches a plateau. Thus in practice, we keep a medium dictionary size $p =128$ for all experiments.

6.3 Regularized ℓ^1-Graph

6.3.1 *Regularization of ℓ^1-Graph by Fixed Graph Laplacian*

In many real applications, high-dimensional data always reside on or close to a intrinsically low dimensional manifold embedded in the high-dimensional ambient space. Clustering the data according to its underlying manifold structure is important and challenging in machine learning. Moreover, the effectiveness of graph-based clustering methods, such as spectral clustering, motivates researchers to build the graph which reflects the manifold structure of the data. ℓ^1-graph [Cheng *et al.* (2010)], which builds the graph weight matrix by reconstructing each datum from the remaining data and the noise term through sparse representation, has been shown to be robust to noise and capable of finding datum-adaptive neighborhood for the graph construction. Also, the sparse manifold clustering method [Elhamifar and Vidal (2011)] points out that the sparse graph is useful for recovering the intrinsic manifold structure in the data.

However, ℓ^1-graph performs sparse representation for each datum separately without considering the geometric information and manifold structure of the entire data. Previous research shows that the data representations which respect the manifold structure of the data produce superior results in various clustering and classification tasks [Belkin *et al.* (2006); He *et al.* (2011)]. Inspired by ℓ^1-graph and manifold learning, we present a Laplacian Regularized ℓ^1-Graph (LRℓ^1-Graph) for data clustering in this section. In accordance with the manifold assumption, the sparse representations of LRℓ^1-Graph are regularized using the proper graph Laplacian. As a result, the sparse representations are smoothed along the geodesics on the data manifold where nearby datums have similar sparse representations. Furthermore, motivated by the fact that the sparse representations of the ℓ^1-Graph lead to a pairwise similarity matrix for spectral clustering

with satisfactory empirical performance, we discuss an iterative regularization scheme which utilizes the regularized sparse representations from the
previous iteration to build the graph Laplacian for the current iteration of
regularization for the LRℓ^1-Graph. The iterative regularization scheme
produces superior clustering performance shown in our experimental
results.

6.3.1.1   *The Laplacian Regularized ℓ^1-Graph*

Given the data $\mathbf{X} = \{x_1\}_{l=1}^n \in \mathbb{R}^d$, ℓ^1-graph seeks for the robust sparse
representation for each datum by solving the ℓ^1-norm optimization problem

$$\|x_i - \mathbf{B}\alpha^i\|_2^2 + \lambda\|\alpha^i\|_1, i = 1, 2, \dots, n \tag{6.28}$$

where matrix $\mathbf{B} = [x_1, \dots, x_n, \mathbf{I}] \in \mathbb{R}^{d \times (n+d)}$, λ is the weighting parameter
controlling the sparsity of the sparse representation, $\mathbf{I}$ is the identity matrix,
$\alpha^i = \{\alpha_j^i\}_{j=1}^{n+d}$ is the sparse representation for x_i under the dictionary $\mathbf{B}$.
We denote by α the $(n+d) \times n$ coefficient matrix with elements $\alpha_{ij} = \alpha_i^j, 1 \leq$
$i \leq n+d, 1 \leq j \leq n$. To avoid trivial solution that $\alpha_{ii} = 1$, it is required
that $\alpha_{ii} = 0$ for $1 \leq i \leq n$. Let $G = (\mathbf{X}, \mathbf{W})$ be the ℓ^1-graph where the
data $\mathbf{X}$ are the vertices, $\mathbf{W}$ is the graph weight matrix and $\mathbf{W}_{ij}$ indicates
the similarity between x_i and x_j. Interpreting α_{ji} as the directed similarity
between x_i and x_j, ℓ^1-graph [Cheng *et al.* (2010)] builds the symmetric
pairwise similarity matrix $\mathbf{W}$ using the sparse representations as below:

$$\mathbf{W} = (\alpha_{[1:n]} + \alpha_{[1:n]}^T)/2 \tag{6.29}$$

where $\alpha_{[1:n]}$ is the first n rows of α. $\mathbf{W}$ is then fed into the spectral
clustering method to produce the clustering result.

The pairwise similarity matrix using the sparse representations α plays
an essential role for the performance of ℓ^1-graph based clustering. In order to obtain the sparse representations that account for the geometric
information and manifold structure of the data, we employ the manifold
assumption [Belkin *et al.* (2006)] which in our case requires that nearby
data points x_i and x_j in the data manifold exhibit similar sparse representations with respect to the dictionary $\mathbf{B}$. In other words, α varies smoothly
along the geodesics in the intrinsic geometry. Given a pairwise similarity
matrix $\hat{\mathbf{W}}$, the sparse representations α that capture the geometric structure of the data according to the manifold assumption should minimize the
following objective function $\frac{1}{2} \sum_{i=1}^n \sum_{j=1}^n \hat{\mathbf{W}}_{ij}\|\alpha^i - \alpha^j\|_2^2 = \mathrm{Tr}\left(\alpha \mathbf{L} \alpha^\mathbf{T}\right)$ where
$\mathbf{L} = \hat{\mathbf{D}} - \hat{\mathbf{W}}$ is the graph Laplacian matrix, and $\hat{\mathbf{D}}$ is a diagonal matrix

given by $\hat{\mathbf{D}}_{ii} = \sum_{j=1}^{n} \hat{\mathbf{W}}_{ij}$. Incorporating the regularization term $\mathrm{Tr}\left(\alpha L \alpha^{\mathbf{T}}\right)$ into (6.28), we obtain the objective function for LRℓ^1-graph as below:

$$\min_{\alpha} \sum_{i=1}^{n} \|x_i - \mathbf{B}\alpha^i\|_2^2 + \lambda\|\alpha^i\|_1 + \gamma \mathrm{Tr}(\alpha L \alpha^{\mathbf{T}}) \qquad (6.30)$$

$$s.t. \quad \alpha_{ii} = 0, 1 \leq i \leq n$$

As suggested in the manifold regularization framework [Belkin *et al.* (2006)], the pairwise similarity matrix $\hat{\mathbf{W}}$ is constructed by Gaussian kernel. We use coordinate descent to optimize the objective function (6.30). Since (6.30) is convex, the global minimum is guaranteed. In each step of coordinate descent, we minimize (6.30) with respect to α^i with fixed $\alpha^{-i} = \left[\alpha^1, ...\alpha^{i-1}, \alpha^{i+1}, ...\alpha^n\right]$. Namely, we optimize the following objective function in terms of α^i by coordinate descent:

$$\min_{\alpha^i} \|x_i - \mathbf{B}\alpha^i\|^2 + \lambda\|\alpha^i\|_1 + \gamma \mathbf{L}_{ii}(\alpha^i)^T \alpha^i + 2(\alpha^i)^T \sum_{j \neq i} L_{ij}\alpha^j$$

$$s.t. \quad \alpha_{ii} = 0 \qquad (6.31)$$

(6.31) can be optimized using the efficient feature-sign search algorithm [Lee *et al.* (2006)]. In addition, ℓ^1-Graph uses the sparse representations to build the pairwise similarity matrix (6.29) for spectral clustering and obtains satisfactory clustering results. It inspires us to design an iterative regularization scheme, where the regularized sparse representation from the previous iteration is used to construct the graph Laplacian for the current iteration of regularization. Algorithm 6.4 describes the learning procedure for LRℓ^1-Graph.

6.3.1.2 *Experimental Results*

The coefficient matrix α obtained from the learning procedure for LRℓ^1-Graph is used to construct the pairwise similarity matrix $\mathbf{W}$ by (6.29), and then $\mathbf{W}$ is fed into the spectral clustering algorithm to produce the clustering result. We compare our algorithm to K-means (KM), Spectral Clustering (SC), ℓ^1-Graph and Sparse Manifold Clustering and Embedding (SMCE). The clustering results on several real data sets, i.e. UCI Wine, UCI Breast Tissue (BT) and ORL face database, are shown in Table 6.12 where the clustering performance is measured by Accuracy (AC) and the Normalized Mutual Information (NMI). ORL-k denotes the first k samples in the ORL face database. We use fixed empirical value $\lambda = 0.1, \gamma = 30, M = 2$

Algorithm 6.4 Learning Procedure for LRℓ^1-Graph.

Input:

The data set $\mathbf{X} = \{x_1\}_{l=1}^n$, the number of iterations M for iterative regularization, the initial graph Laplacian $\mathbf{L} = \hat{\mathbf{D}} - \hat{\mathbf{W}}$ computed with Gaussian kernel, the parameters λ and γ.

1: $m = 1$, initialize the coefficient matrix $\alpha = \mathbf{0}$

2: **while** $m \leq M$ **do**

3:     Use coordinate descent algorithm with current $\mathbf{L}$ to optimize (6.30) and obtain the coefficient matrix α.

4:     Build the graph Laplacian $\mathbf{L} = \mathbf{D} - \mathbf{W}$, where $\mathbf{W} = (\alpha_{[1:n]} + \alpha_{[1:n]}^T)/2$, $\mathbf{D}$ is a diagonal matrix such that $\mathbf{D}_{ii} = \sum_j \mathbf{W}_{ij}$. $m = m + 1$.

5: **end while**

Output: The coefficient matrix (i.e. the sparse representations) α.

---

throughout the experiments, and tune λ between $[0.1, 1]$ for ℓ^1-Graph and SMCE. We observe that LRℓ^1-Graph outperforms other clustering methods by the iterative regularization scheme.

Table 6.12   Clustering results on real data sets.

Data Set	Measure	KM	SC	ℓ^1-Graph	SMCE	LRℓ^1-Graph
Wine	AC	0.7022	0.5618	0.6629	0.7135	**0.8371**
	NMI	0.4287	0.3522	0.4070	0.4317	**0.5903**
BT	AC	0.3396	0.4057	0.4434	0.4528	**0.7547**
	NMI	0.3265	0.3563	0.3104	0.4131	**0.6437**
ORL-100	AC	0.5817	0.3813	0.7100	0.7200	**0.9113**
	NMI	0.6188	0.5154	0.7653	0.7517	**0.9011**
ORL-200	AC	0.5310	0.3812	0.7267	0.7050	**0.7873**
	NMI	0.6654	0.5631	0.8239	0.8114	**0.8617**
ORL	AC	0.5304	0.4479	0.6958	0.7050	**0.7547**
	NMI	0.7299	0.6710	0.8446	0.8362	**0.8754**

6.3.2   *Regularization of ℓ^1-Graph by Learnt Sparse Codes*

In this section we present another regularized ℓ^1-Graph method for data clustering. Clustering is a common and important unsupervised data analysis method which partitions data into a set of self-similar clusters, and the clustering results always serve as indispensable input to other algorithms in machine learning and computer vision, or the clusters themselves reveal important patterns of the data.

Most clustering algorithms fall into two categories: similarity-based and model-based clustering methods. Model-based clustering methods usually statistically model the data by a mixture of parametric distributions, and the parameters of the distributions are estimated via fitting the statistical model to the data [Fraley and Raftery (2002)]. The representative model-based clustering is Gaussian Mixture Model (GMM), which assumes that the data are generated from a mixture of Gaussians and the parameters of the Gaussian distributions are estimated by Maximum Likelihood through the Expectation-Maximization algorithm [Fraley and Raftery (2002); Bishop *et al.* (2006)]. GMM-based clustering achieves satisfactory results and it has been broadly applied to machine learning, pattern recognition and computer vision [He *et al.* (2011); Yan *et al.* (2008); Zhou *et al.* (2009b); Povey *et al.* (2010)].

Although model-based clustering methods possess clear statistical interpretations, it is difficult to estimate parameters of the distributions for high dimensional data, which is the case in many real applications. In addition, the real data may not be generated from the assumed statistical models. In contrast, similarity-based clustering methods partition the data based on the similarity function and alleviate the difficult parameter estimation in case of high dimensionality. K-means [Duda *et al.* (2000)] finds a local minima of sum of within-cluster dissimilarities, and spectral clustering [Ng *et al.* (2002)] identifies clusters of complex shapes lying on some low dimensional manifolds. ℓ^1-graph [Yan and Wang (2009); Cheng *et al.* (2010)], which builds the graph by reconstructing each datum with all the other data, has been shown to be robust to noise and capable of producing superior results for high dimensional data, compared to K-means and spectral clustering. Compared to k-nearest-neighbor graph and ϵ-ball graph, ℓ^1-graph adaptively determines the neighborhood of each datum by solving sparse representation problem locally. We introduce sparse coding and ℓ^1-graph in the sequel.

6.3.2.1 *Sparse Coding and ℓ^1-Graph for Clustering*

The aim of sparse coding is to represent an input vector by only a few sparse coefficients, called the sparse code, over a dictionary which is usually over-complete. It has been widely applied in machine learning and signal processing, and extensive literature has demonstrated the convincing performance of sparse code as a discriminative and robust feature representation [Yang *et al.* (2009c)]. Denote the data by $\mathbf{X} = [\mathbf{x}_1, \mathbf{x}_2, \ldots, \mathbf{x}_n]$, where $\mathbf{x}_i$ lies in the d-dimensional Euclidean space $\mathbb{R}^d$, and let the dictionary matrix be $\mathbf{D} = [\mathbf{d}_1, \mathbf{d}_2, \ldots, \mathbf{d}_p] \in \mathbb{R}^{d \times p}$ with each $\mathbf{d}_m$ $(m = 1, \ldots, p)$

being the atom or the basis vector of the dictionary. Sparse coding method searches for the linear sparse representation with respect to the dictionary $\mathbf{D}$ for each datum $\mathbf{x}_i$. Sparse coding is performed by the following convex optimization

$$\alpha^i = \arg\min_{\alpha^i} \|\alpha^i\|_1 \quad s.t. \quad \mathbf{x}_i = \mathbf{D}\alpha^i \quad i = 1, \ldots, n$$

In [Cheng *et al.* (2010)], the authors applied the idea of sparse coding to data clustering and subspace learning applications, and constitute the ℓ^1-graph. Given the data $\mathbf{X} = [\mathbf{x}_1, \ldots, \mathbf{x}_n] \in \mathbb{R}^{d \times n}$, ℓ^1-graph seeks for the robust sparse representation for the entire data by solving the ℓ^1-norm optimization problem for each data point:

$$\min_{\alpha^i} \|\alpha^i\|_1 \quad s.t. \ \mathbf{x}_i = \mathbf{X}\alpha^i \quad i = 1, \ldots, n \tag{6.32}$$

where $\alpha^i \in \mathbb{R}^{n \times 1}$, and we denote by α the coefficient matrix $\alpha = [\alpha^1, \ldots, \alpha^n] \in \mathbb{R}^{n \times n}$ with the element $\alpha_{ij} = \alpha_i^j$. To avoid trivial solution that $\alpha = \mathbf{I}_n$ ($n \times n$ identity matrix), it is required that the diagonal elements of α be zero, i.e. $\alpha_{ii} = 0$ for $1 \leq i \leq n$. ℓ^1-graph features robustness to data noise and an adaptive neighborhood, specified by the non-zero entries in the sparse codes, for each datum. Let $G = (\mathbf{X}, \mathbf{W})$ be the ℓ^1-graph where $\mathbf{X}$ is the set of vertices, $\mathbf{W}$ is the graph weight matrix and $\mathbf{W}_{ij}$ indicates the similarity between $\mathbf{x}_i$ and $\mathbf{x}_j$. ℓ^1-graph sets the $n \times n$ matrix $\mathbf{W}$ as

$$\mathbf{W} = (|\alpha| + |\alpha^T|)/2 \tag{6.33}$$

where $|\alpha|$ is the matrix whose elements are the absolute values of α, and then feed $\mathbf{W}$ as the pairwise similarity matrix into the spectral clustering algorithm to get the clustering result. It achieves better performance than spectral clustering with pairwise similarity matrix set by Gaussian kernel which is widely used in a variety of machine learning tasks. It should be emphasized that the pairwise similarity matrix (6.33) constructed by the coefficient matrix α leads to the superior performance of ℓ^1-graph based clustering.

However, ℓ^1-graph performs sparse representation for each datum separately and it sacrifices the potential of the geometric structure of the data especially in case of high dimensionality. In the next section, we introduce Regularized ℓ^1-Graph, which incorporates the information of the manifold structure of the data into the construction of the sparse graph.

6.3.2.2 *Regularized ℓ^1-Graph*

High-dimensional data always lie on or close to a submanifold of low intrinsic dimension, and clustering the data according to its underlying manifold structure is important and challenging in computer vision and machine learning. While ℓ^1-graph demonstrates better performance than many traditional similarity-based clustering methods, it performs sparse representation for each datum independently without considering the geometric information and manifold structure of the entire data. In order to obtain the sparse representations that account for the geometric information and manifold structure of the data, we can employ the manifold assumption [Belkin *et al.* (2006)] and use a novel Regularized ℓ^1-Graph (Rℓ^1-Graph). The manifold assumption in this case requires that if two points $\mathbf{x}_i$ and $\mathbf{x}_j$ are close in the intrinsic geometry of the submanifold, their corresponding sparse codes α^i and α^j are also expected to be similar to each other. In other words, α varies smoothly along the geodesics in the intrinsic geometry (See Figure 6.10). Based on the spectral graph theory [Chung (1997)], extensive literature uses graph Laplacian to impose local smoothness of the embedding to preserve the local manifold structure [Belkin *et al.* (2006); Liu *et al.* (2010); He *et al.* (2011); Zheng *et al.* (2011); Gao *et al.* (2013)]. Given a proper pairwise similarity matrix $\mathbf{W}$, the sparse code α that captures the local geometric structure of the data in accordance with the manifold assumption should minimize the following regularization term:

$$\frac{1}{2}\sum_{i=1}^{n}\sum_{j=1}^{n}\mathbf{W}_{ij}\|\alpha^i - \alpha^j\|_2^2 = \mathrm{Tr}(\alpha\mathbf{L_W}\alpha^T) \tag{6.34}$$

where $\mathbf{L_W}$ is defined as

$$\mathbf{L_W} = \frac{1}{2}(\mathbf{D_W} + \tilde{\mathbf{D}}_{\mathbf{W}}) - \mathbf{W} \tag{6.35}$$

wherein $\mathbf{D_W}$ and $\tilde{\mathbf{D}}_{\mathbf{W}}$ are diagonal matrices with diagonal elements $(\mathbf{D_W})_{ii} = \sum_{j=1}^{n}\mathbf{W}_{ij}$ and $(\tilde{\mathbf{D}}_{\mathbf{W}})_{ii} = \sum_{j=1}^{n}\mathbf{W}_{ji}$. $\mathbf{L_W}$ is the graph Laplacian using the symmetric pairwise similarity matrix $\mathbf{W}$, and (6.35) also allows for nonsymmetric $\mathbf{W}$. Let $\mathbf{A}$ be a KNN adjacency matrix, and $\mathbf{A}_{ij} = 1$ if and only if either $\mathbf{x}_i$ is among the K-nearest neighbors of $\mathbf{x}_j$. The KNN adjacency matrix $\mathbf{A}$ encourages local smoothness of the sparse codes in a neighborhood of each data point without considering data that are far away from each other. Motivated by the local smoothness of the embedding and the effectiveness of the pairwise similarity matrix constructed by the sparse codes (6.33) in clustering, we can use $\mathbf{W} = (\mathbf{A} \circ |\alpha| + \mathbf{A}^T \circ |\alpha^T|)/2$ in the regularization term (6.34), and $\circ$ indicates the entrywise product.

It should be emphasized that our regularization term uses the graph Laplacian constructed by the sparse codes, which exhibits superior clustering performance compared to the Laplacian regularization used by previous works [He *et al.* (2011); Gao *et al.* (2013)] including Laplacian regularized sparse coding [Gao *et al.* (2013)]. In Laplacian regularization, the pairwise similarity matrix $\mathbf{W}$ is set by the Gaussian kernel. In contrast, the pairwise similarity matrix constructed by the sparse codes enables $R\ell^1$-Graph to learn the sparse codes that are optimal in both sparsely representing the data and modeling the pairwise similarity between the data. The resultant sparse codes leads to better clustering performance evidenced by our experimental results. By incorporating the Laplacian regularizer (6.34) into the

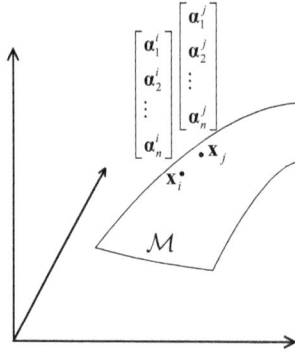

Fig. 6.10 Illustration of the manifold assumption used in our $R\ell^1$-Graph. This figure shows an example of a two-dimensional submanifold $\mathcal{M}$ in the three-dimensional ambient space. Two neighboring points $\mathbf{x}_i$ and $\mathbf{x}_j$ in the submanifold are supposed to have similar sparse codes, i.e. $\alpha^i = [\alpha_1^i, \ldots, \alpha_n^i]^T$ and $\alpha^j = [\alpha_1^j, \ldots, \alpha_n^j]^T$, according to the manifold assumption.

ℓ^1-graph scheme, we obtain the following objective function for $R\ell^1$-Graph:

$$\min_{\alpha, \mathbf{W}} \sum_{i=1}^{n} \|\mathbf{x}_i - \mathbf{X}\alpha^i\|_2^2 + \lambda \|\alpha^i\|_1 + \gamma \mathrm{Tr}(\alpha \mathbf{L}_{\mathbf{W}} \alpha^T) \qquad (6.36)$$

$$s.t. \ \mathbf{W} = (\mathbf{A} \circ |\alpha| + \mathbf{A}^T \circ |\alpha^T|)/2 \quad \alpha \in S$$

where $S = \{\alpha \in \mathbb{R}^{n \times n} | \alpha_{ii} = 0, 1 \leq i \leq n\}$, $\lambda > 0$ is the weight controlling the sparsity of the coefficients, and $\gamma > 0$ is the weight of the regularization term.

We further reformulate the optimization problem (6.36) into the following optimization problem with simplified equality constraint:

$$\min_{\alpha, \mathbf{W}} \sum_{i=1}^{n} \|\mathbf{x}_i - \mathbf{X}\alpha^i\|_2^2 + \lambda \|\alpha^i\|_1 + \gamma \text{Tr}(\alpha \mathbf{L}_{\mathbf{A}\circ|\mathbf{W}|}\alpha^T) \qquad (6.37)$$

$$s.t. \ \mathbf{W} = \alpha \quad \alpha \in S$$

Note that $\text{Tr}(\alpha \mathbf{L}_{\mathbf{A}\circ|\mathbf{W}|}\alpha^T) = \frac{1}{2}\sum_{i=1}^{n}\sum_{j=1}^{n} \mathbf{A}_{ij}|\mathbf{W}_{ij}|\|\alpha^i - \alpha^j\|_2^2$. Proposition 6.1 establishes the equivalence between the problem (6.37) and problem (6.36).

Prop 6.1. The solution α^* to the problem (6.37) is also the solution to the problem (6.36), and vice versa.

The proof is shown in A.2.2. The equality constraint of the new formulation (6.37) removes the $|\cdot|$ operator and the transpose of the coefficient matrix α. (6.37) leads to a more tractable augmented Lagrangian function than its preliminary form (6.36), which facilitates the optimization algorithm shown in the next section.

6.3.2.3 *Optimization Algorithm*

We employ Alternating Direction Method of Multipliers (ADMM) [Bertsekas (1999); Boyd *et al.* (2011)] to solve the nonconvex optimization problem (6.37). ADMM decomposes the original problem (6.37) into a sequence of tractable subproblems which can be solved efficiently. ADMM iteratively minimizes the augmented Lagrangian with respect to each primal variable, and the augmented Lagrangian function for the constrained optimization (6.37) is

$$\mathcal{L}(\alpha, \mathbf{W}, \mathbf{Y}) = \sum_{i=1}^{n} \|\mathbf{x}_i - \mathbf{X}\alpha^i\|_2^2 + \lambda \|\alpha^i\|_1$$

$$+ \gamma \text{Tr}(\alpha \mathbf{L}_{\mathbf{A}\circ|\mathbf{W}|}\alpha^T) + \langle \mathbf{Y}, \mathbf{W} - \alpha \rangle + \frac{\beta}{2}\|\mathbf{W} - \alpha\|_F^2 \quad (6.38)$$

where $\langle \mathbf{A}, \mathbf{B} \rangle = \text{Tr}(\mathbf{A}^T\mathbf{B})$ is the Frobenius inner product, $\mathbf{Y}$ is the dual variable or the Lagrangian multiplier, and β is a pre-set small positive constant called penalty parameter.

By ADMM, the optimization of (6.37) consists of the following iterative optimizations:

$$\alpha^{(k)} = \text{argmin}_\alpha \mathcal{L}(\alpha, \mathbf{W}^{(k-1)}, \mathbf{Y}^{(k-1)}) \tag{6.39}$$

$$\mathbf{W}^{(k)} = \text{argmin}_\mathbf{W} \mathcal{L}(\alpha^{(k)}, \mathbf{W}, \mathbf{Y}^{(k-1)}) \tag{6.40}$$

$$\mathbf{Y}^{(k)} = \mathbf{Y}^{(k-1)} + \beta(\mathbf{W}^{(k)} - \alpha^{(k)}) \tag{6.41}$$

where the superscript $k \geq 1$ is the current iteration index. From (6.41) we can see that the penalty parameter β is also the step size for updating the Lagrangian multiplier $\mathbf{Y}$. We explain the subproblems (6.39) and (6.40) in detail in the sequel, and we also remove the superscript k for simplicity of the presentation without confusion.

- Subproblem (6.39): update α while fixing $\mathbf{W}$ and $\mathbf{Y}$

$$\min_{\alpha \in S} \sum_{i=1}^{n} \|\mathbf{x}_i - \mathbf{X}\alpha^i\|_2^2 + \lambda\|\alpha^i\|_1 + \gamma\text{Tr}(\alpha\mathbf{L}_{\mathbf{A}\circ|\mathbf{W}|}\alpha^T) - \langle\mathbf{K},\alpha\rangle + \frac{\beta}{2}\langle\alpha,\alpha\rangle$$

$$\tag{6.42}$$

where $\mathbf{K} = \mathbf{Y} + \beta\mathbf{W}$. We denote by $F(\alpha)$ the objective function (6.42), and use coordinate descent algorithm to solve problem (6.42). In each step of the coordinate descent, we optimize $F(\alpha^i)$ with $[\alpha^1, \ldots, \alpha^{i-1}, \alpha^{i+1}, \ldots, \alpha^n]$ fixed:

$$\min_{\alpha^i \in \mathbb{R}^n} F(\alpha^i) = \frac{1}{2}\alpha^{iT}\mathbf{P}_i\alpha^i + \mathbf{b}_i^T\alpha^i + \lambda\|\alpha^i\|_1 \tag{6.43}$$

$$s.t. \ \alpha_{ii} = 0$$

where $\mathbf{P}_i = 2\mathbf{X}^T\mathbf{X} + (\gamma(\sum_{j\neq i}\mathbf{A}_{ij}|\mathbf{W}_{ij}| + \mathbf{A}_{ji}|\mathbf{W}_{ji}|) + \beta)\mathbf{I}_n$ which is a positive definite matrix, $\mathbf{b}_i = -2\mathbf{X}^T\mathbf{x}_i - \gamma\sum_{j\neq i}(\mathbf{A}_{ij}|\mathbf{W}_{ij}| + \mathbf{A}_{ji}|\mathbf{W}_{ji}|)\alpha_j - \mathbf{K}^i$, $\mathbf{K}^i$ is the i-th column of $\mathbf{K}$. Problem (6.43) is a Lasso problem and it is also solved efficiently by ADMM, where the resultant subproblems have closed-form solutions. We leave the details in A.2.3. The optimal solution to (6.42) is obtained by iteratively solving (6.43) for $i = 1 \ldots n$ until convergence. We adopt a warm start technique that effectively reduces the iteration number of coordinate descent. Warm start initializes $\alpha^{(k)}$ in the current iteration by the solution $\alpha^{(k-1)}$ obtained in the previous iteration. In our experiments we observe that the iteration number of coordinate descent is less than 5 in most cases.

Algorithm 6.5 Data Clustering by Regularized ℓ^1-Graph (Rℓ^1-Graph).

Input:
   The data set $\mathbf{X} = \{\mathbf{x}_i\}_{i=1}^n$, the number of clusters c, the parameters λ, the regularization parameter γ, the ADMM penalty parameters β and μ, the threshold ε_1, ε_2 and the maximum iteration number M.
1: $k = 0$, initialize the coefficient matrix, the matrix $\mathbf{W}$ and the Lagrangian multiplier as $\mathbf{0}$, i.e. $\alpha^{(0)} = \mathbf{W}^{(0)} = \mathbf{Y}^{(0)} = \mathbf{0}$.
2: Begin the ADMM iterations:
3: **while** $k \leq M$ **do**
4:    Solve subproblems (6.39), (6.40) and (6.41) according to the details explained in Section 6.3.2.3 to obtain $\alpha^{(k+1)}$, $\mathbf{W}^{(k+1)}$ and $\mathbf{Y}^{(k+1)}$.
5:    **if** $k \geq 1$ and $(\|\alpha^{(k)} - \alpha^{(k-1)}\|_F < \varepsilon_1$ and $\|\mathbf{W}^{(k)} - \alpha^{(k)}\|_F < \varepsilon_2)$ **then**
6:       print
7:    **else**
8:       $k = k + 1$.
9:    **end if**
10: **end while**
11: Obtain the optimal coefficient matrix α^* when the ADMM algorithm converges or maximum iteration number is achieved.
12: Build the pairwise similarity matrix by symmetrizing α^*: $\mathbf{W}^* = \frac{|\alpha^*| + |\alpha^*|^T}{2}$, compute the corresponding normalized graph Laplacian $\mathbf{L}^* = (\mathbf{D}^*)^{-\frac{1}{2}}(\mathbf{D}^* - \mathbf{W}^*)(\mathbf{D}^*)^{-\frac{1}{2}}$, where $\mathbf{D}^*$ is a diagonal matrix with $\mathbf{D}_{ii}^* = \sum_{j=1}^n \mathbf{W}_{ij}^*$
13: Construct the matrix $\mathbf{v} = [\mathbf{v}_1, \ldots, \mathbf{v}_c] \in \mathbb{R}^{n \times c}$, where $\{\mathbf{v}_1, \ldots, \mathbf{v}_c\}$ are the c eigenvectors of $\mathbf{L}^*$ corresponding to its c smallest eigenvalues. Treat each row of $\mathbf{v}$ as a data point in $\mathbb{R}^c$, and run K-means clustering method to obtain the cluster labels for all the rows of $\mathbf{v}$.

Output: The cluster label of $\mathbf{x}_i$ is set as the cluster label of the i-th row of $\mathbf{v}$, $1 \leq i \leq n$.

- Subproblem (6.40): update $\mathbf{W}$ while fixing α and $\mathbf{Y}$

$$\min_{\mathbf{W}} \gamma \mathrm{Tr}(\alpha \mathbf{L}_{\mathbf{A} \circ |\mathbf{W}|} \alpha^T) + \langle \mathbf{Y}, \mathbf{W} \rangle - \beta \langle \mathbf{W}, \alpha \rangle + \frac{\beta}{2} \langle \mathbf{W}, \mathbf{W} \rangle$$

which is equivalent to

$$\min_{\mathbf{W}} \sum_{i,j=1}^n \frac{\beta}{2}(\mathbf{W}_{ij} - \frac{\beta \alpha_{ij} - \mathbf{Y}_{ij}}{\beta})^2 + \gamma \mathbf{Q}_{ij}^\alpha |\mathbf{W}_{ij}| \tag{6.44}$$

(6.44) can be solved for each $\mathbf{W}_{ij}$ separately by soft thresholding as below:

$$\mathbf{W}_{ij} = \max\{0, |\beta\alpha_{ij} - \mathbf{Y}_{ij}| - \gamma\mathbf{Q}_{ij}^{\alpha}\} \cdot \frac{\text{sign}(\beta\alpha_{ij} - \mathbf{Y}_{ij})}{\beta} \quad 1 \leq i,j \leq n$$

$$(6.45)$$

where $\mathbf{Q}^{\alpha}$ is a $n \times n$ matrix with elements $\mathbf{Q}_{ij}^{\alpha} = \frac{1}{2}\mathbf{A}_{ij}\|\alpha^i - \alpha^j\|_2^2$, and the sign function $\text{sign}(\cdot)$ is defined as

$$\text{sign}(x) = \begin{cases} 1 & : \ x > 0 \\ 0 & : \ x = 0 \\ -1 & : \ x < 0 \end{cases} \tag{6.46}$$

Given the initialization $\alpha^{(0)} = \mathbf{W}^{(0)} = \mathbf{Y}^{(0)} = \mathbf{0}$, the ADMM algorithm solves three subproblems (6.39), (6.40) and (6.41) iteratively until convergence or the maximum iteration number is achieved. With the obtained optimal coefficient matrix α^*, we build a pairwise similarity matrix $\mathbf{W}^* = \frac{|\alpha| + |\alpha^T|}{2}$ and then use spectral clustering method to obtain the clustering result, as suggested in ℓ^1-Graph [Cheng et al. (2010)]. Algorithm 6.5 describes our data clustering algorithm using $R\ell^1$-Graph in detail.

Suppose the maximum iteration number of ADMM is N_1, and the maximum iteration number of the coordinate descent for solving subproblem (6.42) is N_2, then the overall time complexity for solving the optimization Problem (6.37) by ADMM is $\mathcal{O}(N_1 n^{2.376} + N_1 N_2 n^2)$. We leave the details in A.2.4. It is known that ADMM converges and achieves globally optimal solution for a class of convex problems [Boyd et al. (2011)]. Although our optimization problem (6.37) is nonconvex, we observe that ADMM for (6.37) always converges in less than 15 iterations for all the experiments we conduct.

6.3.2.4 *Experimental Results*

We demonstrate the performance of $R\ell^1$-Graph with comparison to other competing methods in this section.

Data Set

We conduct clustering experiments on various real data sets, which are summarized in Table 6.13. Three data sets are image data sets, i.e the ORL face database, the Yale face database and the MNIST handwritten digits data set. The ORL face database contains facial images for 40 subjects, and each subject has 10 images. The images are taken at different times with varying lighting and facial expressions. The subjects are all in an upright, frontal position with a dark homogeneous background. The Yale face database contains 165 grayscale images of 15 individuals. The MNIST database of handwritten digits has a total number of 70000 samples ranging from 0 to 9. The digits are normalized and centered in a fixed-size image. We also choose four data sets from UCI machine learning repository [A. Asuncion (2007)], i.e. Heart, Breast Tissue (BT) and Breast Cancer (Breast).

Table 6.13 Real data sets used in experiments.

	ORL	Yale	MNIST	Heart	BT	Breast
# of instances	400	168	70000	270	106	569
Dimension	1024	1024	784	13	9	30
# of classes	40	15	10	2	6	2

Evaluation Metric

We use two measures to evaluate the performance of the clustering methods, i.e. the accuracy and the Normalized Mutual Information(NMI) [Zheng *et al.* (2004)]. Suppose the predicted label of the datum $\mathbf{x}_i$ is $\hat{y}_i$ which is produced by the clustering method, and y_i is its ground truth label. The accuracy is defined as

$$Accuracy = \frac{\mathbf{1}_{\Phi(\hat{y}_i) \neq y_i}}{n} \quad (6.47)$$

where $\mathbf{1}$ is the indicator function, the mapping function Φ is the best permutation mapping function obtained by the Kuhn-Munkres algorithm [Plummer and Lovász (1986)]. Based on (6.47), we can see that the more predicted labels match the ground truth ones, the more accuracy value is obtained.

On the other hand, suppose the clusters obtained from the predicted labels $\{\hat{y}_i\}_{i=1}^n$ and the ground truth labels $\{y_i\}_{i=1}^n$ are $\hat{C}$ and C respectively. The mutual information between $\hat{C}$ and C is

$$MI(\hat{C},C) = \sum_{\hat{c}\in\hat{C},c\in C} p(\hat{c},c)\log_2\left(\frac{p(\hat{c},c)}{p(\hat{c})\,p(c)}\right) \tag{6.48}$$

where $p(\hat{c})$ and $p(c)$ are the probabilities that a data point belongs to the clusters $\hat{c}$ and c respectively, and $p(\hat{c},c)$ is the probability that a data point jointly belongs to clusters $\hat{c}$ and c. The normalized mutual information(NMI) is defined as follows:

$$NMI(\hat{C},C) = \frac{MI(\hat{C},C)}{\max\{H(\hat{C}),H(C)\}} \tag{6.49}$$

where $H(\hat{C})$ and $H(C)$ is the entropy of $\hat{C}$ and C. It can be verified that the normalized mutual information takes values in $[0,1]$. The accuracy and the normalized mutual information has been widely used for evaluate the performance of the clustering methods [Zheng *et al.* (2011); Cheng *et al.* (2010); Zheng *et al.* (2004)].

Clustering Result

We compare our algorithm to K-means (KM), Spectral Clustering (SC) and ℓ^1-Graph. Moreover, in order to demonstrate the superiority of the regularization term (6.34) using the pairwise similarity matrix constructed by the sparse code instead of the Gaussian kernel, we derive Laplacian regularized ℓ^1-Graph (Lℓ^1-Graph). Lℓ^1-Graph is equivalent to the subproblem (6.42) of Rℓ^1-Graph except that $\mathbf{W}$ is set by the Gaussian kernel. For MNIST data set, we randomly select 6 digits out of the 10 digits, and then randomly choose 100 samples for each chosen digit, resulting in a subset comprsing 600 samples. We perform this process for 20 times and report the average clustering performance on the 20 runs. The clustering results on various data sets are shown in Table 6.14. More results are show in A.2.5. By the manifold assumption that imposes local smoothness of the sparse

Table 6.14   Clustering results on real data sets.

Data Set	Measure	KM	SC	ℓ^1-Graph	$L\ell^1$-Graph	$R\ell^1$-Graph
ORL	AC	0.5333	0.4385	0.6964	0.6925	**0.7489**
	NMI	0.7317	0.6604	0.8410	0.8367	**0.8731**
Yale	AC	0.3974	0.2093	0.5339	0.5307	**0.5673**
	NMI	0.4525	0.2067	0.5731	0.5731	**0.5906**
MNIST	AC	0.6276	0.4422	0.6419	0.6425	**0.6617**
	NMI	0.5243	0.3358	0.6207	0.6156	**0.6288**
Heart	AC	0.5889	0.5519	0.6370	0.6333	**0.6407**
	NMI	0.0182	0.0032	0.0534	0.0507	**0.0573**
BT	AC	0.3396	0.4057	0.4434	0.4123	**0.5094**
	NMI	0.3265	**0.3563**	0.2762	0.2658	0.3608
Breast	AC	0.8541	0.6292	0.9016	**0.9051**	**0.9051**
	NMI	0.4223	0.0026	0.5172	**0.5249**	**0.5249**

codes in the data submanifold, $R\ell^1$-Graph obtains better performance than ℓ^1-Graph and SMCE. Moreover, the regularization term using the sparse codes achieves better performance than that using Gaussian kernel.

Parameter Setting

We set $\lambda = 0.1$, $\gamma = 0.5$, and choose $K \in \{5, 15\}$ empirically throughout all the experiments here. There are two parameters that influence the regularization term in $R\ell^1$-Graph, namely the weight of the regularization γ and the number of nearest neighbors K of the KNN adjacency matrix. The regularization term imposes stronger smoothness constraint on the sparse codes with larger γ and K, and vice versa. We investigate how the clustering performance on ORL face database changes when varying these two parameters, and illustrate the result in Figure 6.11 and Figure 6.12 respectively. We observe that the performance of $R\ell^1$-Graph is much better than other algorithms over a large range of both γ and K, revealing the robustness of our algorithm.

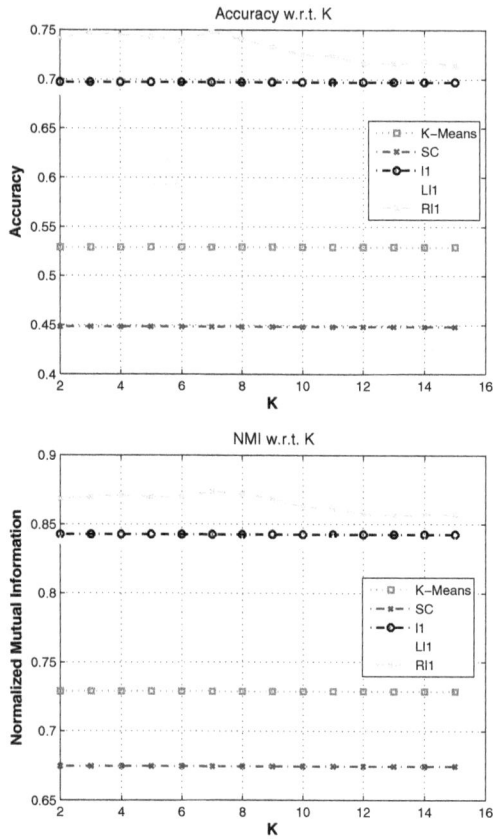

Fig. 6.11   Clustering performance with different values of K, i.e. the number of nearest neighbors, on ORL face database when $\gamma = 0.5$. Left: Accuracy; Right: NMI.

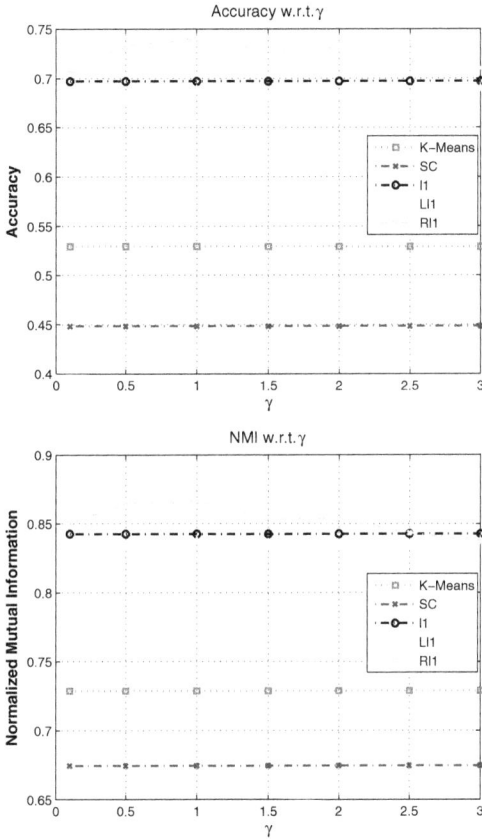

Fig. 6.12 Clustering performance with different values of γ, i.e. the weight of the regularization term, on ORL face database when $K = 5$. Left: Accuracy; Right: NMI.

Chapter 7

Object Recognition

Sparse coding approximates the input signal in terms of a sparse linear combination of the given overcomplete bases or dictionary. Such sparse representations are usually derived by linear programming as an ℓ^1 norm minimization problem [Donoho (2006b)]. Many efficient algorithms aiming to find such a sparse representation have been proposed in the past several years [Donoho *et al.* (2007); Lee *et al.* (2006); Friedman *et al.* (2008)]. A number of empirical algorithms are also proposed to seek dictionaries which allow sparse representations of the signals [Aharon *et al.* (2006); Lee *et al.* (2006)].

The sparse representation has been successfully applied to many inverse problems, e.g., image restoration [Mairal *et al.* (2008c); Yang *et al.* (2008)], and also well applied to classification tasks [Wright *et al.* (2009); Bradley and Bagnell (2008); Yang *et al.* (2009c)]. Wright *et al.* [Wright *et al.* (2009); Wagner *et al.* (2009)] cast the recognition problem as one of finding a sparse representation of the test image in terms of the training set as a whole, up to some sparse error due to occlusion. The algorithm achieves impressive results on public datasets, but fails to handle practical face variations such as alignment and pose. Both [Wright *et al.* (2009)] and [Wagner *et al.* (2009)] utilize the training set as the dictionary for sparse coding, and the sparse representation is modeled directly as the classifier. Others tried to train a compact dictionary for sparse coding [Bradley and Bagnell (2008); Yu *et al.* (2009)], and the sparse representations of the signals are used as image features trained latter with some classifier, e.g., SVM. These holistical sparse coding algorithms on the entire image, on one hand, hold robustness to corruptions such as noise and occlusions, as shown in [Wright *et al.* (2009)]. On the other hand, the underlying linear subspace assumption considerably limits the applications and performances of these approaches, e.g., face expression is known to be nonlinear.

Instead of sparse coding holistically on the entire image, learning sparse representations for local descriptors has also been explored for classification purposes. Raina *et al.* [Raina *et al.* (2007)] described an approach using sparse coding to construct high-level features, showing that sparse representations perform much better than conventional representations, e.g., raw image patches. Yang *et al.* [Yang *et al.* (2009c)] proposed a stage structure where sparse coding model is applied over the hand crafted SIFT features, followed by spatial pyramid max pooling. Applied to general image classification tasks, the proposed approach achieves *state-of-the-art* performance on several benchmarks with a simple linear classifier. However, the method is based on dictionaries trained in a reconstructive manner, which is optimal for reconstruction, but not necessarily for classification. Different network structures were also proposed for fast inference for sparse coding algorithms [Ranzato *et al.* (2007b); Jarrett *et al.* (2009); Lee *et al.* (2009)]. However, these models are difficult to train and the supervised training can not guarantee the sparsity of the data representation.

Recent research on dictionary learning for sparse coding has been targeted at learning discriminant sparse models [Mairal *et al.* (2008a); Bradley and Bagnell (2008)] instead of the purely reconstructive ones. Mairal *et al.* [Mairal *et al.* (2008a)] generalized the reconstructive sparse dictionary learning process by optimizing the sparse reconstruction jointly with a linear prediction model. Bradley and Bagnell [Bradley and Bagnell (2008)] proposed a novel differentiable sparse prior rather than the conventional ℓ_1 norm, and employed a backpropagation procedure to train the dictionary for sparse coding in order to minimize the training error. These approaches need to explicitly associate each data sample, either an image or image patch, with a label in order for the supervised training to proceed. In [Yang *et al.* (2009c)] and [Raina *et al.* (2007)], the local descriptors can belong to multiple classes.

In the sequel, we will address the problem of learning a discriminant dictionary for both sparse data representation and classification. Both local and global image descriptors are considered.

7.1 Supervised Translation-Invariant Sparse Coding

In this section, we discuss a supervised hierarchical sparse coding model, based on images represented by *bag-of-features*, where a local image descriptor may belong to multiple classes. We train the dictionary for local descriptors through back-propagation, by minimizing the training error of the image level features, which are extracted by max pooling over the sparse codes within a spatial pyramid [Yang *et al.* (2009c)]. The achieved dictionary is remarkably more effective than the unsupervised one in terms of classification. And the max pooling procedure over different spatial scales equips the presented model with local translation-invariance similar to the convolutional network [Lee *et al.* (2009)]. Our hierarchical structure can be trained with many classifiers, but here we specifically take linear SVM as our prediction model. For linear SVM, the framework has a computation complexity linear to the data size in training and a constant in testing, and thus will be of particular interest in real applications.

The rest of the section is organized as follows. Sec. 7.1.1 introduces the notations used in our presentation. Sec. 7.1.2 presents the hierarchical translation-invariant sparse coding structure. And Sec. 7.1.3 talks about the supervised dictionary training. We further sketch a justification for our sparse coding model in Sec. 7.1.4. And experiments are evaluated in Sec. 7.1.5.

7.1.1 *Notations*

Bold uppercase letters, $\mathbf{X}$, denote matrices and bold lowercase letters, $\mathbf{x}$, denote column vectors. For both matrices and vectors, bold subscripts $\mathbf{X}_m$ and $\mathbf{x}_n$ are used for indexing, while plain subscripts, such as X_{ij} and x_k, denote the element respectively. When both matrix indexing and element indexing exist, we use the superscripts as matrix indexing and lowerscripts as element indexing. For example, X_{ij}^m denotes the matrix element at the i-th row and j-th column of the m-th matrix $\mathbf{X}^m$. The same case with vectors for mixed indexing.

7.1.2 *Hierarchical Translation-Invariant Sparse Coding Structure*

This section introduces the hierarchical model based on sparse coding on local descriptors for image classification. Given the dictionary, the image level feature extracted is of translation-invariance property, and thus is robust to image misalignment [1].

---

[1] This is different from [Kavukcuoglu *et al.* (2009)], where the sparse coding model is robust to feature misalignment, i.e., the sparse feature won't change much if the feature itself shifts a little.

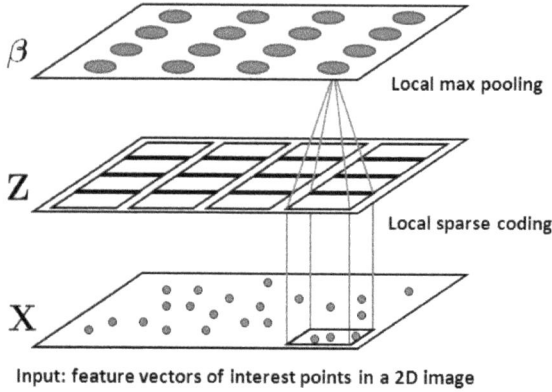

Fig. 7.1   An example architecture of convolutional sparse coding.

7.1.2.1 *Convolutional Sparse Coding*

In our hierarchical model, an image is represented by a local descriptor set $\mathbf{X} = [\mathbf{x}_1, \mathbf{x}_2..., \mathbf{x}_N] \in \mathbb{R}^{d \times N}$, where $\mathbf{x}_i$ denotes the ith local descriptor of the image in column vector. Suppose we are given a dictionary $\mathbf{B} \in \mathbb{R}^{d \times K}$ that can sparsely represent these local descriptors, where K is the size of the dictionary and is typically greater than $2d$. The sparse representations of a descriptor set are computed as

$$\hat{\mathbf{Z}} = \arg\min_{\mathbf{Z}} \|\mathbf{X} - \mathbf{BZ}\|_{\ell_2}^2 + \gamma \|\mathbf{Z}\|_{\ell_1}, \qquad (7.1)$$

where $\hat{\mathbf{Z}} \in \mathbb{R}^{K \times N}$ contains the sparse representations in columns for the descriptors in X. In order for classification, where we need fixed length feature vectors, we define the image level feature over the sparse representation matrix $\hat{\mathbf{Z}}$ by *max pooling*

$$\beta = \xi_{max}(\hat{\mathbf{Z}}), \qquad (7.2)$$

where ξ_{max} is defined on each row of $\hat{\mathbf{Z}} \in \mathbb{R}^{K \times N}$, returning a vector $\beta \in \mathbb{R}^K$ with the i-th element being

$$\beta_i = \max \left\{ |\hat{Z}_{i1}|, |\hat{Z}_{i2}|, ..., |\hat{Z}_{iN}| \right\}. \qquad (7.3)$$

The feature vector β defined in such a way is called *global pooling feature*, because the pooling function is evaluated on the whole descriptor set, discarding all spatial information of the local descriptors. Max pooling has been widely used in neural network algorithms and is also shown to be biological plausible. As we show in Sec. 7.1.4, max pooling is critical for the success of our sparse coding model.

To consider the spatial information and also to achieve regional invariance of the local descriptors to translations, we do convolutional coding [2] by dividing the whole image into $m \times m$ non-overlapping spatial cells. The image level feature is then defined by a concatenation of the max pooling features defined on m^2 spatial cells:

$$\beta = \bigcup_{c=1}^{m^2} \left[\xi_{max}(\hat{\mathbf{Z}}_{I_c}) \right] \tag{7.4}$$

where β is in $\mathbb{R}^{m^2 K}$, $\bigcup[\star]$ denotes the vector concatenation operator, and I_c is the index set for the local descriptors falling into the receptive field of c-th spatial cell. Fig. 7.1 illustrates the structure of our convolutional sparse coding scheme. In the figure, the image is divided into 4×4 spatial cells. The max pooling feature is invariant to translations of the local descriptors within each cell, while on the other hand still retains coarse spatial information as a whole image.

7.1.2.2 *Multi-Scale Convolutional Sparse Coding*

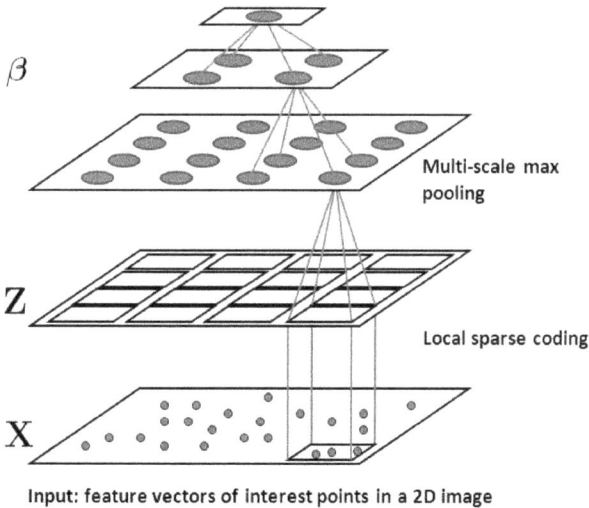

Fig. 7.2 The architecture of the unsupervised hierarchical sparse coding on multiple spatial scales. Three scales are shown.

---

[2]The convolutional coding is not done by weight sharing as in the conventional case, e.g., [Lee *et al.* (2009)], but performed by sparse coding with the same dictionary on local descriptors shifting across the image.

The max pooling feature from convolutional sparse coding achieves a trade off between translation invariance and the spatial information of the local image descriptor. In one extreme, if we use 1×1 cell, i.e., the global pooling, the max pooling feature is most invariant to local descriptor translations, but we lose the informative spatial information totally. In the other extreme, if we divide the image into so many cells that each cell contains only a single descriptor, the spatial information is totally retained, by we lose the translation invariance. Therefore, to achieve both translation invariance and spatial information of the max pooling feature, we can combine convolutional sparse coding on different scales of spatial cell structures, resulting in a hierarchical model similar to the Convolutional Neural Network (CNN) and the spatial pyramid [Yang *et al.* (2009c)]. Fig. 7.2 shows the multi-scale convolutional sparse coding structure we used in our implementation. The higher level of the max pooling feature, the more translation invariant, while the lower level, the more spatial information retained. The final image level feature derived from such a structure is the concatenation of max pooling features from different spatial cells on different convolutional scales.

Suppose we model the image in R spatial scales. In each scale s, the image is divided into $2^{s-1} \times 2^{s-1}$ non-overlapping cells. The multi-scale convolutional max pooling feature $\boldsymbol{\beta}$ is expressed as

$$\boldsymbol{\beta} = \bigcup_{s=1}^{R} [\boldsymbol{\beta}^s] = \bigcup_{s=1}^{R} \left[\bigcup_{c=1}^{2^{s-1}} \boldsymbol{\beta}_c^s \right], \tag{7.5}$$

where $\boldsymbol{\beta}_c^s$ denotes the set-level max pooling feature for the c-th spatial cell on the s-th scale. Eqn. 7.5 is the final feature vector as the input to latter classifiers such as linear SVM.

7.1.3 *Supervised Dictionary Learning for Hierarchical Sparse Coding*

In the previous section, the dictionary $\mathbf{B}$ for sparse coding is used as given. In practice, the dictionary $\mathbf{B}$ is usually trained over a large set of local descriptors $\mathbb{X} = \left[\mathbf{x}^1, \mathbf{x}^2, ..., \mathbf{x}^m \right]$ [3] by an ℓ_1 minimization [Lee *et al.* (2006)]

$$\min_{\{\mathbf{z}^i\}, \mathbf{B}} \sum_{i=1}^{m} \left\{ \|\mathbf{x}^i - \mathbf{B}\mathbf{z}^i\|_{\ell_2}^2 + \gamma \|\mathbf{z}^i\|_{\ell_1} \right\}, \tag{7.6}$$

---

[3] In our context, $\mathbb{X}$ contains local descriptors from many images.

which aims to learn a dictionary that can sparsely represent each local descriptor. The optimization problem in Eqn. 7.6 is not convex in $\mathbf{B}$ and $\{\mathbf{z}_i\}_{i=1}^m$ simultaneously, but is convex in one once the other fixed. Therefore, the optimization is done in an alternative coordinate descent fashion between $\mathbf{B}$ and $\{\mathbf{z}_i\}_{i=1}^m$, which guarantees to converge to a local minimum. Obviously, such a reconstructive learning process is not necessarily optimal for discriminant analysis we are interested in. The following discussions will introduce a discriminant dictionary training procedure based on back-propagation for our hierarchical sparse coding structure.

7.1.3.1 *Back-Propagation*

In retrospect, the previous system in Sec. 7.1.2 defines implicit feature transformations from the descriptor-set represented image $\mathbf{X}_k$ to the hierarchical max pooling feature $\boldsymbol{\beta}_k$. The transformations are achieved by two steps.

Step 1:

$$\mathbf{Z}_k = \varphi\left(\mathbf{X}_k, \mathbf{B}\right) \qquad (7.7)$$

denoting the transformation defined by Eqn. 7.1, and
Step 2:

$$\boldsymbol{\beta}_k = \xi_{max}^*\left(\mathbf{Z}_k\right), \qquad (7.8)$$

where we use ξ_{max}^* to denote the multilevel max pooling function, to differentiate from ξ_{max}. Combining these two steps we have

$$\boldsymbol{\beta}_k = \phi\left(\mathbf{X}_k, \mathbf{B}\right). \qquad (7.9)$$

For classification tasks, with a predictive model $f(\boldsymbol{\beta}_k, \mathbf{w}) \equiv f(\phi(\mathbf{X}_k, \mathbf{B}), \mathbf{w})$, a class label y_k of the image, and a classification loss $\ell(y_k, f(\phi(\mathbf{X}_k, \mathbf{B}), \mathbf{w}))$, we desire to train the whole system with respect to the predictive model parameters $\mathbf{w}$ and $\mathbf{B}$ given n training images:

$$\min_{\mathbf{w}, \mathbf{B}} \left\{ \sum_{k=1}^{n} \ell\left(y_k, f\left(\phi(\mathbf{X_k}, \mathbf{B}), \mathbf{w}\right)\right) + \lambda\|\mathbf{w}\|_{\ell^2}^2 \right\}, \qquad (7.10)$$

where λ is used to regularize the predictive model. For ease of presentation, denote

$$E\left(\mathbf{B}, \mathbf{w}, \{\mathbf{X_k}\}_{k=1}^n\right) = \sum_{k=1}^{n} \ell\left(y_k, f\left(\phi(\mathbf{X}_k, \mathbf{B}), \mathbf{w}\right)\right) + \lambda\|\mathbf{w}\|_{\ell_2}^2. \qquad (7.11)$$

Minimizing $E\left(\mathbf{B},\mathbf{w},\{\mathbf{X_k}\}_{k=1}^n\right)$ over $\mathbf{B}$ and $\mathbf{w}$, the learned dictionary will be more closely tightened with the classification model, and therefore more effective for classification [4]. The problem can be approached by optimizing alternatively over $\mathbf{B}$ and $\mathbf{w}$. Given the dictionary $\mathbf{B}$ fixed, optimization over $\mathbf{w}$ is simply training the classifier with the multi-scale max pooling features. Given the classifier $\mathbf{w}$, to optimize E over $\mathbf{B}$, we have to compute the gradient of E with respect to $\mathbf{B}$ using the chain rule:

$$\begin{aligned}
\frac{\partial E}{\partial \mathbf{B}} &= \sum_{k=1}^{n} \frac{\partial \ell}{\partial \mathbf{B}} = \sum_{k=1}^{n} \frac{\partial \ell}{\partial f}\frac{\partial f}{\partial \mathbf{B}} = \sum_{k=1}^{n} \frac{\partial \ell}{\partial f}\frac{\partial f}{\partial \beta_k}\frac{\partial \beta_k}{\partial \mathbf{B}} \\
&= \sum_{k=1}^{n} \frac{\partial \ell}{\partial f}\frac{\partial f}{\partial \beta_k}\frac{\partial \beta_k}{\partial \mathbf{Z}_k}\frac{\partial \mathbf{Z}_k}{\partial \mathbf{B}}.
\end{aligned} \tag{7.12}$$

Therefore, the problem is reduced to computing the gradients of the sparse representation matrix $\mathbf{Z}_k$ with respect to the dictionary $\mathbf{B}$, which can be calculated by investigating the gradient of each individual sparse code $\mathbf{z}$ (a column of $\mathbf{Z}_k$) with respect to $\mathbf{B}$. The difficulty of computing such a gradient is that there is no analytical link between $\mathbf{z}$ and the dictionary $\mathbf{B}$, which we overcome by using implicit differentiation on the fixed point equations.

7.1.3.2 *Implicit Differentiation*

In order to establish the relationship between a sparse code $\mathbf{z}$ and $\mathbf{B}$, we first find the fixed point equations by computing the gradient with respect to $\mathbf{z}$ on Eqn. 7.1 at its minimum $\hat{\mathbf{z}}$ as suggested by [Bradley and Bagnell (2008)]:

$$\triangledown\left(\|\mathbf{x}-\mathbf{Bz}\|_{\ell^2}^2\right)\big|_{\mathbf{z}=\hat{\mathbf{z}}} = -\triangledown\left(\|\mathbf{z}\|_{\ell^1}\right)\big|_{\mathbf{z}=\hat{\mathbf{z}}}, \tag{7.13}$$

leading to

$$2(\mathbf{B}^T\mathbf{Bz}-\mathbf{B}^T\mathbf{x})\big|_{\mathbf{z}=\hat{\mathbf{z}}} = -\gamma\cdot\text{sign}(\mathbf{z})\big|_{\mathbf{z}=\hat{\mathbf{z}}}, \tag{7.14}$$

where $\text{sign}(\mathbf{z})$ is a vector functioning on each element of vector $\mathbf{z}$, and $\text{sign}(0) = 0$. Note that Eqn. 7.13 and 7.14 hold only under the condition of $\mathbf{z} = \hat{\mathbf{z}}$. In the following derivations, we will admit the condition without the symbol $\big|_{\mathbf{z}=\hat{\mathbf{z}}}$ unless otherwise mentioned.

---

[4]In theory, a reconstructive term should be added in Eq. 7.11 to ensure the learned $\mathbf{B}$ can represent the data well. In practice, we initialize $\mathbf{B}$ with its unsupervised version, and then perform supervised training to refine it, which runs much faster.

In Eqn. 7.14, $\mathbf{z}$ is not linked with $\mathbf{B}$ explicitly. To calculate the gradient of $\mathbf{z}$ with respect to $\mathbf{B}$, we use implicit differentiation by taking derivative of $\mathbf{B}$ on both sides of Eqn. 7.14:

$$\frac{\partial\{2(\mathbf{B}^T\mathbf{B}\mathbf{z} - \mathbf{B}^T\mathbf{x})\}}{\partial B_{mn}} = \frac{\partial\{-\gamma \cdot \text{sign}(\mathbf{z})\}}{\partial B_{mn}}. \tag{7.15}$$

The "sign" function on the right side is not continuous at zero. However, since the left side of Eqn. 7.15 cannot be infinite, $\partial\{-\gamma \cdot \text{sign}(\mathbf{z})\}/\partial B_{mn} = 0$.[5] Since the gradient $\partial z_i/\partial B_{mn}$ is not well defined for $z_i = 0$, we set them to be zero and only care about the gradients where $z_i \neq 0$ [6]. Denote $\tilde{\mathbf{z}}$ as the nonzero coefficients of $\hat{z}$, and $\tilde{\mathbf{B}}$ being the corresponding bases (the supports selected by $\hat{z}$). From Eqn. 7.15, we have

$$\frac{\partial\{2(\tilde{\mathbf{B}}^T\tilde{\mathbf{B}}\tilde{\mathbf{z}} - \tilde{\mathbf{B}}^T\mathbf{x})\}}{\partial B_{mn}} = 0, \tag{7.16}$$

which gives

$$\frac{\partial\tilde{\mathbf{B}}^T\tilde{\mathbf{B}}}{\partial B_{mn}}\tilde{\mathbf{z}} + \tilde{\mathbf{B}}^T\tilde{\mathbf{B}}\frac{\partial\tilde{\mathbf{z}}}{\partial B_{mn}} - \frac{\partial\tilde{\mathbf{B}}^T\mathbf{x}}{\partial B_{mn}} = 0, \tag{7.17}$$

Therefore, the desired gradient can be solved by

$$\frac{\partial\tilde{\mathbf{z}}}{\partial B_{mn}} = \left(\tilde{\mathbf{B}}^T\tilde{\mathbf{B}}\right)^{-1}\left(\frac{\partial\tilde{\mathbf{B}}^T\mathbf{x}}{\partial B_{mn}} - \frac{\partial\tilde{\mathbf{B}}^T\tilde{\mathbf{B}}}{\partial B_{mn}}\tilde{\mathbf{z}}\right). \tag{7.18}$$

Since the number of non-zero coefficients is generally far smaller than the descriptor dimension d, the inverse $\left(\tilde{\mathbf{B}}^T\tilde{\mathbf{B}}\right)^{-1}$ is well-conditioned.

7.1.3.3 *Multi-Scale Gradient*

Now we are ready to compute the gradient of the multi-scale max pooling feature β in Eqn. 7.5 with respect to $\mathbf{B}$. To show the details of derivation, we first examine the simplest case where $\beta_0 = \xi(\hat{\mathbf{Z}})$, the global pooling feature $\hat{\mathbf{Z}}$.

$$\frac{\partial\beta_0}{\partial B_{mn}} = \text{sign}(\hat{\mathbf{z}}^{max}) \odot \frac{\partial\hat{\mathbf{z}}^{max}}{\partial B_{mn}} \tag{7.19}$$

where $\hat{\mathbf{z}}^{max}$ is a vector composed of the elements with the largest absolute values in each row of $\hat{\mathbf{Z}}$. Similarly, the gradient of the final multi-scale max

---

[5]Otherwise, if a small change of $\mathbf{B}$ causes sign change of $\mathbf{z}$, the right side of Eqn. 7.15 will be ∞.

[6]In practice, such a procedure works well.

pooling feature β with respect to **B** is computed as

$$\frac{\partial \beta}{\partial B_{mn}} = \frac{\partial \bigcup_{s=1}^{R}\left[\bigcup_{c=1}^{2^{s-1}}\beta_c^s\right]}{\partial B_{mn}} = \bigcup_{s=1}^{R}\left[\bigcup_{c=1}^{2^{s-1}}\left[\frac{\partial \beta_c^s}{\partial B_{mn}}\right]\right] \tag{7.20}$$

where I_s^c again indicates the index set of the local descriptors in receptive field of c-th cell on the s-th scale. With $\partial\beta/\partial B_{mn}$ calculated, the quantity of 7.12 can be evaluated through the chain rules, and the dictionary **B** can be updated iteratively for toward optimal for classification.

7.1.4 *Interpretation as Sparse Subspace Modeling*

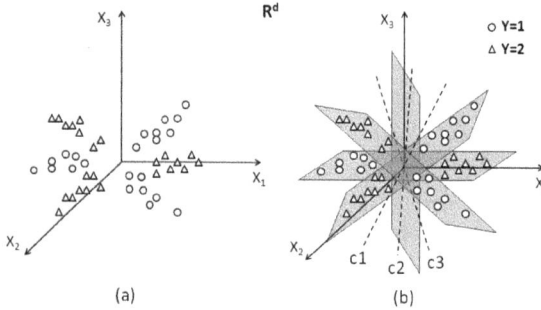

Fig. 7.3   The rationale behind our hierarchical sparse coding model. Left: the local descriptors from two classes $Y = 1, 2$ in the original space; Right: sparse coding discovers the linear subspace structure of the local descriptors. Simple linear classifiers are sufficient to separate two classes within each linear subspace.

Assume the local image descriptors are sparse signals with respect to a dictionary **B**. To simply the analysis, suppose these local descriptors reside in a union of M linear subspaces with non-sharing bases. Sparse coding clusters each local image descriptor into a linear subspace and projects it into the corresponding sub-coordination system, in which the nonzero coefficients of its sparse codes represent its coordinates. Within each sub-coordinate system, a simple linear classifier is likely to separate the projected local descriptors from the two classes. Concatenating these linear classifiers produces a linear classifier on the sparse codes of these local descriptors. Equivalently, training a linear classifier in the sparse feature space produces linear classifiers within each sub-coordinate systems. Fig. 7.3 illustrates this idea in the original descriptor space, where good linear separation is possible for descriptors from two classes within each subspace discovered by sparse coding, and overall a good nonlinear separation in the descriptor space is achieved.

Since sparse coding functions as a means of efficient descriptor space partition, which is determined by the dictionary, the supervised dictionary training can be explained as seeking the descriptor space partitions where the local image descriptors from two classes are most separable given the classifier.

7.1.5 *Experiment Results*

We verify the performance of the presented algorithm on several benchmark tasks including face recognition (CMU PIE [Sim *et al.* (2001)], CMU Multi-PIE [Gross *et al.* (2008)]), handwritten digit recognition (MNIST) [LeCun *et al.* (1998)] and gender recognition (FRGC [Philips *et al.* (2006)]). In each task, we report the prediction accuracies for our model with unsupervised and supervised dictionaries to show the benefits from supervised training. We also compare our algorithm with *state-of-the-art* algorithms specifical for each dataset under the same experiment settings.

7.1.5.1 *Implementation Details*

For all the tasks we test, the local descriptors are simply the raw image patches, densely sampled from the image on a regular grid with step size of 1 pixel. These raw image patches are pre-normalized to be unit vectors before sparse coding. Tab. 7.1 summaries the experiment settings for all the datasets. In our experiments, image size, patch size, the sparsity regularization γ, and dictionary size all affects the performance of our hierarchical sparse coding model. These parameters are set empirically, without searching for optimal settings. The dictionaries **B**'s are initialized by the corresponding unsupervised ones for supervised training.

Table 7.1 Parameter settings for the datasets we use. We set these parameters empirically, without testing for optimal settings.

dataset	image size	patch size	γ	dictionary size
CMU PIE	32×32	8×8	0.1	128
Multi-PIE	30×40	8×8	0.1	128
MNIST	28×28	12×12	0.2	256
FRGC	32×32	8×8	0.1	128

The optimization usually converges within 10 iterations. The following depicts some details regarding the supervised training.

(1) **Predictive model**: the predictive model we use in Eqn. 7.10 for discriminant dictionary training is linear SVM. But we modify the traditional hinge loss function to a differentiable squared hinge loss. The model regularization parameter λ is set to be 0.1 for all datasets.
(2) **Feature**: instead of the multi-scale max pooling feature, we use the *global max pooling feature* for the dictionary training process. As we will see in the later experiment results, the performance of our hierarchical model with unsupervised dictionary is already fairly decent. Therefore, minimizing the training error with the max pooling feature is more effective than that of the multi-scale pooling feature.
(3) **Optimization**: the optimization in Eqn. 7.10 is implemented in a stochastic way with gradient descent. The initial learning rate is set as 0.001, which decays in a manner similar to the neural network:

$$r = \frac{r_0}{\sqrt{n/N + 1}} \qquad (7.21)$$

where r_0 is the initial learning rate, r is the current learning rate, n is the incremental count of the current example and N is the size of the dataset.

To show the effectiveness of the supervised training procedure used here, we report the validation performance on each test set for both unsupervised dictionary and supervised dictionary. Note that the feature we use here is only the global max pooling feature, to be consistent with the optimization process. For datasets CMU PIE and Multi-PIE, where we have multiple testing settings, we only report one as an example. Tab. 7.2 shows the performance comparisons for the two dictionaries on all the datasets. In terms of error reduction, the supervised model improves the performance significantly. Without further notification, in the latter experiments, the performances reported are all obtained with the multi-scale max pooling feature for both unsupervised and supervised dictionaries. To make notation uncluttered, we specifically use "U-SC" and "S-SC" to denote the hierarchical model using unsupervised dictionary and supervised dictionary respectively.

7.1.5.2   *Face Recognition*

We first apply the presented algorithm to the face recognition problem. We evaluate the algorithm's performance on two database: CMU PIE [Sim *et al.* (2001)] and CMU Multi-PIE [Gross *et al.* (2008)].

Table 7.2   Error rate for both unsupervised and supervised dictionary on different datasets. Supervised training improvements are reported in terms of error reduction. Note that the feature used is the global pooling feature.

Dataset	Unsupervised	Supervised	Improvements
CMU PIE	11.5	2.3	80.0%
Multi-PIE	32.3	21.9	32.2%
MNIST	2.8	1.1	60.7%
FRGC	11.9	6.4	46.2%

The database consists of 41,368 images of 68 people, each person under 13 poses, 43 different illumination conditions and with 4 different expressions. We use a subset of the database same as in [Cai *et al.* (2007, 2008)] for fair comparison.The subset only contains five near frontal poses (C05, C07, C09, C27, C29) and all the images under different illuminations and expressions. Therefore, there are 170 images for each individual. A random subset of p ($p = 30, 50, 70, 90, 130$) images per person are selected as the training set and the rest of the database is considered as the testing set.

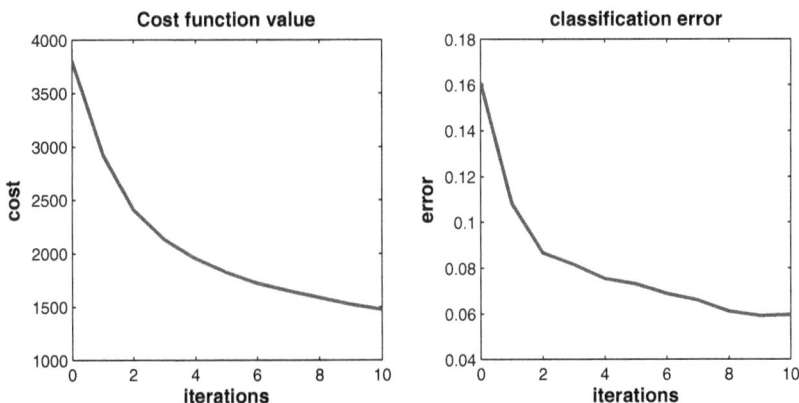

Fig. 7.4   The supervised optimization process on CMU PIE for 10 iterations.

Fig. 7.4 shows the optimization process of supervised training for 10 iterations for $p = 50$ experiment setting. For each iteration, we record its cost function value, and also evaluate the performance with current learned dictionary on the test set. As expected, the classification error decreases as the cost function value decreases. Tab.7.3 shows the performance comparisons with the literature on this dataset. "Improvements" shows the improvement from unsupervised dictionary to supervised dictionary. As shown, both our unsupervised and supervised sparse coding algorithm significantly outperform S-LDA [Cai *et al.* (2008)], reported as *state-of-the-art* performance algorithm on this database, reducing the error rate by more than 10 times.

Table 7.3   Classification error (%) on CMU PIE database for different algorithms. 'Improve' shows the improvements from unsupervised sparse coding (U-SC) to supervised sparse coding (S-SC) in terms of reducing error rate.

Training	30	50	70	90	130
LDA	7.9	4.8	4.0	3.4	2.9
R-LDA [Cai *et al.* (2007)]	5.0	3.9	3.5	3.2	3.0
S-LDA [Cai *et al.* (2008)]	3.6	2.5	2.1	1.8	1.6
U-SC	0.81	0.26	0.22	0.11	0.037
S-SC	**0.49**	**0.15**	**0.12**	**0.037**	**0**
Improvements	39.5%	42.3%	45.5%	66.4%	100%

The second experiment on face recognition is conducted on the large scale CMU Multi-PIE database [Gross *et al.* (2008)]. The database contains 337 subjects across simultaneous variations in pose, expression, and illumination. In order to compare with [Wagner *et al.* (2009)] fairly, we use the same experiment settings for face recognition. Of these 337 subjects, 249 subjects present in Session 1 are used as the training set. Session 2, 3 and 4 are used as testing. The remaining 88 subjects are considered "outliers" or invalid images in [Wagner *et al.* (2009)] for face verification, and in this work we neglect them and only care about face recognition. For the training set, [Wagner *et al.* (2009)] only included 7 frontal extreme illuminations, taken with neutral expression. We use exactly the same training set. For the test set, all 20 illuminations from Sessions 2-4 are used, which were recorded at distinct times over a period of several months. The dataset is challenging due to the large number of subjects, and due to natural variation in subject appearance over time.

Tab. 7.4 shows our results compared with those reported in the [Wagner *et al.* (2009)] for Linear Discriminant Analysis (LDA) [Belhumeur *et al.* (1997)], Nearest Neighbor (NN), Nearest Subspace (NS) [Lee *et al.* (2005)], and Sparse Representation (SR). LDA, NN and NS are used as the baseline algorithms in [Wagner *et al.* (2009)]. The SR algorithm, unifying face alignment and face recognition in the same framework, performs much better compared to these baseline algorithms, reporting the top classification accuracy on this dataset. To compare with the SR algorithm, we make two

Table 7.4 Face recognition error (%) on large-scale Multi-PIE. 'Improvements' row shows the improvements due to supervised training.

Rec. Rates	Session 2	Session 3	Session 4
LDA	50.6	55.7	52.1
NN	32.7	33.8	37.2
NS	22.4	25.7	26.6
SR	8.6	9.7	9.8
U-SC	5.4	9.0	7.5
S-SC	**4.8**	**6.6**	**4.9**
Improvements	11.1%	26.7%	34.7%

noteworthy comments:

(1) The linear combination model of SR is known to be good at handling illuminations. The training set is chosen as to minimize its size.
(2) The SR algorithm models the sparse representation as the classifier directly, which is highly nonlinear. Our model simply uses a linear SVM trained by *one-vs-all*, dividing the feature space into 249 parts.

And yet, our supervised sparse coding strategy significantly reduce the error rates of SR by 41.9%, 32.0% and 50.0% for session 2, 3 and 4 respectively.

7.1.5.3 *Handwritten Digit Recognition*

We also test our algorithm on the benchmark MNIST handwritten digits dataset [LeCun *et al.* (1998)]. The database consists of 70,000 handwritten digits, of which 60,000 digits are modeled as training and 10,000 as testing. The digits have been size-normalized and centered in a fixed-size image. The supervised training optimization process converges quickly and we stop by 5 iterations. Tab. 7.5 shows the performance comparisons with other methods reported on the dataset. "L1 sparse coding" and "Local coordinate coding" methods denote the holistical sparse coding scheme on the entire image with trained compact dictionaries, with the latter enforcing locality constraints. Our patch-based hierarchical model performs much better than the above holistical methods. The supervised training reduces the error of the unsupervised model by 14.3% and we achieve similar performance as CNN under the same condition, which is known as the best algorithm on the MNIST dataset.

Table 7.5   Classification error (%) comparison with *state-of-the-art* algorithms in the literature on MNIST.

Algorithms	Error Rate
SVM (RBF)	1.41
L1 sparse coding (linear SVM)	2.02
Local coordinate coding (linear SVM) [Yu *et al.* (2009)]	1.90
Deep belief network	1.20
CNN [Yu *et al.* (2008)]	0.82
U-SC (linear SVM)	0.98
S-SC (linear SVM)	**0.84**
Improvements	14.3%

7.1.5.4   *Gender Recognition*

Our gender recognition experiment is conducted on the FRGC 2.0 dataset [Philips *et al.* (2006)]. This dataset contains 568 individuals, totally 14714 face images under various lighting conditions and backgrounds. Besides person identities, each image is annotated with gender and ethnicity. For gender recognition, we fix 114 persons' 3014 images (randomly chosen) as the testing set, and the rest 451 individuals' 11700 images as our training images. Comparisons are performed with the *state-of-the-art* algorithms on FRGC in the same experiment setting as reported in Tab. 7.6. The supervised sparse coding strategy boosts the performance by 22.1% error reduction compared with the unsupervised version, outperforming the top performance algorithm CNN.

Table 7.6   Classification error (%) comparison with *state-of-the-art* gender recognition algorithms in the literature on FRGC.

Algorithms	Error Rate
SVM (RBF)	8.6
CNN [Yu *et al.* (2008)]	5.9
Unsupervised Sparse Coding	6.8
Supervised Sparse Coding	**5.3**
Improvements	22.1%

7.2   Max-Margin Sparse Representation Classifier

Sparse Representation-based Classification (SRC) distinguishes signals from different classes according to the sparse coding reconstruction errors under different hypotheses. The dictionary used in SRC serves as the parameter for both representation and classification, and therefore is the key to attain high recognition accuracy. Over the years, various methods have been explored to design dictionaries for SRC, including generative approaches [Engan *et al.* (1999); Aharon *et al.* (2006); Lee *et al.* (2006); Mairal *et al.* (2009a)] as well as discriminative approaches [Yang *et al.* (2011c); Ramirez *et al.* (2010); Qiu *et al.* (2011); Jiang *et al.* (2011); Mairal *et al.* (2012)].

In this section, we present a margin-based perspective towards SRC and and a maximum margin performance metric that is specifically designed for learning the dictionaries of SRC [Wang *et al.* (2013)]. Based on the local stability of sparse code support, we show that the decision boundary of SRC is a continuous piecewise quadratic surface, and the margin of a sample is approximated as its distance to the tangent plane of the decision function. Following the idea of Support Vector Machine (SVM), we can use the hinge loss of approximated margin as a metric for better classification performance and generalization capability of SRC.

7.2.1 *Local Decision Boundary for SRC*

Suppose our data sample $\mathbf{x}$ lies in the high dimensional space $\mathbb{R}^m$ and comes from one of the C classes with label $y \in \{1...C\}$. In SRC, a dictionary $\mathbf{D} \in \mathbb{R}^{m \times n}$ with n atoms is composed of C class-wise sub-dictionaries $\mathbf{D}_c \in \mathbb{R}^{m \times n_c}$ such that $\mathbf{D} = [\mathbf{D}_1, ..., \mathbf{D}_C] = [\mathbf{d}_1, ..., \mathbf{d}_n]$. The associated sparse code can be decomposed into C sub-codes as $\alpha = [\alpha_1; ...; \alpha_C]$, where each α_c corresponds to the coefficients for sub-dictionary $\mathbf{D}_c$. SRC makes classification decision based on the residual of signal approximated by the sub-code of each class: $r_c = \|\mathbf{e}_c\|_2^2$, where $\mathbf{e}_c = \mathbf{D}_c \alpha_c - \mathbf{x}$ is the reconstruction error vector for class c.

To perform margin-based analysis for SRC, we first need to find its classification decision boundary. Consider two classes c_1 and c_2, and assume the dictionary $\mathbf{D}$ is given. The decision function at sample $\mathbf{x}$ is simply defined as $f(\mathbf{x}) = r_{c_2} - r_{c_1} \gtrless 0$. $f(\mathbf{x})$ can be expanded as:

$$f(\mathbf{x}) = 2(\mathbf{D}_{c_1} \alpha_{c_1} - \mathbf{D}_{c_2} \alpha_{c_2})^T \mathbf{x} - \|\mathbf{D}_{c_1} \alpha_{c_1}\|^2 + \|\mathbf{D}_{c_2} \alpha_{c_2}\|^2. \quad (7.22)$$

Eq. (7.22) could be regarded as a linear hyper-plane in the space of data $\mathbf{x}$, if the sparse code α was fixed. What complicates things here is that α is also determined by $\mathbf{x}$ through the sparse coding model in (1.4), and the hyper-plane in (7.22) will change with any small change in $\mathbf{x}$. Expressing α analytically as a function of $\mathbf{x}$ is not possible in general, unless we know *a priori* the support and sign vector of α. In the latter case, the non-zero part of α can be found according to the optimal condition of LASSO solution [Zou *et al.* (2007)]:

$$\alpha_\Lambda = (\mathbf{D}_\Lambda^T \mathbf{D}_\Lambda)^{-1}(\mathbf{D}_\Lambda^T \mathbf{x} - \frac{\lambda}{2}\mathbf{s}_\Lambda), \tag{7.23}$$

where $\Lambda = \{j|\alpha_j \neq 0\}$ is the active set of sparse coefficients with cardinality $|\Lambda| = \|\alpha\|_0 = s$, $\alpha_\Lambda \in \mathbb{R}^s$ contains the sparse coefficients at these active locations, $\mathbf{D}_\Lambda \in \mathbb{R}^{m \times s}$ is composed of the columns in $\mathbf{D}$ corresponding to Λ, and $\mathbf{s}_\Lambda \in \mathbb{R}^s$ carries the signs (± 1) of α_Λ. Although the active set Λ and sign vector $\mathbf{s}_\Lambda$ also depend on $\mathbf{x}$, it can be shown that they are locally stable if $\mathbf{x}$ changes by a small amount of $\Delta\mathbf{x}$ satisfying the following stability conditions:

$$\begin{cases} |\mathbf{d}_j^T\{\mathbf{e} + [\mathbf{D}_\Lambda(\mathbf{D}_\Lambda^T\mathbf{D}_\Lambda)^{-1}\mathbf{D}_\Lambda^T - \mathbf{I}]\Delta\mathbf{x}\}| \leq \frac{\lambda}{2}, \forall j \notin \Lambda \\ \mathbf{s}_\Lambda \odot [(\mathbf{D}_\Lambda^T\mathbf{D}_\Lambda)^{-1}\mathbf{D}_\Lambda^T\Delta\mathbf{x}] > -\mathbf{s}_\Lambda \odot \alpha_\Lambda \end{cases}, \tag{7.24}$$

where $\odot$ denotes element-wise multiplication, and $\mathbf{e} = \mathbf{D}_\Lambda \alpha_\Lambda - \mathbf{x}$ is the global reconstruction error. All the conditions in (7.24) are linear inequalities for $\Delta\mathbf{x}$. Therefore, the local neighborhood around $\mathbf{x}$ where the active set (and signs[7]) of signal's sparse code remains stable is a convex polytope.

Now substitute the sparse code terms in (7.22) with (7.23), and after some manipulations we obtain a quadratic local decision function $f_\Lambda(\mathbf{x})$ which is defined for any $\mathbf{x}$ whose sparse code corresponds to active set Λ:

$$\begin{aligned} f_\Lambda(\mathbf{x}) = &\mathbf{x}^T \mathbf{\Phi}_{c_2}^T \mathbf{\Phi}_{c_2} \mathbf{x} + 2\nu_{c_2}^T \mathbf{\Phi}_{c_2} \mathbf{x} + \nu_{c_2}^T \nu_{c_2} \\ &- (\mathbf{x}^T \mathbf{\Phi}_{c_1}^T \mathbf{\Phi}_{c_1} \mathbf{x} + 2\nu_{c_1}^T \mathbf{\Phi}_{c_1} \mathbf{x} + \nu_{c_1}^T \nu_{c_1}), \end{aligned} \tag{7.25}$$

where

$$\mathbf{\Phi}_c = \mathbf{D}_\Lambda \mathbf{P}_c(\mathbf{D}_\Lambda^T \mathbf{D}_\Lambda)^{-1} \mathbf{D}_\Lambda^T - \mathbf{I}, \tag{7.26}$$

$$\nu_c = -\frac{\lambda}{2}\mathbf{D}_\Lambda \mathbf{P}_c(\mathbf{D}_\Lambda^T \mathbf{D}_\Lambda)^{-1} \mathbf{s}_\Lambda, \tag{7.27}$$

and $\mathbf{P}_c$ is an $s \times s$ diagonal matrix with 1 at positions corresponding to class c in the active set and 0 otherwise. The above analysis leads to the following proposition for the decision function of SRC.

Proposition 7.1. *The decision function of SRC is a piecewise quadratic function of input signal with the form of*

$$f(\mathbf{x}) = f_\Lambda(\mathbf{x}), \tag{7.28}$$

for any $\mathbf{x}$ in the convex polytope defined by Eq. (7.24) where the active set Λ of its sparse code is stable.

---

[7]In the following, the concept of sign vector $\mathbf{s}_\Lambda$ is included by default when we refer to "active set" or "Λ".

Since there are a set of quadratic decision functions each devoted to a local area of $\mathbf{x}$, SRC is capable of classifying data which cannot be linearly or quadratically separated in a global sense. The decision boundary of SRC can be adapted to each local area in the most discriminative and compact way, which shares a similar idea with locally adaptive metric learning [Domeniconi *et al.* (2002)]. On the other hand, these quadratic functions as well as the partition of local areas cannot be adjusted individually; they are all tied via a common model $\mathbf{D}$. This is crucial to reduce model complexity and enhance information sharing among different local regions, considering there could be as many as 3^n regions[8] out of the partition of the entire signal space.

To find the decision boundary of SRC, we simply need to check at what values of $\mathbf{x}$, $f(\mathbf{x})$ will vary from positive to negative, as the decision threshold is 0. It has been show in [Zou *et al.* (2007)] that the sparse code α is a continuous function of $\mathbf{x}$. Thus we can easily see that $f(\mathbf{x})$ is also continuous over the entire domain of $\mathbf{x}$, and the points on the decision boundary of SRC have to satisfy $f(\mathbf{x}) = 0$, which is stated in the following proposition.

Proposition 7.2. *The decision boundary of SRC is a piecewise quadratic hypersurface defined by $f(\mathbf{x}) = 0$.*

7.2.2 *Margin Approximation for SRC*

For linear classifiers, the margin of a sample is defined as its distance from the decision hyperplane. In the context of SRC, we similarly define the margin of a sample $\mathbf{x}_0$ as its distance to the closest point on the decision boundary: $\min_{f(\mathbf{x})=0} \|\mathbf{x}_0 - \mathbf{x}\|_2$. Unfortunately, due to the complexity of SRC's decision function $f(\mathbf{x})$, it is difficult to evaluate the associated margin directly.

Instead, we estimate $\mathbf{x}_0$'s margin by approximating $f(\mathbf{x})$ with its tangent plane at $\mathbf{x}_0$. Such approximation is appropriate only when gradient $\nabla f(\mathbf{x})$ does not change too much as $f(\mathbf{x})$ descents from $f(\mathbf{x}_0)$ to 0, which is generally true based on the following observations. First, within each polytope for a stable active set Λ, $\nabla f_\Lambda(\mathbf{x})$ is a linear function of $\mathbf{x}$ and will not change a lot if $\mathbf{x}_0$ lies close to the boundary. Second, as implied by the empirical findings in Fig. 7.5, if we have two contiguous polytopes corresponding respectively to two stable active sets, Λ_1 and Λ_2, which are

---

[8]Each atom can be assigned with a positive, negative, or zero coefficient.

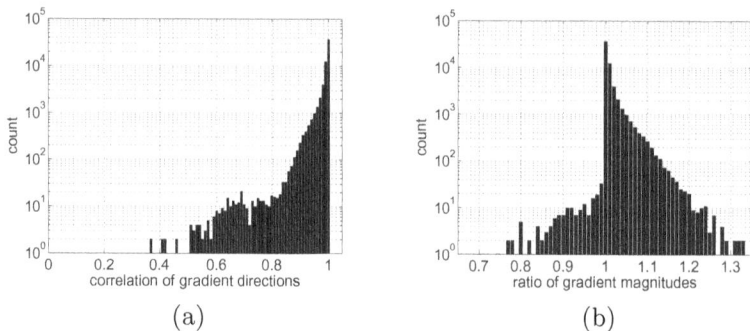

Fig. 7.5　The histograms of the (a) correlation and (b) magnitude ratio between the decision function gradients ∇f_{Λ_1} and ∇f_{Λ_2} on the MNIST data set. ∇f_{Λ_1} is the gradient at original data $\mathbf{x}$, and ∇f_{Λ_2} is the gradient at data with a small perturbation $\Delta \mathbf{x}$ from $\mathbf{x}$, such that only one of the conditions in Eq. (7.24) is violated. Both (a) and (b) are highly peaked around 1.

the same except for one entry, then with a high probability the gradient of decision function in the two polytopes will be approximately the same near their border: $\nabla f_{\Lambda_1} \approx \nabla f_{\Lambda_2}$. This observation allows us to approximate the decision function over a number of polytopes with a common tangent plane. Third, as will be discussed in Sec. 7.2.3, we are more interested in the data samples near the decision boundary when optimizing a large margin classifier. Thus, those faraway samples whose margins cannot be accurately approximated can be safely ignored. Therefore, our approximation is also suitable for the use with margin maximization.

Once the decision function $f(\mathbf{x})$ is linearly approximated, the margin γ of $\mathbf{x}_0$ is simply its distance (with sign) to the hyperplane $f(\mathbf{x}) = 0$:

$$
\begin{aligned}
\gamma(\mathbf{x}_0) &= \frac{f(\mathbf{x}_0)}{\|\nabla f(\mathbf{x}_0)\|_2} = \frac{f(\mathbf{x}_0)}{\|\nabla f_{\Lambda}(\mathbf{x}_0)\|_2} \\
&= \frac{r_{c_2} - r_{c_1}}{2\|\boldsymbol{\Phi}_{c_2}^T \mathbf{e}_{c_2} - \boldsymbol{\Phi}_{c_1}^T \mathbf{e}_{c_1}\|_2},
\end{aligned} \tag{7.29}
$$

where we use the relationship $\mathbf{e}_c = \boldsymbol{\Phi}_c \mathbf{x} + \nu_c$ to simplify the expression in (7.29); all the $\boldsymbol{\Phi}_c$'s and ν_c's are calculated according to (7.26) and (7.27) with the active set Λ of $\mathbf{x}_0$'s sparse code. It should be noted that the decision function gradient ∇f is not defined on the borders of convex polytopes with different active sets. In such a case, we just replace $\|\nabla f\|_2$ with the largest directional derivative evaluated in all the pertinent polytopes.

In SRC, all data samples are usually normalized onto the unit ball such that $\|\mathbf{x}\|_2 = 1$. In this way, the change of $f(\mathbf{x})$ in the direction of $\mathbf{x}_0$ itself

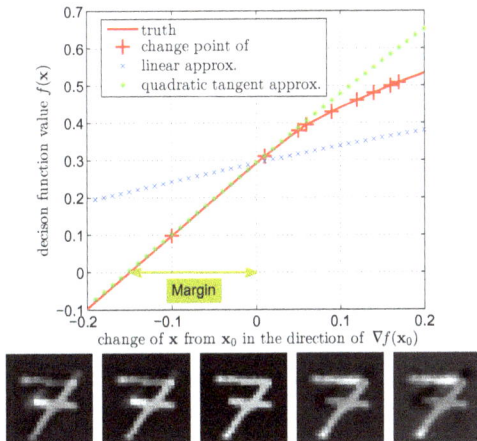

Fig. 7.6 Top: decision function $f(\mathbf{x})$ for class "7" against class "4" in the MNIST data set and its approximations, where $\mathbf{x}$ changes in the 1D neighborhood of a sample $\mathbf{x}_0$ in the direction of gradient $\nabla f(\mathbf{x}_0)$. Bottom: the images of $\mathbf{x}$ as it moves in the direction of $\nabla f(\mathbf{x}_0)$ (from left to right). The central image corresponds to the original sample $\mathbf{x}_0$.

should not be taken into account when we calculate the margin of $\mathbf{x}_0$. The margin expression can be further amended as

$$\gamma(\mathbf{x}_0) = \frac{f(\mathbf{x}_0)}{\|\mathbf{M}\nabla f(\mathbf{x}_0)\|_2} = \frac{r_{c_2} - r_{c_1}}{2\|\mathbf{M}(\mathbf{\Phi}_{c_2}^T \mathbf{e}_{c_2} - \mathbf{\Phi}_{c_1}^T \mathbf{e}_{c_1})\|_2}, \tag{7.30}$$

where $\mathbf{M} = (\mathbf{I} - \mathbf{x}_0 \mathbf{x}_0^T)$.

Fig. 7.6 graphically illustrates our margin approximation approach for one image sample $\mathbf{x}_0$ from class "7" in the MNIST digits data set. We evaluate the ground truth value of decision function $f(\mathbf{x})$ at a series of data points $\mathbf{x}$ in a 1D interval generated by shifting $\mathbf{x}_0$ along the direction of $\nabla f(\mathbf{x}_0)$, and record all the points where the active set of sparse code changes. We can see that the piecewise smooth $f(\mathbf{x})$ (plotted as a red curve) can be well approximated by the tangent of local quadratic decision function (green asterisk) in a neighborhood where the active set (whose stable region is delimited by red plus) does not change too much. However, the linear approximation (blue cross) suggested by Eq. (7.22) is much less accurate, though they all intersect at point $\mathbf{x}_0$. The margin (indicated by golden arrow) we find for this example is very close to its true value. Fig. 7.6 also shows how the appearance of the image signal is distorted to the imposter class "4" from its true class "7" as it moves along the gradient of decision function.

7.2.3 *Maximum-Margin Dictionary Learning*

The concept of maximum margin has been widely employed in training classifiers, and it serves as the cornerstone of many popular models including SVM. The classical analysis on SVM [Vapnik (1999)] established the relationship between the margin of the training set and the classifier's generalization error bound. Recently, a similar effort has been made for sparsity-based linear predictive classifier [Mehta and Gray (2013)], which motivates us to design the dictionary for SRC from a perspective based on the margin analysis given in the previous section.

Suppose we have a set of N labeled training data samples: $\{\mathbf{x}_i, y_i\}_{i=1...N}$. Learning a discriminative dictionary $\mathbf{D}^*$ for SRC can be generally formulated as the following optimization problem:

$$\mathbf{D}^* = \arg \min_{\mathbf{D} \in \mathcal{D}} \frac{1}{N} \sum_i \mathcal{L}(\mathbf{x}_i, y_i; \mathbf{D}). \tag{7.31}$$

where $\mathcal{D}$ denotes $\mathbb{R}^{m \times n}$ dictionary space with unit-norm atoms. To maximize the margin of a training sample close to the decision boundary of SRC, we follow the similar idea in SVM and define the loss function $\mathcal{L}(\mathbf{x}, y; \mathbf{D})$ using a multi-class hinge function:

$$\mathcal{L}(\mathbf{x}, y; \mathbf{D}) = \sum_{c \neq y} \max\{0, -\gamma(\mathbf{x}, y, c) + b\}, \tag{7.32}$$

where b is a non-negative parameter controlling the minimum required margin between classes, and

$$\gamma(\mathbf{x}, y, c) = \frac{r_c - r_y}{2\|\mathbf{M}(\mathbf{\Phi}_c^T \mathbf{e}_c - \mathbf{\Phi}_y^T \mathbf{e}_y)\|_2}, \tag{7.33}$$

is the margin of sample $\mathbf{x}$ with label y calculated against a competing class $c \neq y$, which is adopted from Eq. (7.30). The loss function in (7.32) is zero if the sample margin is equal or greater than b; otherwise, it gives penalty linearly proportional to negative margin. Different from what is defined in SVM, the margin we use here is unnormalized since the unit dictionary atom constraint ensures the objective function is bounded. Moreover, (7.32) promotes multi-class margin by summing over all possible imposter classes c and optimizing the single parameter $\mathbf{D}$ that is shared by all classes. This offers an advantage over a set of one-versus-rest binary classifiers whose margins can only be optimized separately.

According to the numerator in (7.33), the residual difference between the correct and incorrect classes, $r_c - r_y$, should be maximized to achieve a large margin. Such requirement is consistent with the classification scheme in (2.2), and it has also been enforced in other dictionary learning algorithms such as [Mairal *et al.* (2008b)]. In addition, we further introduce a novel term in the denominator of (7.33), which normalizes the nonuniform gradient of SRC decision function in different local regions and leads to a better estimation to the true sample margin.

We solve the optimization problem in Eq. (7.31) using an online algorithm based on stochastic gradient descent method, which is usually favored when the objective function is an expectation over a large number of training samples [Mairal *et al.* (2009a)]. In our algorithm, the dictionary is first initialized with a reasonable guess $\mathbf{D}^0$ (which can be the concatenation of sub-dictionaries obtained by applying K-means or random selection to each class). Then we go through the whole data set multiple times and iteratively update the dictionary with decreasing step size until convergence. In the t-th iteration, a single sample $(\mathbf{x}, y)$ is drawn from the data set randomly and the dictionary is updated in the direction of the gradient of its loss function:

$$\mathbf{D}^t = \mathbf{D}^{t-1} - \rho^t [\nabla_{\mathbf{D}} \mathcal{L}(\mathbf{x}, y; \mathbf{D}^{t-1})]^T, \qquad (7.34)$$

where ρ^t is the step size at iteration t. It is selected as $\rho^t = \dfrac{\rho^0}{\sqrt{(t-1)/N+1}}$ with initial step size ρ^0. The gradient of our loss function is

$$\nabla_{\mathbf{D}} \mathcal{L}(\mathbf{x}, y; \mathbf{D}) = - \sum_{c \in \mathcal{C}(\mathbf{x}, y)} \nabla_{\mathbf{D}} \gamma(\mathbf{x}, y, c) \qquad (7.35)$$

where $\mathcal{C}(\mathbf{x}, y) = \{c | c \neq y, \gamma(\mathbf{x}, y, c) < b\}$. We ignore those competing classes with zero margin gradient ($\gamma(\mathbf{x}, y, c) > b$) or zero sub-gradient ($\gamma(\mathbf{x}, y, c) = b$). The latter case occurs with very low probability in practice and thus will not affect the convergence of stochastic gradient descent as long as a suitable step size is chosen [Bottou (2004)].

All that remains to be evaluated is $\nabla_{\mathbf{D}} \gamma(\mathbf{x}, y, c)$, which can be obtained by taking derivative of Eq. (7.33) with respect to $\mathbf{D}$. We realize from the results in [Mehta and Gray (2013)] that the active set Λ for any particular sample $\mathbf{x}$ is stable when there is a small perturbation applied to dictionary $\mathbf{D}$. Since the approximation of margin is also based on a locally stable Λ, we can safely deduce that $\gamma(\mathbf{x}, y, c)$ is a differentiable function of $\mathbf{D}$. In this way, we circumvent the trouble of indifferentiability when directly taking derivative of sparse code with respect to $\mathbf{D}$ as has been done in [Mairal *et al.* (2012); Yang *et al.* (2012b)]. In addition, since (7.33) depends only on $\mathbf{D}_\Lambda$, we just need to update those dictionary atoms corresponding to the active set Λ of each sample $\mathbf{x}$. The dictionary updating rule in (7.34) can be rewritten as:

$$\mathbf{D}_\Lambda^t = \mathbf{D}_\Lambda^{t-1} + \rho^t \cdot [\nabla_{\mathbf{D}_\Lambda}\gamma(\mathbf{x}, y, c)]^T, \qquad (7.36)$$

which is repeated for all $c \in \mathcal{C}(\mathbf{x}, y)$. Once the dictionary is updated in the current iteration, all its atoms are projected to the unit ball to comply with the constraint that $\mathbf{D} \in \mathcal{D}$.

7.2.4   *Experiments*

7.2.4.1   *Algorithm Analysis*

To get a better understanding of the aforementioned method, we first conduct some analysis on its behavior in this section using a subset of 20,000 training samples from the MNIST [LeCun *et al.* (1998)] digits data set.

The accuracy of SRC margin approximation, which is key to the effectiveness of our method, is first investigated. Because it is impossible to find the exact margin of a sample $\mathbf{x}_0$, we use the shortest distance between $\mathbf{x}_0$ and the decision boundary *in the gradient direction* $\nabla f(\mathbf{x}_0)$ as a surrogate to the ground truth margin. Such "directional margin" is found by a line search and plotted in Fig. 7.7 against the estimated margin $\gamma(\mathbf{x}_0)$ using Eq. (7.30) for all the samples. A strong linear relationship is observed between the directional and estimated margin, especially for those samples with small margins which are indeed to the interest of our algorithm. We also plot the distribution of residual difference $r_{c_2} - r_{c_1}$, which shows a weaker correlation with the directional margin. This justifies that maximizing $\gamma(\mathbf{x})$ as defined in (7.33) is a better choice than simply maximizing $r_{c_2} - r_{c_1}$ for large-margin optimization.

The behavior of our MMDL algorithm is examined in Fig. 7.8. The objective function value over the training samples decreases steadily and converges in about 70 iterations. At the same time, the recognition accuracy on a separate test set is remarkably improved during the iterations, indicating a good correspondence between our margin-based objective function and SRC's generalized performance [9].

The minimum required margin b in Eq. (7.32) is an important parameter in MMDL, whose effect on recognition performance is shown in Table 7.7.

---

[9]We do observe some small fluctuations on the testing accuracy, which is caused by the stochastic gradient descent.

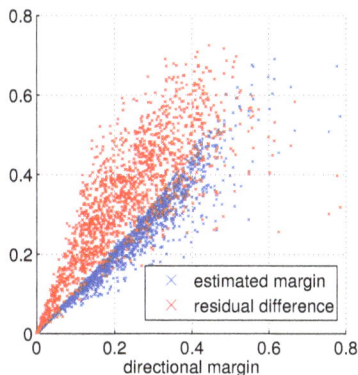

Fig. 7.7 Distributions of estimated margin $\gamma(\mathbf{x})$ and residual different $r_{c_2} - r_{c_1}$ plotted against directional margin measured in the gradient direction $\nabla f(\mathbf{x})$.

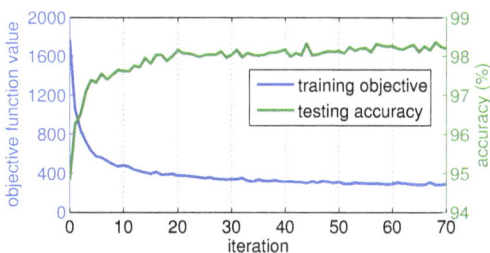

Fig. 7.8 The objective function on training set and recognition accuracy on test set during the iterations of MMDL algorithm.

Table 7.7 The effect of parameter b on classification accuracy.

b	0	0.05	0.1	0.15	0.2
train acc.	100.00	100.00	99.44	98.45	97.39
test acc.	96.78	98.01	**98.13**	97.36	96.77

A too small value of b leads to over-fitting to training set, while a too large value leads to bias of the classification objective. We find $b = 0.1$ is generally a good choice on different data sets, and gradually reducing b during the iterations can help the algorithm focus more on those hard samples near decision boundary.

The image patterns of some dictionary atoms obtained using MMDL are shown in Fig. 7.9, together with those obtained using unsupervised sparse

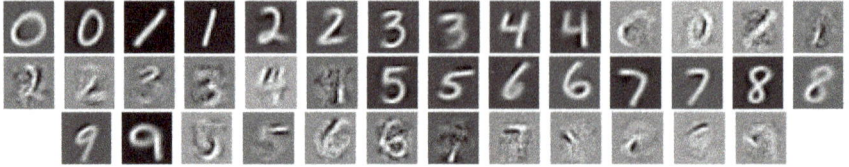

Fig. 7.9 Dictionary atoms for MNIST digits data, learned using unsupervised sparse coding (row 1, 3) and MMDL (row 2, 4).

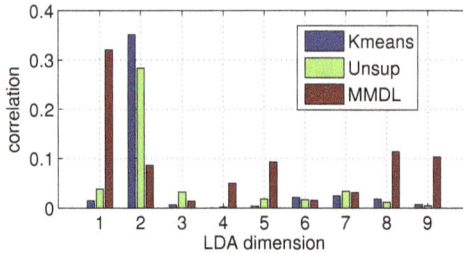

Fig. 7.10 Correlation between the first principal component of atoms from different dictionaries and the LDA directions of the MNIST training data.

coding [Lee *et al.* (2006)], which were used to initialize the dictionary in MMDL. The discriminative atoms trained with MMDL look quite different from their initial reconstructive appearances, and place more emphasis on local edge features that are unique to each class. The discriminative power of our learned dictionary can be further demonstrated in Fig. 7.10, which shows that, compared with K-means and unsupervised sparse coding, the MMDL algorithm learns dictionary atoms whose first principle component has a much higher correlation with most of the LDA directions (especially the first one) of the training data. Although LDA directions may not be optimal for SRC, our dictionary atoms appear to be more devoted to discriminative features instead of reconstructive ones.

7.2.4.2 *Recognition Performance Evaluation*

Now we report the recognition performance of the presented method on several benchmark data sets. SRC is most well known for face recognition task, therefore we first test on two face data sets: extended YaleB [Georghiades *et al.* (2001)] and AR face [Martinez and Benavente (1998)]. We use 2,414 face images of 38 subjects from the extended YaleB data set, and a subset containing 2,600 images of 50 female and 50 male subjects from the

Table 7.8   Recognition accuracies (%) on face databases.

Method	Extended YaleB	AR Face
Full	**97.34**	96.50
Subsample	91.20	73.17
KSVD [Aharon *et al.* (2006)]	88.63	90.00
Kmeans	95.44	90.00
Unsup [Lee *et al.* (2006)]	96.35	90.33
LC-KSVD [Jiang *et al.* (2011)]	95.00	93.70
MMDL	**97.34**	**97.33**
Error reduction (%)	27.12	72.39

Table 7.9   Performance of SRC on the MNIST digits database.

Training method / Size of **D**	Accuracy (%)
Subsample / 30000	98.05
Subsample / 150	82.19
Kmeans / 150	94.19
Unsup [Lee *et al.* (2006)] / 150	94.84
Ramirez *et al.* [Ramirez *et al.* (2010)] / 800	98.74
MMDL / 150	**98.76**
Error reduction (%)	75.97

AR face data set. We follow the procedure in [Jiang *et al.* (2011)] to split the training and test data, and obtain random projected face features of 504(540)-dimension for extended YaleB(AR face). For both data sets, we compare the performance of SRC with dictionaries obtained from the full training set ("Full"), random subsampling of training set ("Subsample"), KSVD [Aharon *et al.* (2006)], K-means ("Kmeans"), unsupervised sparse coding ("Unsup") [Lee *et al.* (2006)], and our MMDL algorithm. Comparison with the state-of-the-art results of LC-KSVD [Jiang *et al.* (2011)] is also given, which employs a linear classification model on space codes. For extended YaleB(AR face), 15(5) atoms per subject are used for all the dictionaries expect for "Full", and λ is set as 0.01(0.005). As shown in Table 7.8, MMDL achieves the highest accuracies on both data sets, and outperforms the "Full" SRC on AR face using a much smaller dictionary. The huge reduction in the error rate of MMDL with respect to its initialization value given by "Unsup" further confirms the effectiveness of our learning algorithm.

Our method is also evaluated on the full MNIST data set, which contains 60,000 images for training and 10,000 for testing. We use PCA to reduce the dimension of each image such that 99% energy is preserved, and set $\lambda = 0.1$.

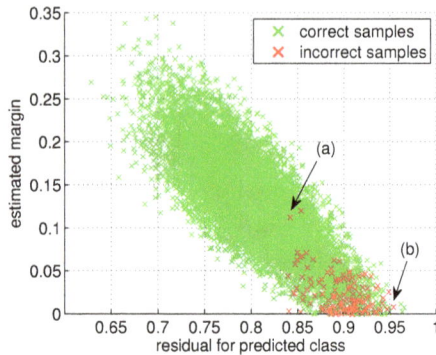

Fig. 7.11 Distributions of correctly and incorrectly classified test samples plotted against estimated margin and reconstruction residual using the atoms from predicted class.

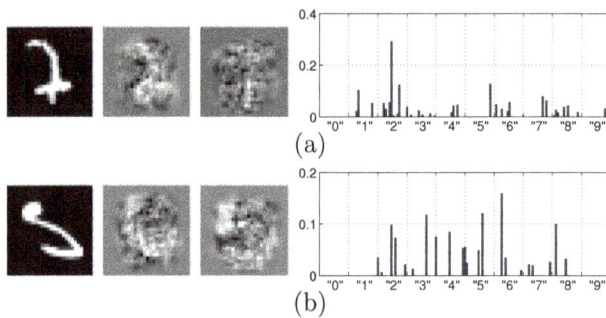

Fig. 7.12 Two misclassified samples corresponding to the red crosses marked by (a) and (b) in Fig. 7.11. From left to right: original sample; reconstruction with atoms of predicted class; reconstruction with atoms of truth class; sparse coefficients.

Table 7.9 lists the classification accuracies of SRC with dictionaries trained using various methods and with different sizes. MMDL is shown to be advantageous over other methods in terms of both accuracy and dictionary compactness, the latter of which implies higher efficiency in computation as well as storage. Note that we are unable to evaluate SRC with the "Full" setting because the memory required for the operation on such a huge dictionary exceeds our system capacity (32GB).

Fig. 7.11 reveals the distinct distributions of correctly and incorrectly classified samples in terms of estimated margin and reconstruction residual with predicted class. The incorrect samples are observed to have higher residuals and smaller margins, which is expected since hard samples typically can not be well represented by the corresponding classes and lie close to the boundary of imposter classes. This provides another evidence to show the accuracy of our margin estimation. Therefore, the estimated margin can also serve as a metric of classification confidence, based on which the classification results could be further refined. Two cases of failed test samples are illustrated in Fig. 7.12. The digit "7" in (a) is misclassified as "2" with a large margin due to the strong inter-class similarity and high intra-class variation insufficiently captured by the training set. The digit "5" in (b) cannot be faithfully represented by any class; such an outlier has a very small margin and thus can be potentially detected for special treatment.

Chapter 8

Hyper-Spectral Image Modeling

The spectral information contained in hyperspectral imagery allows characterization, identification, and classification of land-covers with improved accuracy and robustness. However, several critical issues should be addressed in the classification of hyperspectral data, among which are the following [Swain (1978); Plaza *et al.* (2009)]: 1) small amount of available labeled data; 2) high dimensionality of each spectral sample; 3) spatial variability of spectral signatures; 4) high cost of sample labeling. In particular, the large number of spectral channels and small number of labeled training samples pose the problem of the curse of dimensionality and as a consequence resulting in the risk of overfitting the training data. For these reasons, desirable properties of a hyperspectral image classifier should be its ability to produce accurate land-cover maps when working within a high-dimensional feature space, low-sized training datasets, and high levels of spatial spectral signature variability.

Many supervised and unsupervised classifiers have been developed to tackle the hyperspectral data classification problem [RichardsJA (1999)]. Classical supervised methods, such as artificial neural networks [Bischof and Leonardis (1998); Yang (1999)] and support vector machines (SVMs) [Schölkopf and Smola (2002); Belkin *et al.* (2006)], were readily revealed to be inefficient when dealing with a high number of spectral bands and lack of labeled data. In [Gómez-Chova *et al.* (2008)], SVM was regularized with an unnormalized graph Laplacian, thus leading to the Laplacian SVM (LapSVM) that adopts the manifold assumption for semi-supervised classification. Another framework based on neural network was presented in [Ratle *et al.* (2010)]. It consists of adding a flexible embedding regularizer to the loss function used for training neural networks, and leads to improvements in both classification accuracy and scalability on several hyperspectral image classification problems. In recent years, kernel-based methods have often been adopted for hyperspectral image classification [Camps-Valls *et al.* (2006, 2004); Camps-Valls and Bruzzone (2005)]. They are certainly able to handle efficiently the high-dimensional input feature space and deal with the noisy samples in a robust way [Shawe-Taylor and Cristianini (2004)]. More recently, sparse representation has been increasingly popular for image classification. The sparse representation-based classification (SRC) [Wright *et al.* (2009)] is mainly based on the observation that despite the high dimensionality of natural signals, signals belonging to the same class usually lie in a low-dimensional subspace. In [Chen *et al.* (2011)], a SRC-based algorithm for hyperspectral classification was presented, that utilizes the sparsity of the input sample with respect to a given over-complete training dictionary. It is based on a sparsity model where a test spectral pixel is approximately represented by a few training samples (atoms) among the entire atoms from a dictionary. The weightings associated with the atoms are called the sparse code. The class label of the test pixel is then determined by the characteristics of the recovered sparse code. Experimental results show remarkable improvements in discriminative effects. However, the main difficulty with all supervised methods is that the learning process heavily depends on the quality of the training dataset. Even worse, labeled hyperspectral training samples are only available in a very limited number due to the cost of sample labeling. On the other hand, unsupervised methods are not sensitive to the number of labeled samples since they operate on the whole dataset, but the relationships between clusters and class labels are not ensured [Bidhendi *et al.* (2007)]. Moreover, typically in hyperspectral classification, a preliminary feature selection/extraction step is undertaken to reduce the high input space dimensionality, which is time-consuming, scenario-dependent, and needs prior knowledge.

As a trade-off, semi-supervised classification methods become a natural alternative to yield better performance. In semi-supervised learning literature, the algorithms are provided with some available supervised information in the form of labeled data in addition to the wealth of unlabeled data. Such a framework has recently attracted a considerable amount of research in remote sensing, such as the Laplacian SVM (LapSVM) [Belkin *et al.* (2006); Gómez-Chova *et al.* (2008)], transductive SVM [Bruzzone *et al.* (2006)], biased-SVM [Muñoz-Mari *et al.* (2010)] and Graph-based methods [Gu and Feng (2012)]. Even though the above mentioned algorithms exhibit good performance in classifying hyperspectral images, most of them are based on the assumption that spectrally similar instances should share the same label. However in practice, we may have very different spectra corresponding to the same material, which sometimes makes the above strict assumption no longer valid. Moreover, in most recent hyperspectral classification approaches [Li *et al.* (2012); Mathur and Foody (2008)], the spatial information is exploited together with the spectral features, encouraging pixels in the local neighborhood to have similar labels. The spatial smoothness assumption holds well in the homogenous regions of hyperspectral images. However, conventional approaches often fail to capture the spatial variability of spectral signatures, e.g., on the border of regions belonging to different classes.

In this chapter, we present a hyperspectral image classification method [Wang *et al.* (2015a)], tackling the problems imposed by the special characteristics of hyperspectral images, namely, high-input dimension of pixels, low number of labeled samples, and spatial variability of the spectral signatures. To this end, the presented method has the following characteristics and technical contributions:

- **Semi-supervised**: Extending the task-driven dictionary learning formulation in [Mairal *et al.* (2012)] to the semi-supervised framework for hyperspectral classification, the huge number of unlabeled samples in the image are exploited together with a limited amount of labeled samples to improve the classification performance in a task-driven setting.
- **Joint optimization of feature extraction and classification**: Almost all prior research on hyperspectral classifier design can be viewed as the combinations of two independent parts: 1) extraction of features; 2) a training procedure for designing the classifier. Although, in some prior work raw spectral pixels are used directly, it is widely recognized that features extracted from the input pixels, such as the sparse code, often promote a more discriminative and robust classification [Wright *et al.* (2009)]. However, to consider the two stages separately typically leads to a sub-optimal performance, because the extracted features are not optimized for the best performance of the following classification step. Here, we jointly optimize the classifier parameters and dictionary atoms. This is different from the classical data-driven feature extraction approach [Chen *et al.* (2011)] that only tries to reconstruct the training samples well. Our joint task-driven formulation ensures that the learned sparse code features are optimal for the classifier.
- **Incorporation of spatial information**: We incorporate spatial information by adding a spatial Laplacian regularization [Belkin *et al.*

(2006)] to the probabilistic outputs of the classifier, i.e., the likelihood of the predicted labels. This is more flexible than the popular "naive" Laplacian smoothness constraint, that simply enforces all pixels in a local window to have similar learned features.

A novel formulation of bi-level optimization is designed to meet our requirements [Colson *et al.* (2007); Yang *et al.* (2012b)], which is solved by a stochastic gradient descent algorithm [Kushner and Yin (2003)]. The method is then evaluated on three popular datasets and we see an impressive improvement in performance on all of them. Even for quite ill-posed classification problems, i.e., very small number of high dimensional labeled samples, the presented method gains a remarkable and stable improvement in performance over comparable methods.

The rest of this chapter is organized as follows. Section 8.1 manifests a step-by-step construction of our formulation in details, followed by the optimization algorithm to solve it. Section 8.2 discusses the classification results of this method in comparison to several other competitive methods, with a wide range of available labeled samples. It also investigates the influences of both the unlabeled samples and dictionary atoms on the classifier's performance, as well as the discriminability of the obtained dictionary.

8.1 Formulation and Algorithm

8.1.1 *Notations*

Consider a hyperspectral image $\mathbf{X} \in R^{m \times n}$ of n pixels, each of which consists of an m-dimensional spectral vector. Let $\mathbf{X} = [\mathbf{x}_1, \mathbf{x}_2, \cdots, \mathbf{x}_n]$ denote the pixel set in a hyperspectral image, with each spectral pixel $\mathbf{x}_i \in R^{m \times 1}, i = 1, 2, \cdots, n$. For all the corresponding labels $\mathbf{y} = [y_1, y_2, \cdots, y_n]$, we assume l labels $[y_1, y_2, \cdots, y_l]$ are known, constituting a labeled training set $\mathbf{X}_l = [\mathbf{x}_1, \mathbf{x}_2, \cdots, \mathbf{x}_l]$, while making $\mathbf{X}_u = [\mathbf{x}_{l+1}, \mathbf{x}_{l+2}, \cdots, \mathbf{x}_n]$ the unlabeled training set with $u = n - l$. We assume that the number of labeled samples is uniformly selected for each class. This means for a K-class classification, each class has $l_c = \frac{l}{K}$ labeled samples.

Without loss of generality, we let all $y_i \in \{-1, 1\}$ to focus on discussing a binary classification. However, the classifier here can be naturally extended to a multi-class case, by either replacing the binary classifier with the multi-class classifier (e.g., soft-max classifier [Duan *et al.* (2003)]), or adopting the well-known one-versus-one or one-versus-all strategy.

Our goal is to jointly learn a dictionary $\mathbf{D}$ consisting of a set of basis for extracting the sparse code (feature vector), and the classification parameter $\mathbf{w}$ for a binary classifier applied to the extracted feature vector, while guaranteeing them to be optimal to each other.

8.1.2 *Joint Feature Extraction and Classification*

8.1.2.1 *Sparse Coding for Feature Extraction*

In [Chen *et al.* (2011)], the authors suggest that the spectral signatures of pixels belonging to the same class are assumed to approximately lie in a low-dimensional subspace. Pixel can be compactly represented by only a few sparse coefficients (sparse code). Here, we adopt the sparse code as the input features, since extensive literature has examined the outstanding effect of SRC for a more discriminative and robust classification [Wright *et al.* (2009)].

We assume that all the data samples $\mathbf{X} = [\mathbf{x}_1, \mathbf{x}_2, \cdots, \mathbf{x}_n], \mathbf{x}_i \in R^{m \times 1}, i = 1, 2, \cdots, n$, are encoded into their corresponding sparse codes $\mathbf{A} = [\mathbf{a}_1, \mathbf{a}_2, \cdots, \mathbf{a}_n], \mathbf{a}_i \in R^{p \times 1}, i = 1, 2, \cdots, n$, using a learned dictionary $\mathbf{D} = [\mathbf{d}_1, \mathbf{d}_2, \cdots, \mathbf{d}_p]$, where $\mathbf{d}_i \in R^{m \times 1}, i = 1, 2, \cdots, p$ are the learned atoms. It should be noted that the initial dictionary is generated by assigning equal number of atoms to each class. That means for a K-class classification, there are $p_c = \frac{p}{K}$ atoms assigned to each class in a dictionary consisting of p atoms.

The sparse representation is obtained by the following convex optimization

$$\mathbf{A} = \arg\min_{\mathbf{A}} \tfrac{1}{2}||\mathbf{X} - \mathbf{DA}||_F^2 + \lambda_1 \sum_i ||\mathbf{a}_i||_1 + \lambda_2 ||\mathbf{A}||_F^2, \qquad (8.1)$$

or rewritten in a separate form for each $\mathbf{x}_i$

$$\mathbf{a}_i = \arg\min_{\mathbf{a}_i} \tfrac{1}{2}||\mathbf{x}_i - \mathbf{Da}_i||_2^2 + \lambda_1 ||\mathbf{a}_i||_1 + \lambda_2 ||\mathbf{a}_i||_2^2. \qquad (8.2)$$

Note $\lambda_2 > 0$ is necessary for proving the differentiability of the objective function (see Lemma A.2.1). However, setting $\lambda_2 = 0$ proves to work well in practice [Mairal *et al.* (2012)].

Obviously, the effect of sparse coding (8.1) largely depends on the quality of dictionary $\mathbf{D}$. The authors in [Chen *et al.* (2011)] suggest to construct the dictionary by directly selecting atoms from the training samples. More sophisticated methods are widely used in SRC literature, discussing on how to learn a more compact and effective dictionary from a given training dataset, e.g., the K-SVD algorithm [Aharon *et al.* (2006)].

We recognize that many structured sparsity constraints (priors) [Chen *et al.* (2011); Sun *et al.* (2014)] can also be considered for dictionary learning. They usually exploit the correlations among the neighboring pixels or their features. For example, the SRC dictionary has an inherent group-structured property since it is composed of several class-wise sub-dictionaries, i.e., the atoms belonging to the same class are grouped together to form a sub-dictionary. Therefore, it would be reasonable to enforce each pixel to be compactly represented by groups of atoms instead of individual ones. This could be accomplished by encouraging coefficients of only certain groups to be active, like the Group Lasso [Simon *et al.* (2013)]. While the performance may be improved by enforcing structured sparsity priors, the algorithm will be considerably more complicated. Therefore, we do not take into account any structured sparsity prior here, and leave them for our future study.

8.1.2.2   *Task-Driven Functions for Classification*

Classical loss functions in SRC are often defined by the reconstruction error of data samples [Chen *et al.* (2011); Lee *et al.* (2006)]. The performances of such learned classifiers highly hinge on the quality of the input features, which is only sub-optimal without the joint optimization with classifier parameters. In [Pham and Venkatesh (2008)], the authors study a straightforward joint representation and classification framework, by adding a penalty term to the classification error in addition to the reconstruction error. The authors in [Jiang *et al.* (2011); Zhang *et al.* (2013a)] propose to enhance the dictionary's representative and discriminative power by integrating both the discriminative sparse-code error and the classification error into a single objective function. The approach jointly learns a single dictionary and a predictive linear classifier. However, being a semi-supervised method, the unlabeled data does not contribute much to promoting the discriminative effect in [Zhang *et al.* (2013a)], as only the reconstruction error is considered on the unlabeled set except for an "expansion" strategy applied to a small set of highly-confident unlabeled samples.

In order to obtain an optimal classifier with regard to the input feature, we exploit a task-driven formulation which aims to minimize a classification-oriented loss [Mairal *et al.* (2012)]. We incorporate the sparse codes $\mathbf{a}_i$, which are dependent on the atoms of the dictionary $\mathbf{D}$ that are to be learned, into the training of the classifier parameter $\mathbf{w}$. The logistic loss is used in the objective function for the classifier. We recognize that this formulation can be easily extended to other classifiers, e.g., SVM. The loss function for the labeled samples is directly defined by the logistic loss

$$L(\mathbf{A}, \mathbf{w}, \mathbf{x}_i, y_i) = \sum_{i=1}^{l} \log(1 + e^{-y_i \mathbf{w}^T \mathbf{a}_i}). \tag{8.3}$$

For unlabeled samples, the label of each $\mathbf{x_i}$ is unknown. We introduce the predicted confidence probability p_{ij} that sample $\mathbf{x_i}$ has label y_j (y_j=1 or -1), which is naturally set as the likelihood of the logistic regression

$$p_{ij} = p(y_j | \mathbf{w}, \mathbf{a}_i, \mathbf{x}_i) = \frac{1}{1 + e^{-y_j \mathbf{w}^T \mathbf{a}_i}}, \quad y_j = 1 \quad or \quad -1. \tag{8.4}$$

The loss function for the unlabeled samples then turns into a entropy-like form

$$U(\mathbf{A}, \mathbf{w}, \mathbf{x}_i) = \sum_{i=l+1}^{l+u} \sum_{y_j} p_{ij} L(\mathbf{a}_i, \mathbf{w}, \mathbf{x}_i, y_j), \tag{8.5}$$

which can be viewed as a weighted sum of loss under different classification outputs y_j.

Furthermore, we can similarly define p_{ij} for the labeled sample $\mathbf{x}_i$, that is 1 when y_j is the given correct label y_i and 0 elsewhere. The joint loss functions for all the training samples can thus be written into a unified form

$$T(\mathbf{A}, \mathbf{w}) = \sum_{i=1}^{l+u} \sum_{y_j} p_{ij} L(\mathbf{a}_i, \mathbf{w}, \mathbf{x}_i, y_j). \tag{8.6}$$

A semi-supervised task-driven formulation has also been proposed in [Mairal *et al.* (2012)]. However, it is posed as a naive combination of supervised and unsupervised steps. The unlabeled data are only used to minimize the reconstruction loss, without contributing to promoting the discriminative effect. In contrast, our formulation (8.6) clearly distinguishes itself by assigning an adaptive confidence weight (8.4) to each unlabeled sample, and minimizes a classification-oriented loss over both labeled and unlabeled samples. By doing so, unlabeled samples also contribute to improving the discriminability of learned features and classifier, jointly with the labeled samples, rather than only optimized for reconstruction loss.

8.1.2.3 *Spatial Laplacian Regularization*

We first introduce the weighting matrix $\mathbf{G}$, where G_{ik} characterizes the similarity between a pair of pixels $\mathbf{x}_i$ and $\mathbf{x}_k$. We define G_{ik} in the form of shift-invariant bilateral Gaussian filtering [Tomasi and Manduchi (1998)] (with controlling parameters σ_d and σ_s)

$$G_{ik} = \exp(-\frac{d(\mathbf{x}_i, \mathbf{x}_k)}{2\sigma_d^2}) \cdot \exp(-\frac{||\mathbf{x}_i - \mathbf{x}_k||_2^2}{2\sigma_s^2}), \tag{8.7}$$

which measures both the spatial Euclidean distance ($d(\mathbf{x}_i, \mathbf{x}_k)$) and the spectral similarity between an arbitrary pair of pixels in a hyperspectral image. Larger G_{ik} represents higher similarity and vice versa. Further, rather than simply enforcing pixels within a local window to share the same label, G_{ik} is defined over the whole image and encourages both spatially neighboring and spectrally similar pixels to have similar classification outputs. It makes our spatial constraints much more flexible and effective. Using the above similarity weights, we define the spatial Laplacian regularization function

$$S(\mathbf{A}, \mathbf{w}) = \sum_{i=1}^{l+u} \sum_{y_j} \sum_{k}^{l+u} G_{ik} ||p_{ij} - p_{kj}||_2^2). \qquad (8.8)$$

8.1.3   *Bi-Level Optimization Formulation*

Finally, the objective cost function for the joint minimization formulation can be expressed by the following bi-level optimization (the quadratic term of $\mathbf{w}$ is to avoid overfitting)

$$\begin{aligned} &\min_{\mathbf{D}, \mathbf{w}} \quad T(\mathbf{A}, \mathbf{w}) + S(\mathbf{A}, \mathbf{w}) + \tfrac{\lambda}{2} ||\mathbf{w}||_2^2 \\ &s.t. \quad \mathbf{A} = \arg\min_{\mathbf{A}} \tfrac{1}{2} ||\mathbf{X} - \mathbf{D}\mathbf{A}||_F^2 + \lambda_1 \sum_i ||\mathbf{a}_i||_1 + \lambda_2 ||\mathbf{A}||_F^2. \end{aligned} \qquad (8.9)$$

Bilevel optimization [Colson *et al.* (2007)] has been investigated in both theory and application sides. In [Yang *et al.* (2012b)], the authors propose a general bilevel sparse coding model for learning dictionaries across coupled signal spaces. Another similar formulation has been studied in [Mairal *et al.* (2012)] for general regression tasks.

In the testing stage, each test sample is first represented by solving (8.2) over the learned $\mathbf{D}$. The resulting sparse coefficients are fed to the trained logistic classifier with the previously learned $\mathbf{w}$. The test sample is classified into the class of the highest output probability (8.4).

8.1.4   *Algorithm*

Built on the similar methodologies of [Mairal *et al.* (2012)] and [Yang *et al.* (2012b)], we solve (8.9) using a projected first order stochastic gradient descent (SGD) algorithm, whose detailed steps are outlined in Algorithm 1. At a high level overview, it consists of an outer stochastic gradient descent loop that incrementally samples the training data. It uses each sample to approximate gradients with respect to the classifier parameter $\mathbf{w}$ and the dictionary $\mathbf{D}$, which are then used to update them. Next, we briefly explain a few key technical points of the Algorithm 1.

8.1.4.1 *Stochastic Gradient Descent*

The stochastic gradient descent (SGD) algorithm [Kushner and Yin (2003)] is an iterative, "on-line" approach for optimizing an objective function, based on a sequence of approximate gradients obtained by randomly sampling from the training data set. In the simplest case, SGD estimates the objective function gradient on the basis of a single randomly selected example $\mathbf{x}_t$

$$w_{t+1} = w_t - \rho_t \nabla_w F(\mathbf{x}_t, w_t), \tag{8.10}$$

where F is a loss function, w is a weight being optimized and ρ_t is a step size known as the "learning rate". The stochastic process $\{w_t, t = 1, \cdots\}$ depends upon the sequence of randomly selected examples $\mathbf{x}_t$ from the training data. It thus optimizes the empirical cost, which is hoped to be a good proxy for the expected cost.

Following the derivations in [Mairal *et al.* (2012)], we can show that the objective function in (8.9), denoted as $B(\mathbf{A}, \mathbf{w})$ for simplicity, is differentiable on $\mathbf{D} \times \mathbf{w}$, and that

$$\begin{aligned} \nabla_{\mathbf{w}} B(\mathbf{A}, \mathbf{w}) &= \mathbb{E}_{\mathbf{x}, y}[\nabla_{\mathbf{w}} T(\mathbf{A}, \mathbf{w}) + \nabla_{\mathbf{w}} S(\mathbf{A}, \mathbf{w}) + \lambda \mathbf{w}] \\ \nabla_{\mathbf{D}} B(\mathbf{A}, \mathbf{w}) &= \mathbb{E}_{\mathbf{x}, y}[-\mathbf{D}\beta^* \mathbf{A}^{\mathbf{T}} + (\mathbf{X}_t - \mathbf{DA})\beta^{*T}], \end{aligned} \tag{8.11}$$

where β^* is a vector defined by the following property:

$$\begin{aligned} \beta^*_{S^C} &= 0 \\ \beta^*_S &= (\mathbf{D}_S^T \mathbf{D}_S + \lambda_2 \mathbf{I})^{-1} \nabla_{\mathbf{A}_S}[T(\mathbf{A}, \mathbf{w}) + S(\mathbf{A}, \mathbf{w})], \end{aligned} \tag{8.12}$$

and S are the indices of the nonzero coefficients of $\mathbf{A}$. The proof of the above equations is given in A.3.

8.1.4.2 *Sparse Reconstruction*

The most computationally intensive step in Algorithm 1 is solving the sparse coding (step 3). Here, the Feature-Sign algorithm [Lee *et al.* (2006)] is adopted for efficiently solving the exact solution to the sparse coding problem.

Remark on SGD convergence and sampling strategy: As a typical case in machine learning, we use SGD in a setting where it is not guaranteed to converge in theory, but behaves well in practice, as shown in our experiments. (The convergence proof of SGD [Bottou (1998)] for nonconvex problems indeed assumes three times differentiable cost functions.)

SGD algorithms are typically designed to minimize functions whose gradients have the form of an expectation. While an i.i.d (independent and

---

Algorithm 8.1 Stochastic gradient descent algorithm for solving (8.9).

Require: X, Y; λ, λ_1, λ_2, σ_d and σ_s; $\mathbf{D}_0$ and $\mathbf{w}_0$ (initial dictionary and classifier parameter); ITER (number of iterations); t_0, ρ (learning rate)

1: FOR t=1 to ITER DO
2: Draw a subset $(\mathbf{X}_t, \mathbf{Y}_t)$ from $(\mathbf{X}, \mathbf{Y})$
3: Sparse coding: computer $\mathbf{A}^*$ using Feature-Sign algorithm:
     $\mathbf{A}^* = \arg\min_{\mathbf{A}} \frac{1}{2}||\mathbf{X}_t - \mathbf{DA}||_2^2 + \lambda_1 \sum_i ||\mathbf{a}_i||_1 + \frac{\lambda_2}{2}||\mathbf{A}||_2^2$
4: Compute the active set S (the nonzero support of $\mathbf{A}$)
5: Compute β^*: Set $\beta_{S^C}^* = 0$ and $\beta_S^* = (\mathbf{D}_S^T \mathbf{D}_S + \lambda_2 \mathbf{I})^{-1} \nabla_{\mathbf{A_s}}[T(\mathbf{A}, \mathbf{w}) + S(\mathbf{A}, \mathbf{w})]$
6: Choose the learning rate $\rho_t = \min(\rho, \rho \frac{t_0}{t})$
7: Update $\mathbf{D}$ and $\mathbf{W}$ by a projected gradient step:
     $\mathbf{w} = \prod_{\mathbf{w}}[\mathbf{w} - \rho_t(\nabla_{\mathbf{w}} T(\mathbf{A}, \mathbf{w}) + \nabla_{\mathbf{w}} S(\mathbf{A}, \mathbf{w}) + \lambda \mathbf{w})]$
     $\mathbf{D} = \prod_{\mathbf{D}}[\mathbf{D} - \rho_t(\nabla_{\mathbf{D}}(-\mathbf{D}\beta^* \mathbf{A}^T + (\mathbf{X}_t - \mathbf{DA})\beta^{*T})]$
     where $\prod_{\mathbf{w}}$ and $\prod_{\mathbf{D}}$ are respectively orthogonal projections on the embedding spaces of $\mathbf{w}$ and $\mathbf{D}$.
8: END FOR

Ensure: D and **w**

---

identically distributed) sampling process is required, It cannot be computed in a batch mode. In our algorithm, instead of sampling one per iteration, we adopt a mini-batch strategy by drawing more samples at a time. Authors in [Mairal *et al.* (2012)] further pointed out that solving multiple elastic-net problems with the same dictionary $\mathbf{D}$ can be accelerated by the pre-computation of the matrix $\mathbf{D}^T \mathbf{D}$. In practice, we draw a set of 200 samples in each iteration, which produces steadily good results in all our experiments under universal settings.

Strictly speaking, drawing samples from the distribution of training data should be made i.i.d. (step 2 in Algorithm 1). However, this is practically difficult since the distribution itself is typically unknown. As an approximation, samples are instead drawn by iterating over random permutations of the training set [Bottou (1998)].

8.2   Experiments

In this section, we evaluate the presented method on three popular datasets, and compare it with some related approaches in the literature, including:

- Laplacian Support Vector Machine (LapSVM) [Belkin *et al.* (2006); Gómez-Chova *et al.* (2008)], that is a semi-supervised extension of the SVM and applies the spatial manifold assumption to SVM. The classification is directly executed on raw pixels without any feature extraction, which follows the original setting in [10].
- Semi-supervised Classification (SSC) approach [Wang *et al.* (2012)] that employs a modified clustering assumption.
- Semi-supervised hyperspectral image segmentation that adopts Multinomial Logistic Regression with Active Learning (MLR-AL) [Li *et al.* (2010)]

Regarding parameter choices of the three methods, we try our best to follow the settings in their original papers. For LapSVM, the regularization parameters γ_1, γ_2 are selected from $[10^{-5}, 10^5]$ according to a five-fold cross-validation procedure. In SSC, the width parameter of Gaussian function is tuned using a five-fold cross-validation procedure. The parameter setting in MLR-AL follows that of the original paper [Li *et al.* (2010)].

Besides the above mentioned three algorithms, we also include the following algorithms in the comparison, in order to illustrate the merits of both joint optimization and spatial Laplacian regularization on the classifier outputs:

- Non-joint optimization of feature extraction and classification (Non-Joint). It refers to conducting the following two stages of the optimization sequentially:

  1. **Feature extraction:**
     $\mathbf{A} = \arg\min_{\mathbf{A}} \frac{1}{2}||\mathbf{X} - \mathbf{D}\mathbf{A}||_F^2 + \lambda_1 \sum_i ||\mathbf{a_i}||_1$
     $+\lambda_2||\mathbf{A}||_F^2.$ (8.13)
  2. **Learning a classifier:**
     $\min_{\mathbf{w}} \quad T(\mathbf{A}, \mathbf{w}) + \frac{\lambda}{2}||\mathbf{w}||_2^2.$

  The training of $\mathbf{D}$ is independent of the learning of the classifier parameter $\mathbf{w}$. This is different from the joint optimization of the dictionary and classifier as is done in (8.9) by the task-driven formulation.
- Non-joint optimization of feature extraction and classification, with spatial Laplacian regularization (Non-Joint + Laplacian). It is the same as the Non-Joint method except for adding a spatial Laplacian

regularization term $S(\mathbf{A}, \mathbf{w})$ to the second subproblem:

1. Feature extraction:
$\mathbf{A} = \arg\min_{\mathbf{A}} \frac{1}{2}||\mathbf{X} - \mathbf{DA}||_F^2 + \lambda_1 \sum_i ||\mathbf{a}_i||_1 +$
$\lambda_2 ||\mathbf{A}||_F^2.$ (8.14)

2. Learning a classifier:
$\min_{\mathbf{w}} \quad T(\mathbf{A}, \mathbf{w}) + S(\mathbf{A}, \mathbf{w}) + \frac{\lambda}{2}||\mathbf{w}||_2^2.$

- The joint method without spatial Laplacian regularization (Joint), which is done by dropping the $S(\mathbf{A}, \mathbf{W})$ term in (8.9)

$\min_{\mathbf{D}, \mathbf{W}} \quad T(\mathbf{A}, \mathbf{w}) + \frac{\lambda}{2}||\mathbf{w}||_2^2$

$s.t. \quad \mathbf{A} = \arg\min_{\mathbf{A}} \frac{1}{2}||\mathbf{X} - \mathbf{DA}||_F^2 + \lambda_1 \sum_i ||\mathbf{a}_i||_1$ (8.15)
$+\lambda_2 ||\mathbf{A}||_F^2.$

- The joint method with spatial Laplacian regularization (Joint + Laplacian), by minimizing the bi-level formulation (8.9).

Parameter Setting For the presented method, the regularization parameter λ in (8.9) is fixed to be 10^{-2}, and λ_2 in (8.2) is set to 0 to exploit sparsity. The elastic-net parameter λ_1 in (8.2) is generated by a cross-validation procedure, which is similar to the one in [Mairal *et al.* (2012)]. The values of λ_1 are 0.225, 0.25, and 0.15 for the three experiments in Sections 8.2.1-8.2.3, respectively. σ_d and σ_s in (8.7) are fixed as 3 and 3,000, respectively. The learning rate ρ is set as 1, and maximum number ITER is set as 1000 for all. Although, we have verified that these choices of parameters work well in extensive experiments, we recognize that a finer tuning of them may further improve the performance.

In particular, we would like to mention the initializations of $\mathbf{D}$ and $\mathbf{w}$. For the two non-joint methods, $\mathbf{D}$ is initialized by solving the first subproblem (feature extraction) in (8.13) or (8.14). In this subproblem, for each class, we initialize its sub-dictionary atoms randomly. We then employ several iterations of K-SVD using only the available labeled data for that class, and finally combine all the output class-wise sub-dictionaries into a single initial dictionary $\mathbf{D}$. Next, we solve $\mathbf{A}$ based on $\mathbf{D}$, and continue to feed $\mathbf{A}$ into the second subproblems (learning a classifier) in (8.13) and (8.14) for good initializations of $\mathbf{w}$, for Non-Joint and Non-Joint + Laplacian, respectively. For the two joint methods, we use the results of Non-Joint, and Non-Joint + Laplacian, to initialize $\mathbf{D}$ and $\mathbf{w}$ of Joint and Joint + Laplacian, respectively.

The one-versus-all strategy is adopted for addressing multi-class problems, which means that we train K different binary logistic classifiers with

Table 8.1   Overall classification results (%) for the AVIRIS Indiana Pines data with different numbers of labeled samples per class (u=ALL, $\lambda = 10^{-2}$, λ_1=0.225, λ_2=0, ρ=1, σ_d=3, σ_s=3,000).

l_c	2	3	4	5	6	7	8	9	10
LapSVM [Belkin *et al.* (2006)]	57.80	61.32	63.1	66.39	68.27	69.00	70.15	70.04	70.73
SSC [Wang *et al.* (2012)]	44.61	56.98	58.27	60.56	60.79	64.19	66.81	69.40	70.50
MLR+AL [Li *et al.* (2010)]	52.34	56.16	59.21	61.47	65.16	69.21	72.14	73.89	74.43
Non-Joint ($p_c = 50$)	63.72	69.21	71.87	76.88	79.04	81.81	85.23	87.77	88.54
Non-Joint + Laplacian ($p_c = 50$)	66.89	72.37	75.33	78.78	81.21	84.98	87.25	88.61	89.88
Joint ($p_c = 5$)	69.81	76.03	80.42	82.91	84.81	85.76	86.95	87.54	89.31
Joint + Laplacian ($p_c = 5$)	**76.55**	**80.63**	**84.28**	**86.33**	**88.27**	**90.68**	**91.87**	**92.53**	**93.11**

K corresponding dictionaries for a K-class problem. For each test sample, the classifier with the maximum score will provide the class label. When the class number is large, this one-versus-all approach has proven to be more scalable than learning a single large dictionary with a multi-class loss [Mairal *et al.* (2012)], while providing very good results.

For the two joint methods, we assign only five dictionary atoms per class to initialize the dictionary, which means for a K-class problem we have $p_c = 5$ and $p = 5K$ for the total dictionary size. For the two non-joint methods, fifty dictionary atoms ($p_c = 50$) are assigned per class in the first subproblems of (8.13) and (8.14), respectively. The choices of dictionary sizes for both joint and non-joint methods will be illustrated in Section 8.2.4. The reason why we use the term "atoms per class" are two-fold: 1) we initialize our dictionary by first applying KSVD to each class to obtain a class-wise sub-dictionary. This helps to improve the class discriminability of the learned dictionary more than just applying KSVD to the whole data. Therefore, we need to specify how many atoms are assigned per class in the initialization stage. Note when Algorithm 1 starts, the atoms become all entangled, and further it is impossible to identify how many (and which) atoms are representing a specific class in the final learned dictionary; 2) As each dataset has a different number of classes, and empirically, more classes demand more dictionary atoms to represent. Note, however, if we assign atoms in proportion to the number of samples per class, some minor classes will tend to be severely underrepresented.

In Sections 8.2.1-8.2.3, we use all the unlabeled pixels (denoted as "ALL") from each hyperspectral image for semi-supervised training. In Section 8.2.5, we discuss how unlabeled samples u will influence the classification accuracy. Section 8.2.6 provides a visualized example to manifest that this method indeed leads to a more discriminative dictionary that contributes to a higher classification accuracy.

8.2.1   Classification Performance on AVIRIS Indiana Pines Data

The AVIRIS sensor generates 220 bands across the spectral range from 0.2 to 2.4 μm. In the experiment, the number of bands is reduced to 200 by removing 20 water absorption bands. The AVIRIS Indiana Pines hyperspectral image has the spatial resolution of 20m and 145×145 pixels. It contains 16 classes, most of which are different types of crops (e.g., corns, soybeans, and wheats). The ground-truth classification map is shown in Fig. 8.1(a).

Table 8.1 evaluates the influence of the number of labeled samples per class l_c on the classification of AVIRIS Indiana Pines data, with l_c varying from 2 to 10. The dictionary consists of only $p = 80$ atoms to represent all the 16 classes for the joint methods, and $p = 800$ for the non-joint methods. The bold value in each column indicates the best result among all the seven methods. As can be seen from the table, the classification results improve for all the algorithms with the increase in the number of labeled samples. The last two methods, i.e., "Joint" and "Joint + Laplacian", outperform the other five methods in terms of overall accuracy (OA) significantly. It is also observed that the "Joint + Laplacian" method obtains further improvement over the "Joint" method, showing the advantage of spatial Laplacian regularization. Amazingly, we notice that even when there are as few as three samples per class, the OA of the presented method ("Joint + Laplacian") is still higher than 80%.

Fig. 8.1 demonstrates the classification maps obtained by all the methods when 10 labeled samples are used per class. The presented method, either with or without spatial regularization, obtains much less misclassifications compared with the other methods. What is more, the homogenous areas in (h) are significantly better preserved than that in (g), that again confirms the effectiveness of the spatial Laplacian regularization on the output of the classifier. Fig. 8.2 visually demonstrates that along with the increase of l_c, the classification results gradually improve, and both the regional and scattered misclassifications are reduced dramatically.

8.2.2   Classification Performance on AVIRIS Salinas Data

This dataset is collected over the Valley of Salinas, Southern California, in 1998. This hyperspectral image is of size 217×512, with 16 different classes of objects in total. In our experiment, a nine-class subset is considered,

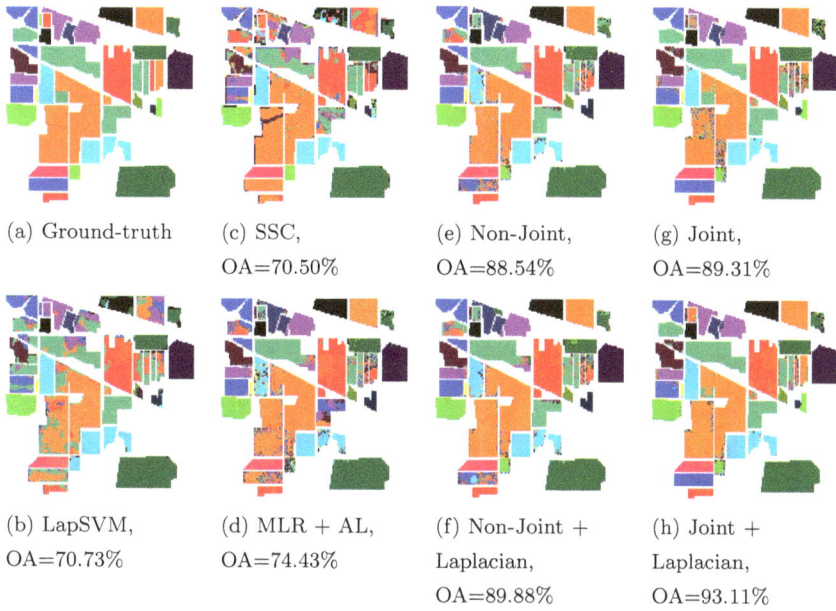

Fig. 8.1   Classification maps for the AVIRIS Indian Pines scene using different methods with 10 labeled samples per class.

Table 8.2   Overall classification results (%) for the AVIRIS Salinas data with different numbers of labeled samples per class (u=ALL, $\lambda = 10^{-2}$, λ_1=0.25, λ_2=0, ρ=1, σ_d=3, σ_s=3,000).

l_c	2	3	4	5	6	7	8	9	10
LapSVM [Belkin *et al.* (2006)]	**90.77**	91.53	**92.95**	93.50	94.77	95.08	96.05	97.17	98.00
SSC [Wang *et al.* (2012)]	59.47	61.84	64.90	67.19	71.04	73.04	72.81	73.51	75.36
MLR+AL [Li *et al.* (2010)]	78.98	82.32	84.31	86.27	85.86	89.41	92.27	93.78	95.66
Non-Joint ($p_c = 50$)	85.88	87.21	89.29	90.76	91.42	92.87	93.95	94.78	95.26
Non-Joint + Laplacian ($p_c = 50$)	87.67	89.28	91.54	92.67	93.93	95.28	96.79	97.83	98.08
Joint ($p_c = 5$)	89.71	90.03	91.42	92.12	93.25	94.54	96.05	97.45	98.90
Joint + Laplacian ($p_c = 5$)	90.65	**91.59**	92.28	**93.63**	**95.22**	**96.58**	**97.81**	**98.53**	**99.40**

including vegetables, bare soils, and vineyard fields. The ground-truth classification map is shown in Fig. 8.3 (a). As AVIRIS Salinas is recognized to be easier for classification than AVIRIS Indian Pines, all methods obtain high OAs as listed in Table 8.2, while the "Joint + Laplacian" method marginally stands out. When we turn to Fig. 8.3 (b)-(h) for the comparison in classification maps, however, the "Joint + Laplacian" method is visually much superior in reducing scattered misclassifications.

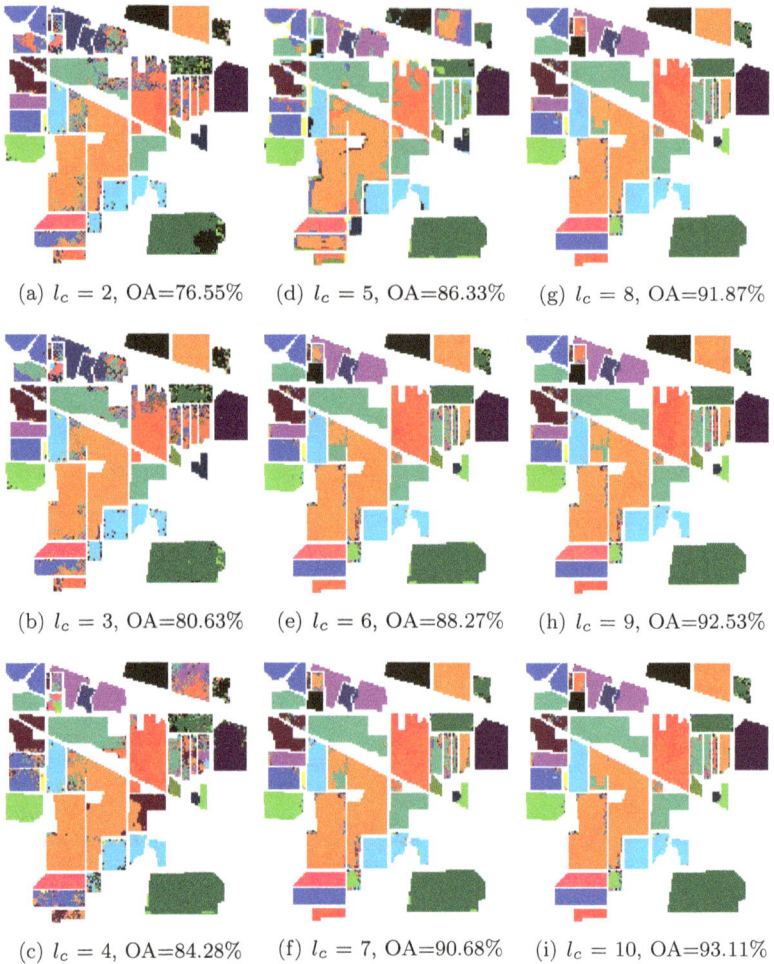

(a) $l_c = 2$, OA=76.55%   (d) $l_c = 5$, OA=86.33%   (g) $l_c = 8$, OA=91.87%

(b) $l_c = 3$, OA=80.63%   (e) $l_c = 6$, OA=88.27%   (h) $l_c = 9$, OA=92.53%

(c) $l_c = 4$, OA=84.28%   (f) $l_c = 7$, OA=90.68%   (i) $l_c = 10$, OA=93.11%

Fig. 8.2   Classification maps for the AVIRIS Indian Pines scene using the presented Joint + Laplacian method with different numbers of labeled samples per class.

8.2.3   *Classification Performance on University of Pavia Data*

The ROSIS sensor collected this data during a flight campaign over the Pavia district in north Italy. 103 spectral bands were used for data acquisition in this dataset, comprising of 610×610 pixel images with a geometric resolution of 1.3m. A few samples contain no information and were discarded before the classification. The ground truth data shows a total of nine

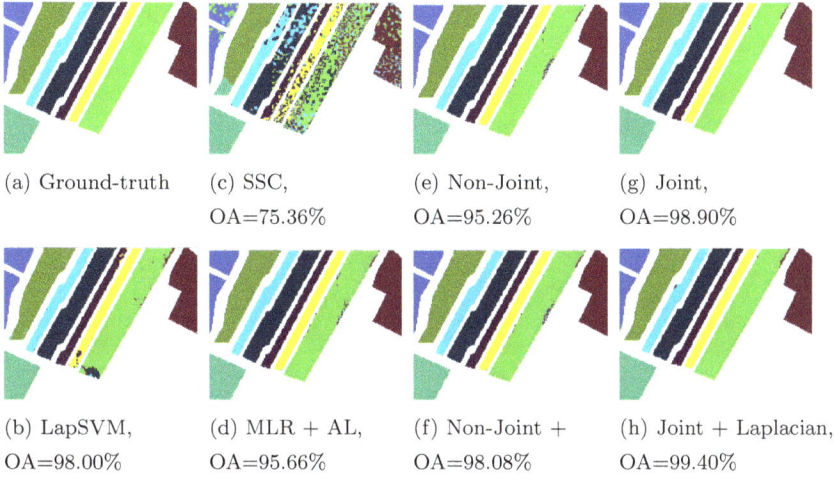

(a) Ground-truth

(c) SSC,
OA=75.36%

(e) Non-Joint,
OA=95.26%

(g) Joint,
OA=98.90%

(b) LapSVM,
OA=98.00%

(d) MLR + AL,
OA=95.66%

(f) Non-Joint +
OA=98.08%

(h) Joint + Laplacian,
OA=99.40%

Fig. 8.3   Classification maps for the AVIRIS Salinas scene using different methods with 10 labeled samples per class.

Table 8.3   Overall classification results (%) for the University of Pavia data with different numbers of labeled samples per class (u=ALL, $\lambda = 10^{-2}$, λ_1=0.15, λ_2=0, ρ=1, σ_d=3, σ_s=3,000).

l_c	2	3	4	5	6	7	8	9	10
LapSVM [Belkin *et al.* (2006)]	64.77	67.83	69.25	71.05	72.97	74.38	76.75	78.17	79.88
SSC [Wang *et al.* (2012)]	69.54	72.84	74.69	76.21	77.24	78.43	79.81	80.25	80.95
MLR+AL [Li *et al.* (2010)]	76.27	78.66	79.30	80.22	81.36	82.41	83.27	84.78	85.53
Non-Joint ($p_c = 50$)	74.21	75.27	76.22	76.83	78.24	79.51	79.67	80.83	81.26
Non-Joint + Laplacian ($p_c = 50$)	**79.23**	80.26	82.58	**84.07**	**86.21**	86.88	87.56	88.23	88.78
Joint ($p_c = 5$)	74.21	76.73	79.24	80.82	82.35	84.54	86.97	87.27	88.08
Joint + Laplacian ($p_c = 5$)	78.56	**80.29**	**82.84**	83.76	85.12	**87.58**	**88.33**	**89.52**	**90.41**

Table 8.4   Overall classification results (%) for the AVIRIS Indiana Pines data with different number of dictionary atoms per class (FIX $l_c = 10$, $u =$ ALL).

p_c	3	5	8	10	20	50	100
Non-Joint	69.21	78.83	81.27	85.45	88.38	88.54	88.91
Non-Joint + Laplacian	72.33	79.22	84.35	88.76	89.27	89.88	90.21
Joint	87.87	89.31	89.27	89.51	89.87	89.95	90.05
Joint + Laplacian	92.42	93.11	93.30	93.53	93.87	93.82	93.67

distinct classes, and has been portrayed visually in Fig. 8.4 (a). Similar conclusions can be attained from both Table 8.3 and Fig. 8.4, that once again verify the merits of both the joint optimization framework and spatial regularization.

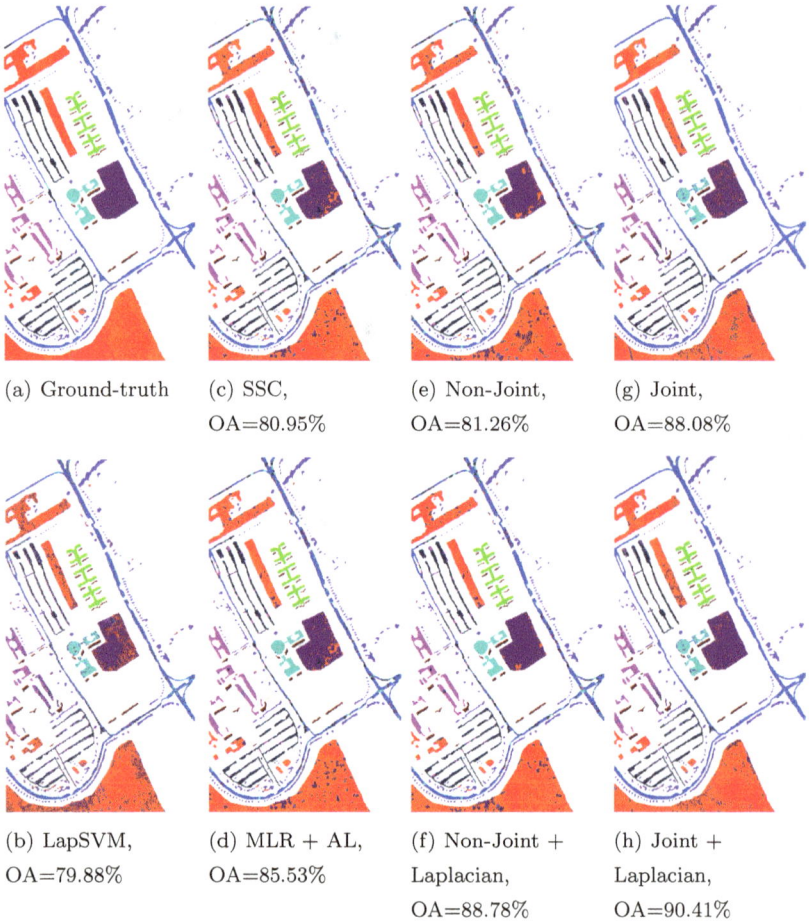

(a) Ground-truth

(c) SSC,
OA=80.95%

(e) Non-Joint,
OA=81.26%

(g) Joint,
OA=88.08%

(b) LapSVM,
OA=79.88%

(d) MLR + AL,
OA=85.53%

(f) Non-Joint +
Laplacian,
OA=88.78%

(h) Joint +
Laplacian,
OA=90.41%

Fig. 8.4   Classification maps for the University of Pavia scene using different methods
with 10 labeled samples per class.

8.2.4   *Influences of Dictionary Size*

To study the influence of the dictionary size, we report the performance
on the AVIRIS Indian Pines dataset for different dictionary sizes, with
both Joint and Joint + Laplacian methods. Moreover, we also include
Non-Joint and Non-Joint + Laplacian methods into the same comparison
experiments, in order to validate their optimal dictionary sizes. It is recognized that a larger dictionary usually means a better performance, but at
a higher computational cost. Setting the size of the dictionary is therefore
often a trade-off between the desired quality of the classification results and

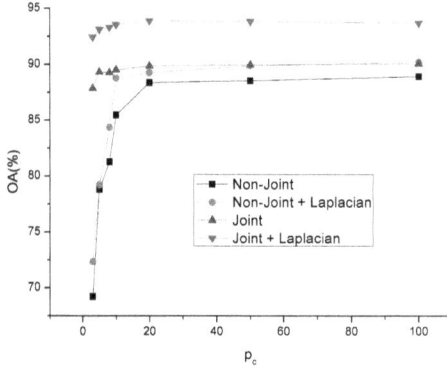

Fig. 8.5 Classification results for the AVIRIS Indian Pines data with different p_c (fix l=160, u =ALL).

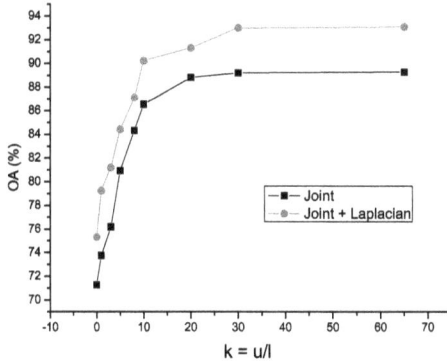

Fig. 8.6 Classification results for the AVIRIS Indian Pines data with different u (fix $l = 160$, $p_c =5$).

computational efficiency of the algorithm.

Table 8.4, as well as Fig. 8.5, proves that the presented method is quite robust to the dictionary size. The performance is only a little bit low even when there are only three dictionary atoms per class (dictionary with $p = 48$ atoms). This is because the overall dictionary is too small to capture all the features in the training data. However, a good classification accuracy can always be achieved with a relatively small dictionary, even with only

Table 8.5   Overall classification results (%) for the AVIRIS Indiana Pines data with different numbers of unlabeled samples (Fix $l = 160$, $p_c = 5$).

$u = kl$	$0l$	$1l$	$3l$	$5l$	$8l$	$10l$	$20l$	$30l$	All
Joint	71.28	73.76	76.20	80.94	84.34	86.54	88.83	89.21	89.31
Joint + Laplacian	75.33	79.25	81.21	84.44	87.12	90.24	91.32	93.02	93.11

five atoms per class (dictionary with $p = 80$ atoms). which indicates that both joint methods can obtain good performance with a computationally reasonable dictionary size. In contrast, the performances of two non-joint methods turn dramatically poorer when the dictionary is highly compact. As the dictionary size is increased and finally turns overcomplete, the performance differences with joint methods become relatively smaller but still quite notable even under $p_c = 100$, where the Joint + Laplacian method maintains a more than 3% advantage in overall accuracy over its counterpart Non-Joint + Laplacian method. While the non-joint methods have to sacrifice computational efficiency (due to a large overcomplete dictionary) for a better accuracy, we can use a compact dictionary and avoid the heavy computational cost in the joint methods.

8.2.5   *Influences of Unlabeled Samples*

In this section, we evaluate how the number of unlabeled samples for training will influence the resulting accuracy, via experiments on AVIRIS Indian Pines dataset as well. In Table 8.5, we demonstrate the influence of changing u, when fixing l_c at 10 in order to have a total of $l = 160$ labeled samples. To be more intuitive, we express u as k times the value of l, i.e., $u = kl$, $k \in Z$, and vary k from 0 (which corresponds to the supervised task-driven case, with Laplacian regularization), until when u reaches the total number of unlabeled samples (denoted as "ALL"). As a consequence, with the same number of labeled samples, increasing the number of unlabeled samples u leads to a monotone increase in the classification accuracy, which validates the advantage of semi-supervised classification. Such an improvement becomes especially remarkable even when the amount of labeled samples is very small, as can also be seen from the plot in Fig. 8.6.

8.2.6   *Discriminability of Dictionary*

In the presented method, we jointly optimize the dictionary and the classifier together. The learned dictionary is thus expected to consist of highly

(a) atom 1   (b) atom 2   (c) atom 3   (d) atom 4   (e) atom 5   (f) atom 6

(a)

(g) atom 1   (h) atom 2   (i) atom 3   (j) atom 4   (k) atom 5   (l) atom 6

(b)

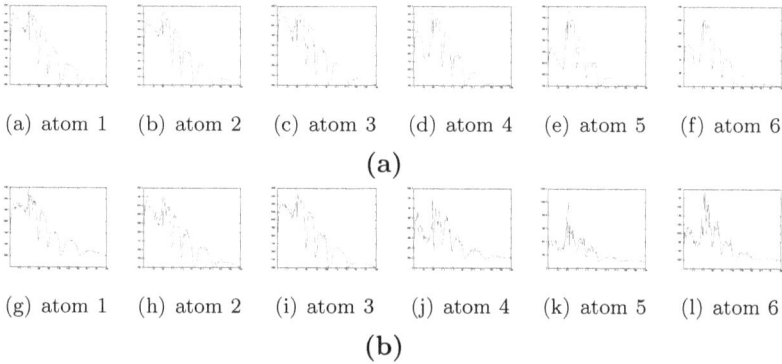

Fig. 8.7   The spectral signatures of (a) the atoms of the K-SVD unsupervised dictionary in the top row (OA=84.45%), and (b) the atoms of the task-driven semi-supervised dictionary in the bottom row (OA=92.05%). For each of the figures, the X-axis and Y-axis stand for the spectral band and radiance value, respectively.

discriminative basis for the classification. This fact has already been implied by the performances in Sections 8.2.1-8.2.3, and here we are going to verify the discriminative property directly by visualizing the dictionary atoms.

We choose two classes, the 3rd class "Corn-min" and the 6th class "Grass/-Trees", from the AVIRIS Indian Pines dataset. Each class has only 10 labeled samples while being abundant in unlabeled samples. We first apply K-SVD to each of the class dataset separately, and obtain a class-wise sub-dictionary of three atoms. Then we concatenate the two sub-dictionaries into a K-SVD dictionary of six atoms, and follow the Non-Joint +Laplacian method (8.14) to do a binary classification. Next, a task-driven dictionary is generated by the presented method (8.9), with the same dictionary size and initialized by the K-SVD dictionary as described previously.

We visualize our results in Fig. 8.7 by plotting the spectral signatures of all the six atoms in the dictionaries. For each figure, the X-axis and Y-axis stand for the spectral band and radiance value, respectively. The atoms generated by K-SVD are plotted in the top row, while the atoms by the presented method are plotted in the bottom row. Comparing to the K-SVD results, the dictionary atoms learned by the presented method looks more "dissimilar" with each other, demonstrating visually a higher discriminability. As a consequence, the classification accuracy of this method achieves 92.05%, which remarkably outperforms the 84.45% accuracy by the Non-Joint +Laplacian method.

Chapter 9

Conclusions

In this monograph, we have an extensive review of the recent development in sparse coding techniques. Both of its supporting theoretical foundation and some novel applications have been covered.

In Chapter 2, a brief overview is given about the latest theatrical results in sparse coding. We discuss different ways to impose sparse prior, infer sparse code, and design sparsifying representation. Although tremendous progress has been made in the past decade, there are still many mysteries about the solution, performance and property of sparse coding. Further explorations are much needed to explain its success in existing applications, and more importantly to guide the discovery of its new utilities.

In Chapter 3, the effectiveness of sparse coding in image SR is demonstrated from several aspects. First, we show this image restoration problem can be formulated in a coupled dictionary learning framework. This framework has been further extended to a recurrent neural network and a joint model incorporating both external and internal examples. Experimental results show that this family of algorithms outperform previous state-of-the-art methods on various test images of different resolutions and scaling factors, and are much more favored by human perception. How to integrate dictionary learning more closely with other domain priors in image SR problem can be a fruitful future direction. Reducing the computational complexity is another important consideration for use on large images. Moreover, the combined strength of sparse coding and neural network is likely to raise the performance bar in other low level and high level image processing problems.

An effective sparse representation based blind image deblurring approach is presented in Chapter 4. This method exploits the sparsity prior of natural images in a proper domain to help alleviating the ill-posed inverse blind deblurring problem. Due to the incorporation of this sparsity regularization, the deblurred image suffers less from the undesirable ringing artifacts as well as noise amplifications. Experimental results under different observation processes demonstrate that this method can generate desirable deblurring results. We further present a joint restoration and recognition method with the sparse representation prior, and demonstrate its application on face recognition from a single blurry image. By combining these two interactive tasks, the algorithm demonstrates significant improvements over the approach treating them separately. In the current model, mild translation misalignment between test and training images can be captured and compensated by the blur kernel. As a future direction, more complex alignment models, *e.g.*, affine transformation, can be incorporated into this framework to further handle more challenging misalignment between the blurry test image and sharp training images with techniques similar to [Wagner *et al.* (2009)] and [Yuan *et al.* (2007)]. Moreover, using learned dictionary rather than the training images directly in the model is also interesting and worthy of investigation in the future.

Chapter 5 is devoted to the investigation of several joint structured sparsity based classification methods for multi-sensor fusion based classification. Several models are developed under different joint structured sparsity assumptions. Besides using the same sparse codes model and common sparse pattern model for joint structured sparsity classification, we also introduce a novel joint dynamic sparsity model for classification. All the joint structured sparsity based classification methods utilized the correlations among all the multiple measurements by enforcing different structured sparsity constraints on the sparse coefficient matrix. Furthermore, for each method, these constraints were explicitly incorporated into the optimization problem. We have also seen the applications to multi-channel acoustic signal based event classification and multi-view face recognition.

The application of sparse coding in clustering is discussed in Chapter 6. First, we present a new graph construction procedure based on the sparse representation of each individual datum with respect to the remaining data samples by ℓ^1-norm minimization, and thus the new graph is called ℓ^1-graph. The ℓ^1-graph is robust to noise, does not have the local neighborhood assumption, and is especially good at modeling high dimensional feature spaces, where, empirically, many data distributions can be well approximated by a union of much lower dimensional linear subspaces. By seeking a sparse representation of each datum in terms of the remaining data samples, we can select the low dimensional linear subspace it lies in. Therefore, the ℓ^1-graph conveys greater discriminating power compared with the conventional graphs based on k-nearest neighbors and ϵ-ball. We show the effectiveness of this ℓ^1-graph in three graph-oriented machine learning tasks, including spectral clustering, subspace learning, and semi-supervised learning. In all cases, the ℓ^1-graph significantly outperforms the corresponding baselines on three different databases.

Second, we introduce a joint framework to optimize sparse coding and discriminative clustering simultaneously. We adopt graph regularized sparse codes as the feature to be learned, and design two clustering-oriented cost functions, by entropy-minimization and maximum-margin principles, respectively. The task-driven bi-level optimization mutually reinforces both sparse coding and clustering steps. Experiments on several benchmark datasets verify the remarkable performance gain as a result of the joint optimization.

We further show how to use regularized ℓ^1-graph for data clustering in this chapter. Complying to the manifold assumption, Rℓ^1-graph encourages the sparse representations of the data to vary smoothly along the geodesics of the intrinsic data submanifold using the graph Laplacian constructed by the sparse codes. Rℓ^1-graph achieves better performance than Laplacian regularized ℓ^1-graph where the graph Laplacian is constructed by Gaussian kernel. Experimental results on real datasets show the effectiveness of the algorithm.

As a generic graph, the ℓ^1-graph can be applied in many other tasks as well, *e.g.*, transfer learning and label propagation, which is open for future exploration.

In Chapter 7, we present a supervised hierarchical sparse coding model for image classification. The hierarchical model is constructed by max pooling over the sparse codes of local image descriptors within a spatial pyramid, and thus the feature is robust to local descriptor translations. The supervised training of the dictionary is done via back-projection where implicit differentiation is used to relate the sparse codes with the dictionary analytically. Experiments on various datasets demonstrate the promising power of the supervised model. We also see an in-depth analysis of the classification margin for SRC in this chapter. The decision boundary of SRC is a continuous piecewise quadratic hypersurface, and it can be approximated by its tangent plane in a local region to facilitate the margin estimation. A learning algorithm based on stochastic gradient descent is derived to maximize the margins of training samples, which generates compact dictionaries with substantially improved discriminative power observed on several datasets.

Future research on discriminative sparse coding could go in several ways. First, current stochastic optimization based on back-propagation is slow. Faster methods should be investigated. Second, it would also be of great interest to establish a strict relationship between the margin and generalization performance of sparse coding based classifier, so that a better knowledge can be gained about under what circumstances is such approach expected to perform best.

Chapter 8 closes the discussion on various applications with a semi-supervised hyperspectral image classification method, which is based on task-driven dictionary learning and spatial Laplacian regularization on the output of a logistic regression classifier. Both the dictionary for feature extraction and the associated classifier are jointly optimized, while both the spectral and spatial information are explored to improve the classification accuracy. Experimental results verify the superior performance of this method on three popular datasets, both quantitatively and qualitatively. A good and stable accuracy is attained in even quite ill-posed problem settings (high dimensional spaces with small number of labeled samples). The application of this algorithm to general image classification and segmentation would be worthy for future exploration.

Appendix A

Appendix

A.1 Joint SR

A.1.1 *Epitomic Matching Algorithm*

We assume an epitome $\mathbf{e}$ of size $M_e \times N_e$, for an input image of size $M \times N$, where $M_e < M$ and $N_e < N$. Similarly to GMMs, $\mathbf{e}$ contains three parameters [Jojic *et al.* (2003); Ni *et al.* (2009); Chu *et al.* (2010)]: μ, the Gaussian mean of size $M_e \times N_e$; ϕ, the Gaussian variance of size $M_e \times N_e$; and π, the mixture coefficients. Suppose Q densely sampled, overlapped patches from the input image, i.e. $\{\mathbf{Z}_k\}_{k=1}^Q$. Each $\mathbf{Z}_k$ contains pixels with image coordinates $\mathbf{S}_k$, and is associated with a hidden mapping $\mathcal{T}_k$ from $\mathbf{S}_k$ to the epitome coordinates. All the Q patches are generated independently from the epitome and the corresponding hidden mappings as below:

$$\prod_{k=1}^Q p(\{\mathbf{Z}_k\}_{k=1}^Q | \{\mathcal{T}_k\}_{k=1}^Q, \mathbf{e}) = \prod_{k=1}^Q p(\mathbf{Z}_k | \mathcal{T}_k, \mathbf{e}) \tag{A.1}$$

The probability $p(\mathbf{Z}_k | \mathcal{T}_k, \mathbf{e})$ in (A.1) is computed by the Gaussian distribution where the Gaussian component is specified by the hidden mapping $\mathcal{T}_k$. $\mathcal{T}_k$ behaves similar to the hidden variable in the traditional GMMs.

Figure A.1 illustrates the role that the hidden mapping plays in the epitome as well as the graphical model illustration for epitome. With all the above notations, our goal is to find the epitome $\mathbf{e}$ that maximizes the log likelihood function $\mathbf{e} = \arg\max_{\hat{\mathbf{e}}} \log p\left(\{\mathbf{Z}_k\}_{k=1}^Q | \hat{\mathbf{e}}\right)$, which can be solved by the Expectation-Maximization (EM) algorithm [Jojic *et al.* (2003); Yang *et al.* (2014a)].

The Expectation step in the EM algorithm which computes the posterior of all the hidden mappings accounts for the most time consuming part of

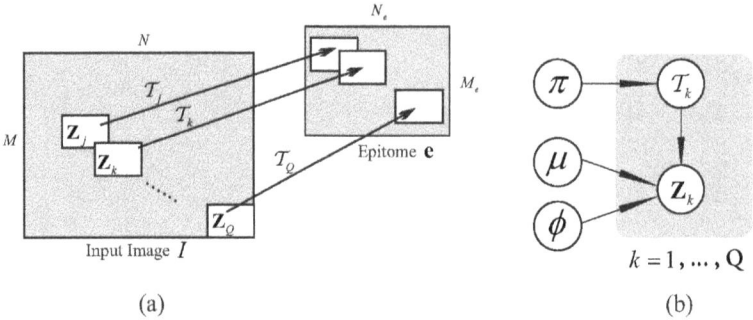

Fig. A.1 (a) The hidden mapping $\mathcal{T}_k$ maps the image patch $\mathbf{Z}_k$ to its corresponding patch of the same size in $\mathbf{e}$, and $\mathbf{Z}_k$ can be mapped to any possible epitome patch in accordance with $\mathcal{T}_k$. (b) The epitome graphical model.

the learning process. Since the posterior of the hidden mappings for all the patches are independent of each other, they can be computed in parallel. Therefore, the learning process can be significantly accelerated by parallel computing.

With the epitome $\mathbf{e}_{\mathbf{Y}'}$ learned from the smoothed input image $\mathbf{Y}'$, the location of the matching patch in the epitome $\mathbf{e}_{\mathbf{Y}'}$ for each patch $\mathbf{X}'^E_{ij}$ is specified by the most probable hidden mapping for $\mathbf{X}'^E_{ij}$:

$$\mathcal{T}^*_{ij} = \arg\max_{\mathcal{T}_{ij}} p\left(\mathcal{T}_{ij} | \mathbf{X}'^E_{ij}, \mathbf{e}\right) \qquad (A.2)$$

The top K patches in $\mathbf{Y}'$ with large posterior probabilities $p\left(\mathcal{T}^*_{ij} | \cdot, \mathbf{e}\right)$ are regarded as the candidate matches for the patch $\mathbf{X}'_{ij}$, and the match $\mathbf{Y}'_{mn}$ is the one in these K candidate patches which has minimum Sum of Squared Distance (SSD) to $\mathbf{X}'^E_{ij}$. Note that the indices of the K candidate patches in $\mathbf{Y}'$ for each epitome patch are pre-computed and stored when training the epitome $\mathbf{e}_{\mathbf{Y}'}$ from the smoothed input image $\mathbf{Y}'$, which makes epitomic matching efficient.

EPI significantly reduces the artifacts and produces more visually pleasing SR results by the dynamic weighting (3.25), compared to the local NN matching method [Freedman and Fattal (2011)].

A.1.2 *Subjective Evaluation Experiment*

The methods under comparison include BIC, CSC, LSE, IER, EPI, JSR. Ground truth HR images are also included when they are available as references. Each of the human subject participating in the evaluation is shown a set of HR image pairs obtained using two different methods for the same LR image. For each pair, the subject needs to decide which one is better than the other in terms of perceptual quality. The image pairs are drawn from all the competitive methods randomly, and the images winning the pairwise comparison will be compared again in the next round until the best one is selected.

We have a total of 101 participants giving 1,047 pairwise comparisons over 6 images with different scaling factors ("Kid"×4, "Chip"×4, "Statue"×4, "Leopard"×3, "Temple"×3 and "Train"×3). Not every participant completed all the comparisons but their partial responses are still useful. All the evaluation results can be summarized into a 7×7 winning matrix $\mathbf{W}$ for 7 methods (including ground truth), based on which we fit a Bradley-Terry [Bradley and Terry (1952)] model to estimate the subjective score for each method so that they can be ranked. In the Bradley-Terry model, the probability that an object X is favored over Y is assumed to be

$$p(X \succ Y) = \frac{e^{s_X}}{e^{s_X} + e^{s_Y}} = \frac{1}{1 + e^{s_Y - s_X}}, \tag{A.3}$$

where s_X and s_Y are the subjective scores for X and Y. The scores $\mathbf{s}$ for all the objects can be jointly estimated by maximizing the log likelihood of the pairwise comparison observations:

$$\max_{\mathbf{s}} \sum_{i,j} w_{ij} \log \left(\frac{1}{1 + e^{s_j - s_i}} \right), \tag{A.4}$$

where w_{ij} is the (i,j)-th element in the winning matrix $\mathbf{W}$, representing the number of times when method i is favored over method j. We use the Newton-Raphson method to solve Eq. (A.4) and set the score for ground truth method as 1 to avoid the scale issue.

A.2 Clustering

A.2.1 *Joint Clustering*

We recall the following lemma [A.2.1] in [Mairal *et al.* (2012)]:

Theorem A.2.1 (Regularity of the elastic net solution). *Consider the formulation in (6.15) (we may drop the last term to obtain the exact elastic net form, without affecting the differentiability conclusions). Let $\lambda_2 > 0$, and $\mathcal{X}$ is assumed to be compact. Then,*

- **a** *is uniformly Lipschitz on* $\mathcal{X} \times \mathcal{D}$
- *Let* $\mathbf{D} \in \mathcal{D}$, σ *be a positive scalar and* **s** *be a vector in* $\{-1, 0, 1\}^p$. *Define* $K_s(\mathbf{D}, \sigma)$ *as the set of vectors* **x** *satisfying for all* j *in* $\{1, ..., p\}$,

$$
\begin{aligned}
|\mathbf{d}_j^T(\mathbf{x} - \mathbf{Da}) - \lambda_2 \mathbf{a}[j]| \le \lambda_1 - \sigma \quad &if \quad \mathbf{s}[j] = 0 \\
\mathbf{s}[j]\mathbf{a}[j] \ge \sigma \quad &if \quad \mathbf{s}[j] \ne 0
\end{aligned} \tag{A.5}
$$

Then there exists $\kappa > 0$ *independent of* $\mathbf{s}, \mathbf{D}$ *and* σ *so that for all* $\mathbf{x} \in K_s(\mathbf{D}, \sigma)$, *the function* **a** *is twice continuously differentiable on* $B_{\kappa\sigma}(\mathbf{x}) \times B_{\kappa\sigma}(\mathbf{D})$, *where* $B_{\kappa\sigma}(\mathbf{x})$ *and* $B_{\kappa\sigma}(\mathbf{D})$ *denote the open balls of radius* $\kappa\sigma$ *respectively centered on* **x** *and* **D**.

A.2.2 *Proof of Proposition 6.1*

The optimization problem in the preliminary form is:

$$
\min_{\alpha, \mathbf{W}} \sum_{i=1}^{n} \|\mathbf{x}_i - \mathbf{X}\alpha^i\|_2^2 + \lambda \|\alpha^i\|_1 + \gamma \mathrm{Tr}(\alpha \mathbf{L_W} \alpha^T) \tag{A.6}
$$

$$
s.t. \ \mathbf{W} = (\mathbf{A} \circ |\alpha| + \mathbf{A}^T \circ |\alpha^T|)/2 \quad \alpha \in S
$$

where $S := \{\alpha \in \mathbb{R}^{n \times n} | \alpha_{ii} = 0, 1 \le i \le n\}$, $\lambda > 0$ is the weight controlling the sparsity of the coefficients, and $\gamma > 0$ is the weight of the regularization term.

We reformulate (A.6) into the following optimization problem with simplified equality constraint:

$$
\min_{\alpha, \mathbf{W}} \sum_{i=1}^{n} \|\mathbf{x}_i - \mathbf{X}\alpha^i\|_2^2 + \lambda \|\alpha^i\|_1 + \mathrm{Tr}(\alpha \mathbf{L}_{\mathbf{A} \circ |\mathbf{W}|} \alpha^T) \tag{A.7}
$$

$$
s.t. \ \mathbf{W} = \alpha \quad \alpha \in S
$$

Proposition 6.1 establishes the equivalence between the problem (A.7) and problem (A.6): the solution α^* to the problem (A.7) is also the solution to the problem (A.6), and vice versa.

Proof. When $\mathbf{W} = \alpha$,

$$
\mathrm{Tr}(\alpha \mathbf{L}_{\mathbf{A} \circ |\mathbf{W}|} \alpha^T) = \frac{1}{2} \sum_{i=1}^{n} \sum_{j=1}^{n} \mathbf{A}_{ij} |\mathbf{W}_{ij}| \|\alpha^i - \alpha^j\|_2^2
$$

$$
= \frac{1}{4} \sum_{i,j=1}^{n} \mathbf{A}_{ij} |\alpha_{ij}| \|\alpha^i - \alpha^j\|_2^2 + \frac{1}{4} \sum_{i,j=1}^{n} \mathbf{A}_{ji} |\alpha_{ji}| \|\alpha^j - \alpha^i\|_2^2
$$

$$
= \frac{1}{2} \sum_{i,j=1}^{n} \frac{\mathbf{A}_{ij} |\alpha_{ij}| + \mathbf{A}_{ji} |\alpha_{ji}|}{2} \|\alpha^i - \alpha^j\|_2^2
$$

Therefore, the objective function of problem (A.7) equals to that of problem (A.6) with their $\mathbf{W}$ determined by the corresponding equality constraints, so these two optimization problems are equivalent to each other. $\qquad\square$

A.2.3 *Solving* (6.43) *with ADMM*

$$\min_{\alpha^i \in \mathbb{R}^n} F(\alpha^i) = \frac{1}{2}\alpha^{iT}\mathbf{P}_i\alpha^i + \mathbf{b}_i^T\alpha^i + \lambda\|\alpha^i\|_1 \qquad (A.8)$$
$$s.t.\ \alpha_{ii} = 0$$

To solve (A.8) by ADMM, (A.8) is rewritten as below by introducing an auxiliary variable $\mathbf{z}$

$$\min_{\alpha^i \in \mathbb{R}^n} F(\alpha^i) = \frac{1}{2}\alpha^{iT}\mathbf{P}_i\alpha^i + \mathbf{b}_i^T\alpha^i + \lambda\|\mathbf{z}\|_1 \qquad (A.9)$$
$$s.t.\ \alpha_i = \mathbf{z}, \mathbf{z}_i = 0$$

Note that α^i is now not involved in the ℓ^1-norm. The advantage of ADMM for the lasso problem is that it transforms the original problem into a sequence of subproblems where closed-form solutions exist, and the lasso problem can be solved efficiently in an iterative manner.

The augmented Lagrangian for the constrained convex optimization problem (A.9) is

$$\mathcal{L}^i(\alpha^i, \mathbf{z}, \mathbf{y}) = \frac{1}{2}\alpha^{iT}\mathbf{P}_i\alpha^i + \mathbf{b}_i^T\alpha^i + \lambda\|\mathbf{z}\|_1 + \mathbf{y}^T(\alpha^i - \mathbf{z}) + \frac{\mu}{2}\|\alpha^i - \mathbf{z}\|_2^2 \qquad (A.10)$$

where $\mathbf{y}$ is the Lagrangian multiplier, μ is the penalty parameter which is a pre-set positive constant. The ADMM iterations for the optimization of (A.9) are listed below, with k being the iteration index:

- Update α^i with fixed $\mathbf{z}$ and $\mathbf{y}$:

$$(\alpha^i)^{(k)} = \min_{\alpha^i} \mathcal{L}^i(\alpha^i, \mathbf{z}^{(k-1)}, \mathbf{y}^{(k-1)}) \qquad (A.11)$$

and (A.11) has closed-form solution

$$(\alpha^i)^{(k)} = (\mathbf{P}_i + \mu\mathbf{I}_n)^{-1}(\mu\mathbf{z}^{(k-1)} - \mathbf{y}^{(k-1)} - \mathbf{b}_i) \qquad (A.12)$$

- Update $\mathbf{z}$ with fixed α^i and $\mathbf{y}$:

$$\mathbf{z}^{(k)} = \min_{\mathbf{z}} \mathcal{L}^i((\alpha^i)^{(k)}, \mathbf{z}, \mathbf{y}^{(k-1)}) \qquad (A.13)$$

By soft thresholding,

$$\mathbf{z}_t^{(k)} = \begin{cases} \max\{0, |\mu(\alpha_t^i)^{(k)} + \mathbf{y}_t^{(k-1)}| - \lambda\} \cdot \frac{\text{sign}(\mu(\alpha_t^i)^{(k)} + \mathbf{y}_t^{k-1})}{\mu} & t \neq i \\ 0 & t = i \end{cases}$$

(A.14)

where the subscript t indicates the t-th element of the vector.

- Update **y**:

$$\mathbf{y}^{(k)} = \mathbf{y}^{(k-1)} + \mu((\alpha^i)^{(k)} - \mathbf{z}^{(k)})$$

(A.15)

The ADMM iterates (A.12), (A.14) and (A.15) until both the primal residual $\|(\alpha^i)^{(k)} - \mathbf{z}^{(k)}\|_2$ and the dual residual $\mu\|\mathbf{z}^{(k+1)} - \mathbf{z}^{(k)}\|_2$ are smaller than a threshold or the iteration number k achieves the pre-set maximum number. It has been proved that ADMM iterations converge to the optimal solution to the convex optimization problem (A.9) [Boyd *et al.* (2011)].

A.2.4 *Time Complexity of ADMM*

Based on the algorithm description in Section 6.3.2.3, the subproblem (6.42) accounts for the most of the time complexity. Suppose the maximum iteration number of ADMM is N_1, and the maximum iteration number of the coordinate descent for solving subproblem (6.42) is N_2. In our implementation, we store the matrix inversion result in equation (A.12), and the time complexity for computing the inversion of a $n \times n$ matrix is $n^{2.376}$ by the Coppersmith-Winograd algorithm, the overall time complexity for solving the optimization Problem (6.37) by ADMM is $\mathcal{O}(N_1 n^{2.376} + N_1 N_2 n^2)$.

A.2.5 *Supplementary Clustering Results*

Figure A.2 shows several examples from the ORL face database.

Fig. A.2   Example images of the ORL face database.

We also examine the changes of the clustering performance on Yale face database with respect to γ and K, and illustrate the result in Figure A.3 and Figure A.4 respectively.

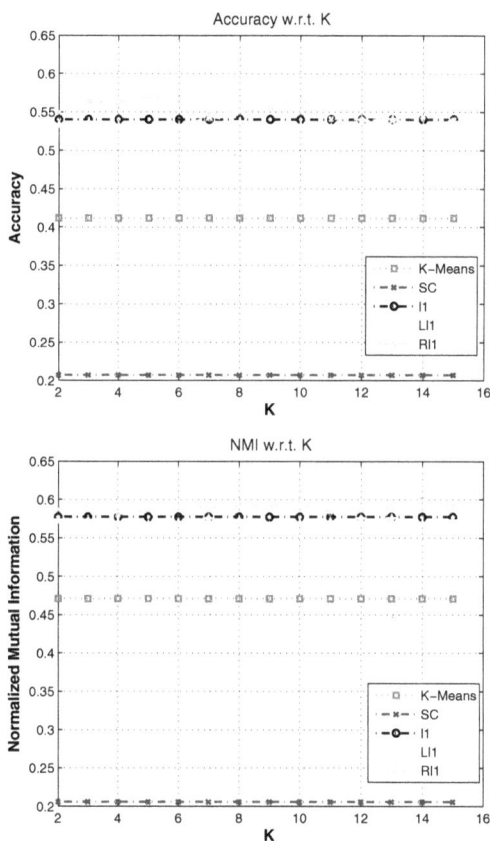

Fig. A.3   Clustering performance with different values of K, i.e. the number of nearest neighbors, on Yale face database when $\gamma = 0.5$. Left: Accuracy; Right: NMI.

The convergence curves of ADMM for ORL face database and Yale face database are shown in Figure A.5.

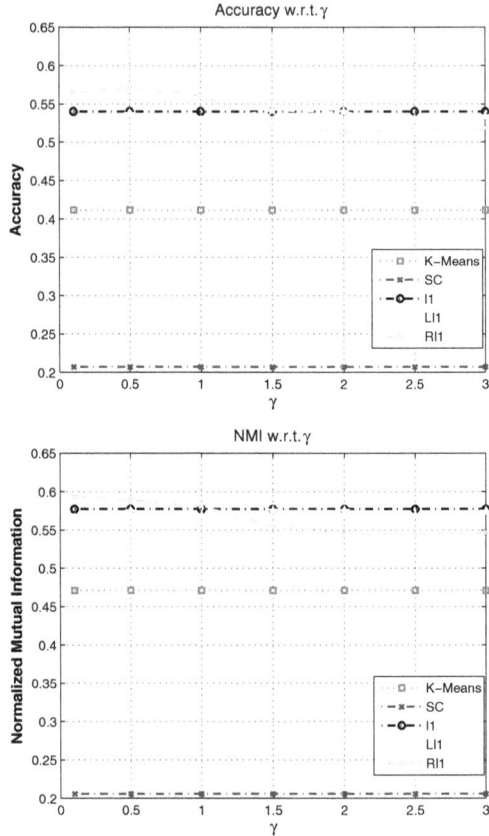

Fig. A.4   Clustering performance with different values of γ, i.e. the weight of the regularization term, on Yale face database when $K = 5$. Left: Accuracy; Right: NMI.

A.3   Derivation of SGD Algorithm (8.10)

Denote $\mathbf{X} \in \mathcal{X}$, $\mathbf{y} \in \mathcal{Y}$ and $\mathbf{D} \in \mathcal{D}$. Let the objective function $B(\mathbf{A}, \mathbf{w})$ in (8.9) denoted as B for short. The differentiability of B with respect to $\mathbf{w}$ is easy to show, using only the compactness of $\mathcal{X}$ and $\mathcal{Y}$, as well as the fact that B is twice differentiable.

We will therefore focus on showing that B is differentiable with respect to $\mathbf{D}$, which is more difficult since $\mathbf{A}$, and thus $\mathbf{a}_i$, is not differentiable everywhere. Without loss of geniality, we use a vector $\mathbf{a}$ instead of $\mathbf{A}$ for simplifying the derivations hereinafter. In some cases, we may equivalently

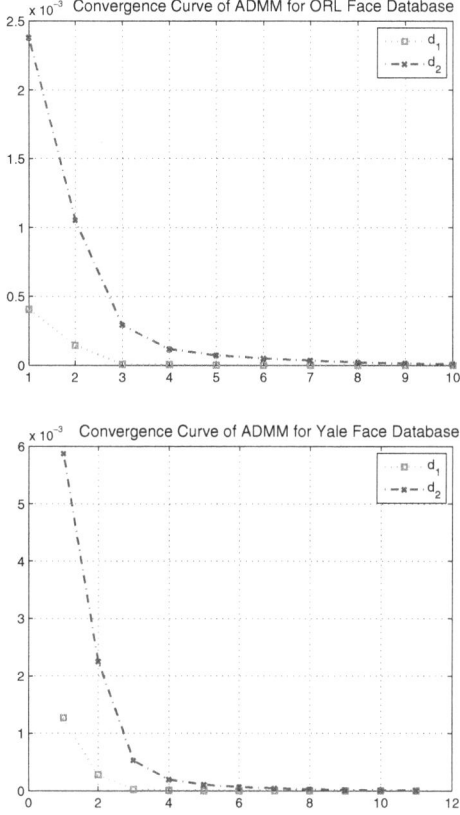

Fig. A.5 Convergence curves of ADMM for ORL (Left) and Yale (Right) face database, $d_1 = \|\mathbf{W} - \alpha\|_F$, $d_2 = \|\alpha^{(k)} - \alpha^{(k-1)}\|_F$.

express $\mathbf{a}$ as $\mathbf{a}(\mathbf{D}, \mathbf{w})$ in order to emphasize the functional dependence.

We recall the lemma [A.2.1] that is proved in [Mairal *et al.* (2009a)] and shown in A.2.1. Built on [A.2.1] and given a small perturbation $\mathbf{E} \in R^{m \times p}$, it follows that

$$
\begin{aligned}
B(\mathbf{a}(\mathbf{D} + \mathbf{E}), \mathbf{w}) - B(\mathbf{a}(\mathbf{D}), \mathbf{w}) = \\
\nabla_{\mathbf{z}} B_{\mathbf{w}}^T(\mathbf{a}(\mathbf{D} + \mathbf{E}) - \mathbf{a}(\mathbf{D})) + O(\|\mathbf{E}\|_F^2)
\end{aligned}
\tag{A.16}
$$

where the term $O(\|\mathbf{E}\|_F^2)$ is based on the fact that $\mathbf{a}(\mathbf{D}, \mathbf{x})$ is uniformly Lipschitz and $\mathcal{X} \times \mathcal{D}$ is compact. It is then possible to show that

$$
\begin{aligned}
B(\mathbf{a}(\mathbf{D} + \mathbf{E}), \mathbf{w}) - B(\mathbf{a}(\mathbf{D}), \mathbf{w}) = \\
Tr(\mathbf{E}^T g(\mathbf{a}(\mathbf{D} + \mathbf{E}), \mathbf{w})) + O(\|\mathbf{E}\|_F^2)
\end{aligned}
\tag{A.17}
$$

where g has the form given in (8.10). This shows that f is differentiable on $\mathcal{D}$, and its gradient with respect to $\mathbf{D}$ is g.

Bibliography

A. Asuncion, D. N. (2007). UCI machine learning repository.

Adler, A., Hel-Or, Y., and Elad, M. (2010). A shrinkage learning approach for single image super-resolution with overcomplete representations, in *The 11th European Conference on Computer Vision*.

Aharon, M., Elad, M., and Bruckstein, A. (2006). K-SVD: An algorithm for designing overcomplete dictionaries for sparse representation, *IEEE Trans. Sig. Proc.* **54**, 11, pp. 4311–4322.

Bach, F. R. (2009). Exploring large feature spaces with hierarchical multiple kernel learning, in *Advances in neural information processing systems*, pp. 105–112.

Baraniuk, R. G., Cevher, V., Duarte, M. F., and Hegde, C. (2010). Model-based compressive sensing, *IEEE Trans. on Information Theory* **56**, 4, pp. 1982–2001.

Barber, D. and Agakov, F. V. (2005). Kernelized infomax clustering, in *Advances in Neural Information Processing Systems*, pp. 17–24.

Belhumeur, P., Hespanda, J., and Kriegman, D. (1997). Eigenfaces vs. fisherfaces: recognition using class specific linear projectoin. *IEEE Transactions on Pattern Analysis and Machine Intelligence (PAMI)*.

Belkin, M., Matveeva, I., and Niyogi, P. (2004). Regularization and semi-supervised learning on large graphs, in *International Conference on Learning Theory*, Vol. 3120, pp. 624–638.

Belkin, M. and Niyogi, P. (2002). Laplacian eigenmaps for dimensionality reduction and data representation, *Neural Computation* **15**, 6, pp. 1373–1396.

Belkin, M., Niyogi, P., and Sindhwani, V. (2006). Manifold regularization: A geometric framework for learning from labeled and unlabeled examples, *The Journal of Machine Learning Research* **7**, pp. 2399–2434.

Bengio, Y., Courville, A., and Vincent, P. (2013). Representation learning: A review and new perspectives, *IEEE Transactions on Pattern Analysis and Machine Intelligence,* **35**, 8, pp. 1798–1828.

Berg, E. V. D. and Friedlander, M. P. (2010). Theoretical and empirical results for recovery from multiple measurements, *IEEE Trans. on Information Theory* **56**, 5, pp. 2516 – 2527.

Bertsekas, D. P. (1999). *Nonlinear Programming*, 2nd edn. (Athena Scientific).

Bevilacqua, M., Roumy, A., Guillemot, C., and Morel, M.-L. A. (2012). Low-complexity single-image super-resolution based on nonnegative neighbor embedding, in *BMVC*.

Bidhendi, S. K., Shirazi, A. S., Fotoohi, N., and Ebadzadeh, M. M. (2007). Material classification of hyperspectral images using unsupervised fuzzy clustering methods, in *Signal-Image Technologies and Internet-Based System, 2007. SITIS'07. Third International IEEE Conference on* (IEEE), pp. 619–623.

Biernacki, C., Celeux, G., and Govaert, G. (2000). Assessing a mixture model for clustering with the integrated completed likelihood, *IEEE Transactions on Pattern Analysis and Machine Intelligence*, **22**, 7, pp. 719–725.

Bischof, H. and Leonardis, A. (1998). Finding optimal neural networks for land use classification, *IEEE transactions on Geoscience and Remote Sensing* **36**, 1, pp. 337–341.

Bishop, C. M. *et al.* (2006). *Pattern recognition and machine learning*, Vol. 1 (springer New York).

Blackard, J. A. and Dean, D. J. (1999). Comparative accuracies of artificial neural networks and discriminant analysis in predicting forest cover types from cartographic variables, *Computers and electronics in agriculture* **24**, 3, pp. 131–151, https://kdd.ics.uci.edu/databases/covertype/covertype.html.

Bottou, L. (1998). Online algorithms and stochastic approximations, in D. Saad (ed.), *Online Learning and Neural Networks* (Cambridge University Press, Cambridge, UK), revised, oct 2012.

Bottou, L. (2004). Stochastic learning, in O. Bousquet and U. von Luxburg (eds.), *Advanced Lectures on Machine Learning*, Lecture Notes in Artificial Intelligence, LNAI 3176 (Springer Verlag), pp. 146–168.

Boyd, S., Parikh, N., Chu, E., Peleato, B., and Eckstein, J. (2011). Distributed optimization and statistical learning via the alternating direction method of multipliers, *Found. Trends Mach. Learn.* **3**, 1, pp. 1–122.

Bradley, D. M. and Bagnell, J. A. (2008). Differential sparse coding, in *Adv. NIPS*, pp. 113–120.

Bradley, R. A. and Terry, M. E. (1952). Rank analysis of incomplete block designs: I. the method of paired comparisons, *Biometrika*, pp. 324–345.

Bruckstein, A. M., Donoho, D. L., and Elad, M. (2009). From sparse solutions of systems of equations to sparse modeling of signals and images.

Bruzzone, L., Chi, M., and Marconcini, M. (2006). A novel transductive svm for semisupervised classification of remote-sensing images, *IEEE Transactions on Geoscience and Remote Sensing*, **44**, 11, pp. 3363–3373.

Buades, A., Coll, B., and Morel, J.-M. (2005). A non-local algorithm for image denoising, in *Computer Vision and Pattern Recognition, 2005. CVPR 2005. IEEE Computer Society Conference on*, Vol. 2 (IEEE), pp. 60–65.

Burger, H. C., Schuler, C., and Harmeling, S. (2013). Learning how to combine internal and external denoising methods, in *Pattern Recognition* (Springer), pp. 121–130.

Cai, D., He, X., and Han, J. (2008). Semi-supervised discriminant analysis, in *IEEE International Conference on Computer Vison (ICCV), 2007*.

Cai, D., He, X., Hu, Y., Han, J., and Huang., T. (2007). Learning a spatially smooth subspace for face recognition, in *CVPR*.

Cai, J.-F., Ji, H., Liu, C., and Shen, Z. (2009). Blind motion deblurring from a single image using sparse approximation, in *CVPR*.

Camps-Valls, G. and Bruzzone, L. (2005). Kernel-based methods for hyperspectral image classification, *Geoscience and Remote Sensing, IEEE Transactions on* **43**, 6, pp. 1351–1362.

Camps-Valls, G., Gómez-Chova, L., Calpe-Maravilla, J., Martin-Guerrero, J. D., Soria-Olivas, E., Alonso-Chordá, L., and Moreno, J. (2004). Robust support vector method for hyperspectral data classification and knowledge discovery, *IEEE Transactions on Geoscience and Remote Sensing*, **42**, 7, pp. 1530–1542.

Camps-Valls, G., Gomez-Chova, L., Muñoz-Mari, J., Vila-Francés, J., and Calpe-Maravilla, J. (2006). Composite kernels for hyperspectral image classification, *Geoscience and Remote Sensing Letters, IEEE* **3**, 1, pp. 93–97.

Candès, E. J. (2006). Compressive sampling, in *Proceedings of the International Congress of Mathematicians*.

Candes, E. J., Romberg, J., and Tao, T. (2006). Robust uncertainty principles: Exact signal reconstruction from highly incomplete frequency information, *IEEE Trans. on Information Theory* **52**, 2, pp. 489–509.

Chatterjee, P. and Milanfar, P. (2010). Is denoising dead? *IEEE Transactions on Image Processing*, **19**, 4, pp. 895–911.

Chen, S., D.Donoho, and Saunders, M. (2001). Atomic decomposition by basis pursuit, *Society for Industrial and Applied Mathematics Review* **43**, 1, pp. 129–159.

Chen, Y., Nasrabadi, N. M., and Tran, T. D. (2010). Sparse subspace target detection for hyperspectral imagery, in *Proc. SPIE, Algorithms and Technologies for Multispectral, Hyperspectral and Ultraspectral Imagery*, Vol. 7695, pp. 769503–769503–8.

Chen, Y., Nasrabadi, N. M., and Tran, T. D. (2011). Hyperspectral image classification using dictionary-based sparse representation, *IEEE Transactions on Geoscience and Remote Sensing*, **49**, 10, pp. 3973–3985.

Chen, Y.-C., Sastry, C. S., Patel, V. M., Phillips, J., and Chellappa, R. (2013). In-plane rotation and scale invariant clustering using dictionaries, *IEEE Transactions on Image Processing*, **22**, 6, pp. 2166–2180.

Cheng, B., Yang, J., Yan, S., Fu, Y., and Huang, T. S. (2010). Learning with l1-graph for image analysis, *IEEE Transactions on Image Processing*, **19**, 4, pp. 858–866.

Childers, D. G., Skinner, D. P., and Kemerait, R. C. (1977). The Cepstrum: A guide to processing, *Proceedings of the IEEE* **65**, pp. 1428–1443.

Cho, S. and Lee, S. (2009). Fast motion deblurring, in *SIGGRAPH ASIA*.

Cho, T. S., Joshi, N., Zitnick, C. L., Kang, S. B., Szeliski, R., and Freeman, W. T. (2010). A content-aware image prior, in *CVPR*.

Chu, X., Yan, S., Li, L., Chan, K. L., and Huang, T. S. (2010). Spatialized epitome and its applications, in *Computer Vision and Pattern Recognition (CVPR), 2010 IEEE Conference on* (IEEE), pp. 311–318.

216   *Sparse Coding and Its Applications in Computer Vision*

Chung, F. R. K. (1997). *Spectral Graph Theory* (American Mathematical Society).
Cohen, A., Daubechies, I., and Feauveau, J.-C. (1992). Biorthogonal bases of compactly supported wavelets, *Communications on pure and applied mathematics* **45**, 5, pp. 485–560.
Colson, B., Marcotte, P., and Savard, G. (2007). An overview of bilevel optimization, *Annals of operations research* **153**, 1, pp. 235–256.
Combettes, P. L. and Pesquet, J.-C. (2011). Proximal splitting methods in signal processing, in *Fixed-point algorithms for inverse problems in science and engineering* (Springer), pp. 185–212.
Cotter, S. F., Rao, B., Engan, K., and Kreutz-Delgado, K. (2005). Sparse solutions to linear inverse problems with multiple measurement vectors, *IEEE Trans. on Signal Processing* **53**, 7, pp. 2477–2488.
Crammer, K. and Singer, Y. (2002). On the algorithmic implementation of multiclass kernel-based vector machines, *The Journal of Machine Learning Research* **2**, pp. 265–292.
Cristianini, N. and Shawe-Taylor, J. (2004). *Kernel Methods for Pattern Analysis* (Cambridge University Press).
Cui, Z., Chang, H., Shan, S., Zhong, B., and Chen, X. (2014). Deep network cascade for image super-resolution, in *ECCV*, pp. 49–64.
Dai, B. and Hu, B. (2010). Minimum conditional entropy clustering: A discriminative framework for clustering. in *ACML*, pp. 47–62.
Das Gupta, M., Rajaram, S., Petrovic, N., and Huang, T. S. (2005). Restoration and recognition in a loop, in *CVPR*.
Daubechies, I., Defrise, M., and De Mol, C. (2003). An iterative thresholding algorithm for linear inverse problems with a sparsity constraint, *arXiv preprint math/0307152*.
Daubechies, I., Defrise, M., and De Mol, C. (2004). An iterative thresholding algorithm for linear inverse problems with a sparsity constraint, *Communications on Pure and Applied Mathematics* **57**, 11, pp. 1413–1457.
Daubechies, I., DeVore, R., Fornasier, M., and Güntürk, C. S. (2010). Iteratively reweighted least squares minimization for sparse recovery, *Communications on Pure and Applied Mathematics* **63**, 1, pp. 1–38.
Domeniconi, C., Peng, J., and Gunopulos, D. (2002). Locally adaptive metric nearest-neighbor classification, *IEEE Trans. PAMI* **24**, 9, pp. 1281–1285.
Dong, C., Loy, C. C., He, K., and Tang, X. (2014). Learning a deep convolutional network for image super-resolution, in *ECCV*, pp. 184–199.
Dong, W., Zhang, L., Shi, G., and Li, X. (2013). Nonlocally centralized sparse representation for image restoration, *IEEE Transactions on Image Processing,* **22**, 4, pp. 1620–1630.
Dong, W., Zhang, L., Shi, G., and Wu, X. (2011). Image deblurring and super-resolution by adaptive sparse domain selection and adaptive regularization, *IEEE Transactions on Image Processing,* **20**, 7, pp. 1838–1857.
Donoho, D. L. (2006a). Compressed sensing, *IEEE Trans. on Information Theory* **52**, 4, pp. 1289–1306.
Donoho, D. L. (2006b). For most large underdetermined systems of linear equations, the minimal ℓ^1-nomr solution is also the sparest solution, *Comm. on*

Pure and Applied Math.

Donoho, D. L., Stodden, V. C., and Tsaig, Y. (2007). *About sparselab*, http:// sparselab.stanford.edu.

Duan, K., Keerthi, S. S., Chu, W., Shevade, S. K., and Poo, A. N. (2003). Multi-category classification by soft-max combination of binary classifiers, in *Multiple Classifier Systems* (Springer), pp. 125–134.

Duarte, M. F., Cevher, V., and Baraniuk, R. G. (2009). Model-based compressive sensing for signal ensembles, in *Proc. of Allerton Conference on Communication, Control, and Computing*, pp. 244–250.

Duarte, M. F., Sarvotham, S., Wakin, M. B., Baron, D., and Baraniuk, R. G. (2005). Joint sparsity models for distributed compressed sensing, in *Workshop on Signal Processing with Adaptative Sparse Structured Representations*.

Duda, R. O., Hart, P. E., and Stork, D. G. (2000). *Pattern Classification (2nd Edition)* (Wiley-Interscience).

Efron, B., Hastie, T., Johnstone, I., Tibshirani, R., *et al.* (2004). Least angle regression, *The Annals of statistics* **32**, 2, pp. 407–499.

Elad, M. and Aharon, M. (2006). Image denoising via sparse and redundant representations over learned dictionaries, *IEEE Transactions on Image Processing*, **15**, 12, pp. 3736–3745.

Elad, M., Figueiredo, M. A. T., and Ma, Y. (2010). On the role of sparse and redundant representations in image processing, *Proc. of IEEE* **98**, 6, pp. 972–982.

Eldar, Y. C. and Mishali, M. (2009). Block sparsity and sampling over a union of subspaces, in *Proc. 16th Int. Conf. on Digital Signal Processing*, pp. 1–8.

Elhamifar, E. and Vidal, R. (2009). Sparse subspace clustering, in *IEEE Conference on Computer Vision and Pattern Recognition* (IEEE), pp. 2790–2797.

Elhamifar, E. and Vidal, R. (2011). Sparse manifold clustering and embedding, in *NIPS*, pp. 55–63.

Engan, K., Aase, S. O., and Hakon Husoy, J. (1999). Method of optimal directions for frame design, in *Proc. ICASSP*, pp. 2443–2446.

Engelberg, S. and Tadmor, E. (2008). Recovery of edges from spectral data with noise-a new perspective, *SIAM Journal on Numerical Analysis* **46**, 5, pp. 2620–2635.

Faktor, T., Eldar, Y. C., and Elad, M. (2012). Exploiting statistical dependencies in sparse representations for signal recovery, *IEEE Trans. on Signal Processing* **60**, 5, pp. 2286–2303.

Fergus, R., Singh, B., Hertzmann, A., Roweis, S. T., and Freeman, W. T. (2006). Removing camera shake from a single photograph, in *SIGGRAPH*.

Fornasier, M. and Rauhut, H. (2011). Compressive sensing, in *Handbook of mathematical methods in imaging* (Springer), pp. 187–228.

Fraley, C. and Raftery, A. E. (2002). Model-Based Clustering, Discriminant Analysis, and Density Estimation, *Journal of the American Statistical Association* **97**, 458, pp. 611–631.

Freedman, G. and Fattal, R. (2011). Image and video upscaling from local self-examples, *ACM Transactions on Graphics (TOG)* **30**, 2, p. 12.

Freeman, W. T., Jones, T. R., and Pasztor, E. C. (2002). Example-based super-resolution, *Computer Graphics and Applications, IEEE* **22**, 2, pp. 56–65.

Friedman, J., Hastie, T., Höfling, H., Tibshirani, R., *et al.* (2007). Pathwise coordinate optimization, *The Annals of Applied Statistics* **1**, 2, pp. 302–332.

Friedman, J., Hastie, T., and Tibshirani, R. (2008). Regularized paths for generalized linear models via coordinate descent.

Fu, W. J. (1998). Penalized regressions: the bridge versus the lasso, *Journal of computational and graphical statistics* **7**, 3, pp. 397–416.

Fukui, K. and Yamaguchi, O. (2005). Face recognition using multi-viewpoint patterns for robot vision, *Springer Tracts in Advanced Robotics* **15**, pp. 192–201.

Gao, S., Tsang, I. W.-H., and Chia, L.-T. (2013). Laplacian sparse coding, hypergraph laplacian sparse coding, and applications, *IEEE Trans. Pattern Anal. Mach. Intell.* **35**, 1, pp. 92–104.

Gemmeke, J. and Cranen, B. (2008). Using sparse representations for missing data imputation in noise robust speech recognition, in *Proc. EUSIPCO*.

Georghiades, A., Belhumeur, P., and Kriegman, D. (2001). From few to many: illumination cone models for face recognition under variable lighting and pose, *IEEE Trans. PAMI* **23**, 6, pp. 643–660.

Glasner, D., Bagon, S., and Irani, M. (2009). Super-resolution from a single image, in *Computer Vision, 2009 IEEE 12th International Conference on* (IEEE), pp. 349–356.

Gómez-Chova, L., Camps-Valls, G., Munoz-Mari, J., and Calpe, J. (2008). Semisupervised image classification with laplacian support vector machines, *Geoscience and Remote Sensing Letters, IEEE* **5**, 3, pp. 336–340.

Gregor, K. and LeCun, Y. (2010). Learning fast approximations of sparse coding, in *ICML*.

Gross, R., Matthews, I., Cohn, J., Kanade, T., and Baker, S. (2008). Multi-PIE, in *IEEE Intl. Conf. Automatic Face and Gesture Recog.*

Grosse, R., Raina, R., Kwong, H., and Ng, A. Y. (2007). Shift-invariant sparse coding for audio classification, in *Twenty-third Conference on Uncertainty in Artificial Intelligence*.

Gu, Y. and Feng, K. (2012). L1-graph semisupervised learning for hyperspectral image classification, in *Geoscience and Remote Sensing Symposium (IGARSS), 2012 IEEE International* (IEEE), pp. 1401–1404.

Harmeling, S., Hirsch, M., and Schölkopf, B. (2010). Space-variant single-image blind deconvolution for removing camera shake, in *NIPS*.

Hastie, T., Tibshirani, R., and Friedman, J. (2008). *The elements of statistical learning*, 2nd edn., Statistics (Springer), ISBN 978-0-387-84857-0.

He, L., Chen, H., and Carin, L. (2010). Tree-structured compressive sensing with variational bayesian analysis, *Signal Processing Letters, IEEE* **17**, 3, pp. 233–236.

He, X., Cai, D., Shao, Y., Bao, H., and Han, J. (2011). Laplacian regularized gaussian mixture model for data clustering, *IEEE Transactions on Knowledge and Data Engineering*, **23**, 9, pp. 1406–1418.

He, X., Cai, D., Yan, S., and Zhang, H. (2005). Neighborhood preserving embedding, in *IEEE International Conference on Computer Vision*, Vol. 2, pp. 1208–1213.

He, X. and Niyogi, P. (2003). Locality preserving projections, in *Advances in Neural Information Processing Systems*, Vol. 16, pp. 585–591.

Hennings-Yeomans, P. H., Baker, S., and Kumar, B. V. (2008). Simultaneous super-resolution and feature extraction for recognition of low-resolution faces, in *CVPR*.

Hu, Z., Huang, J.-B., and Yang, M.-H. (2010). Single image deblurring with adaptive dictionary learning, in *ICIP*.

Huang, J., Zhang, T., and Metaxas, D. (2009). Learning with structured sparsity, in *Proc. Int. Conf. on Machine Learning*.

Huang, K. and Aviyente, S. (2006). Sparse representation for signal classification, in *Advances in Neural Information Processing Systems*, pp. 609–616.

Hull, J. (1994). A database for handwritten text recognition research, *IEEE Transactions on Pattern Analysis and Machine Intelligence* **16**, 5, pp. 550–554.

Jarrett, K., Kavukcuoglu, K., Ranzato, M. A., and LeCun, Y. (2009). What is the best multi-stage architecture for object recognition? in *IEEE International Conference on Computer Vision*.

Ji, S., Xue, Y., and Carin, L. (2008). Bayesian compressive sensing, *IEEE Transactions on Signal Processing*, **56**, 6, pp. 2346–2356.

Jiang, Z., Lin, Z., and Davis, L. S. (2011). Learning a discriminative dictionary for sparse coding via label consistent K-SVD, in *Computer Vision and Pattern Recognition (CVPR), 2011 IEEE Conference on* (IEEE), pp. 1697–1704.

Jojic, N., Frey, B. J., and Kannan, A. (2003). Epitomic analysis of appearance and shape, in *Computer Vision, 2003. Proceedings. Ninth IEEE International Conference on* (IEEE), pp. 34–41.

Joliffe, I. (1986). Principal component analysis, *Springer-Verlag*, pp. 1580–1584.

Kavukcuoglu, K., Ranzato, M. A., Fergus, R., and LeCun, Y. (2009). Learning invariant features through topographic filter maps, in *IEEE Conference on Computer Vision and Pattern Recognition*.

Kim, K. I. and Kwon, Y. (2010). Single-image super-resolution using sparse regression and natural image prior, *IEEE Transactions on Pattern Analysis and Machine Intelligence*, **32**, 6, pp. 1127–1133.

Kokiopoulou, E. and Frossard, P. (2010). Graph-based classification of multiple observation sets, *Pattern Recognition* **43**, 12, pp. 3988–3997.

K.Pillai, J., Patel, V. M., and Chellappa, R. (2009). Sparsity inspired selection and recognition of IRIS images, in *Proc. 3rd IEEE Int. Conf. on Biometrics, Technology And Systems*, pp. 1–6.

Krishnan, D. and Fergus, R. (2009). Fast image deconvolution using hyperlaplacian priors, in *NIPS*.

Krizhevsky, A., Sutskever, I., and Hinton, G. E. (2012). ImageNet classification with deep convolutional neural networks, in *NIPS*, pp. 1097–1105.

Kushner, H. J. and Yin, G. (2003). *Stochastic approximation and recursive algorithms and applications*, Vol. 35 (Springer Science & Business Media).

LeCun, Y., Bottou, L., Bengio, Y., and Haffner, P. (1998). Gradient-based learning applied to document recognition, in *Proceedings of IEEE, vol.86, no.11, pp.2278-2324.*

Lee, C.-P. and Lin, C.-J. (2013). A study on l2-loss (squared hinge-loss) multiclass svm, *Neural computation* **25**, 5, pp. 1302–1323.

Lee, C.-Y., Xie, S., Gallagher, P., Zhang, Z., and Tu, Z. (2014). Deeply-supervised nets, *arXiv preprint arXiv:1409.5185.*

Lee, H., Battle, A., Raina, R., and Ng, A. Y. (2006). Efficient sparse coding algorithms, in *Advances in neural information processing systems*, pp. 801–808.

Lee, H., Grosse, R., Ranganath, R., and Ng, A. Y. (2009). Convolutional deep belief networks for scalable unsupervised learning of hierarchical representations, in *International Conference on Machine Learning.*

Lee, K., Ho, J., and Kriegman, D. (2005). Acquiring linear subspaces for face recognition under variable lighting, *IEEE Transactions on Pattern Analysis and Machine Intelligence* **27**, 5, pp. 684–698.

Levin, A., Fergus, R., Durand, F., and Freeman, W. T. (2007). Deconvolution using natural image priors, Tech. rep., MIT.

Levin, A., Weiss, Y., Durand, F., and Freeman, W. (2009). Understanding and evaluating blind deconvolution algorithms, in *CVPR.*

Li, J., Bioucas-Dias, J. M., and Plaza, A. (2010). Semisupervised hyperspectral image segmentation using multinomial logistic regression with active learning, *IEEE Transactions on Geoscience and Remote Sensing*, **48**, 11, pp. 4085–4098.

Li, J., Bioucas-Dias, J. M., and Plaza, A. (2012). Spectral–spatial hyperspectral image segmentation using subspace multinomial logistic regression and markov random fields, *IEEE Transactions on Geoscience and Remote Sensing,* **50**, 3, pp. 809–823.

Li, S. and Fang, L. (2010). An efficient learned dictionary and its application to non-local denoising, in *Proc. International Conf. on Image Processing.*

Li, X., Zhang, K., and Jiang, T. (2004). Minimum entropy clustering and applications to gene expression analysis, in *Computational Systems Bioinformatics Conference, 2004. CSB 2004. Proceedings. 2004 IEEE* (IEEE), pp. 142–151.

Li, Y.-F., Tsang, I. W., Kwok, J. T., and Zhou, Z.-H. (2009). Tighter and convex maximum margin clustering, in *International Conference on Artificial Intelligence and Statistics*, pp. 344–351.

Ling, Q., Wen, Z., and Yin, W. (2013). Decentralized jointly sparse optimization by reweighted minimization, *IEEE Transactions on Signal Processing,* **61**, 5, pp. 1165–1170.

Liu, J., Cai, D., and He, X. (2010). Gaussian mixture model with local consistency, in *AAAI.*

Liu, J. and Ye, J. (2010). Moreau-Yosida regularization for grouped tree structure learning, in *Advances in Neural Information Processing Systems.*

Lovász, L. and Plummer, M. (2009). *Matching theory*, Vol. 367 (American Mathematical Soc.).

Mairal, J. (2010). *Sparse coding for machine learning, image processing and com-*

puter vision, Ph.D. thesis, Ecole Normale Supérieure de Cachan.

Mairal, J., Bach, F., and Ponce, J. (2012). Task-driven dictionary learning, *IEEE Transactions on Pattern Analysis and Machine Intelligence,* **34**, 4, pp. 791–804.

Mairal, J., Bach, F., Ponce, J., and Sapiro, G. (2008a). Supervised dictionary learning, in *NIPS.*

Mairal, J., Bach, F., Ponce, J., and Sapiro, G. (2009a). Online dictionary learning for sparse coding, in *Proc. ICML*, pp. 689–696.

Mairal, J., Bach, F., Ponce, J., Sapiro, G., and Zisserman, A. (2008b). Discriminative learned dictionaries for local image analysis, in *Proc. CVPR*, pp. 1–8.

Mairal, J., Bach, F., Ponce, J., Sapiro, G., and Zisserman, A. (2009b). Non-local sparse models for image restoration, in *IEEE International Conference on Computer Vision* (IEEE), pp. 2272–2279.

Mairal, J., Elad, M., and Sapiro, G. (2008c). Sparse representation for color image restoration, *IEEE Trans. on Image Processing* **17**, 1, pp. 53 – 69.

Majumdar, A. and Ward, R. K. (2010). Robust classifiers for data reduced via random projections, *IEEE Trans. Sys. Man Cyber. Part B* **40**, pp. 1359–1371.

Malioutov, D., Cetin, M., and Willsky, A. (2005). Sparse signal reconstruction perspective for source localization with sensor arrays, *IEEE Trans. on Signal Processing* **53**, 8, pp. 3010 – 3022.

Mallat, S. (1999). *A wavelet tour of signal processing* (Academic press).

Mallat, S. G. and Zhang, Z. (1993). Matching pursuits with time-frequency dictionaries, *IEEE Transactions on Signal Processing* **41**, 12, pp. 3397–3415.

Martinez, A. and Benavente, R. (1998). The AR face database, CVC Technical Report 24.

Mathur, A. and Foody, G. (2008). Multiclass and binary svm classification: Implications for training and classification users, *Geoscience and Remote Sensing Letters, IEEE* **5**, 2, pp. 241–245.

Mehta, N. and Gray, A. (2013). Sparsity-based generalization bounds for predictive sparse coding, in *Proc. ICML*, accepted.

Meinshausen, N. and Bühlmann, P. (2006). High-dimensional graphs and variable selection with the lasso, *Annals of Statistics* **34**, 3, pp. 1436–1462.

Mirelli, V., Tenney, S., Bengio, Y., Chapados, N., and Delalleau, O. (2009). Statistical machine learning algorithms for target classification from acoustic signature, in *Proc. MSS Battlespace Acoustic and Magnetic Sensors.*

Mishali, M. and Eldar, Y. C. (2008). Reduce and boost: Recovering arbitrary sets of jointly sparse vectors, *IEEE Trans. on Signal Processing* **56**, 10, pp. 4692 – 4702.

Mishali, M. and Eldar, Y. C. (2009). Blind multiband signal reconstruction: Compressed sensing for analog signals, *IEEE Trans. on Signal Processing* **57**, 3, pp. 993 – 1009.

Mosseri, I., Zontak, M., and Irani, M. (2013). Combining the power of internal and external denoising, in *Computational Photography (ICCP), 2013 IEEE International Conference on* (IEEE), pp. 1–9.

Muñoz-Mari, J., Bovolo, F., Gómez-Chova, L., Bruzzone, L., and Camp-Valls, G. (2010). Semisupervised one-class support vector machines for classification of remote sensing data, *IEEE Transactions on Geoscience and Remote Sensing*, **48**, 8, pp. 3188–3197.

Needell, D. and Tropp, J. A. (2009). CoSaMP: Iterative signal recovery from incomplete and inaccurate samples, *Applied and Computational Harmonic Analysis* **26**, 3, pp. 301–321.

Nesterov, Y. *et al.* (2007). Gradient methods for minimizing composite objective function.

Ng, A. Y., Jordan, M. I., Weiss, Y., *et al.* (2002). On spectral clustering: Analysis and an algorithm, *Advances in neural information processing systems* **2**, pp. 849–856.

Ni, K., Kannan, A., Criminisi, A., and Winn, J. (2009). Epitomic location recognition, *IEEE Transactions on Pattern Analysis and Machine Intelligence*, **31**, 12, pp. 2158–2167.

Nishiyama, M., Takeshima, H., Shotton, J., Kozakaya, T., and Yamaguchi, O. (2009). Facial deblur inference to improve recognition of blurred faces, in *CVPR*.

Olshausen, B. and Field, D. (1998). Sparse coding with an overcomplete basis set: A strategy employed by v1? *Vision Research* **37**, 23, pp. 3311–3325.

Osborne, M. R., Presnell, B., and Turlach, B. A. (2000). On the lasso and its dual, *Journal of Computational and Graphical statistics* **9**, 2, pp. 319–337.

Perona, P. and Malik, J. (1990). Scale-space and edge detection using anisotropic diffusion, *IEEE Transactions on Pattern Analysis and Machine Intelligence* **12**, 7, pp. 629–639.

Pham, D.-S. and Venkatesh, S. (2008). Joint learning and dictionary construction for pattern recognition, in *Computer Vision and Pattern Recognition, 2008. CVPR 2008. IEEE Conference on* (IEEE), pp. 1–8.

Philips, P. J., Flynn, P. J., Scruggs, T., Bower, K. W., and Worek, W. (2006). Preliminary face recognition grand challenge results, in *IEEE Conference and Automatic Face and Gesture Recognition*.

Plaza, A., Benediktsson, J. A., Boardman, J. W., Brazile, J., Bruzzone, L., Camps-Valls, G., Chanussot, J., Fauvel, M., Gamba, P., Gualtieri, A., *et al.* (2009). Recent advances in techniques for hyperspectral image processing, *Remote sensing of environment* **113**, pp. S110–S122.

Plummer, D. and Lovász, L. (1986). *Matching Theory*, North-Holland Mathematics Studies (Elsevier Science).

Povey, D., Burget, L., Agarwal, M., Akyazi, P., Feng, K., Ghoshal, A., Glembek, O., Goel, N. K., Karafiát, M., Rastrow, A., Rose, R. C., Schwarz, P., and Thomas, S. (2010). Subspace gaussian mixture models for speech recognition, in *ICASSP*, pp. 4330–4333.

Proakis, J. G. and Manolakis, D. K. (2006). Digital signal processing, principles, algorithms, and applications, 4th edition, *Pentice Hall*.

Qiu, Q., Jiang, Z., and Chellappa, R. (2011). Sparse dictionary-based representation and recognition of action attributes, in *Proc. ICCV*, pp. 707–714.

Raina, R., Battle, A., Lee, H., Packer, B., and Ng, A. Y. (2007). Self-taught learning: Transfer learning from unlabeled data. in *ICML*.

Rakotomamonjy, A. (2010). Surveying and comparing simultaneous sparse approximation (or group lasso) algorithms, Tech. rep., Dept. of Physics, University of Rouen.

Ramirez, I., Sprechmann, P., and Sapiro, G. (2010). Classification and clustering via dictionary learning with structured incoherence and shared features, in *Proc. CVPR*, pp. 3501–3508.

Ranzato, M., Huang, F., Boureau, Y., and LeCun, Y. (2007a). Unsupervised learning of invariant feature hierarchies with applications to object recognition, in *CVPR*.

Ranzato, M. A., Boureau, Y.-L., and LeCun, Y. (2007b). Sparse feature learning for deep belief networks, in *NIPS*.

Ratle, F., Camps-Valls, G., and Weston, J. (2010). Semisupervised neural networks for efficient hyperspectral image classification, *IEEE Transactions on Geoscience and Remote Sensing*, **48**, 5, pp. 2271–2282.

RichardsJA, J. (1999). Remote sensing digital image analysis: An introduction.

Roth, S. and Black, M. J. (2005). Fields of experts: A framework for learning image priors, in *CVPR*.

Roth, V. and Fischer, B. (2008). The group-lasso for generalized linear models: uniqueness of solutions and efficient algorithms, in *Proceedings of the 25th international conference on Machine learning* (ACM), pp. 848–855.

Roth, V. and Lange, T. (2003). Feature selection in clustering problems, in *Advances in neural information processing systems*, p. None.

Roweis, S. and Saul, L. (2000). Nonlinear dimensionality reduction by locally linear embedding, *Science* **290**, 5500, pp. 2323–2326.

Rozell, C. J., Johnson, D. H., Baraniuk, R. G., and Olshausen, B. A. (2008). Sparse coding via thresholding and local competition in neural circuits, *Neural Computation* **20**, 10, pp. 2526–2563.

Rubinstein, R., Bruckstein, A. M., and Elad, M. (2010). Dictionaries for sparse representation modeling, in *Proceedings of IEEE*, Vol. 98.

Rudin, L. I. and Osher, S. (1994). Total variation based image restoration with free local constraints, in *IEEE International Conference Image Processing*, Vol. 1 (IEEE), pp. 31–35.

Schölkopf, B. and Smola, A. J. (2002). *Learning with kernels: Support vector machines, regularization, optimization, and beyond* (MIT press).

Sermanet, P., Eigen, D., Zhang, X., Mathieu, M., Fergus, R., and LeCun, Y. (2013). Overfeat: integrated recognition, localization and detection using convolutional networks, *arXiv preprint arXiv:1312.6229*.

Shan, Q., Jia, J., and Agarwala, A. (2008). High-quality motion deblurring from a single image, in *SIGGRAPH*.

Shawe-Taylor, J. and Cristianini, N. (2004). *Kernel methods for pattern analysis* (Cambridge university press).

Shi, J. and Malik, J. (2000). Normalized cuts and image segmentation, *IEEE Transactions on Pattern Analysis and Machine Intelligence* **22**, 8, pp. 888–905.

Sim, T., Baker, S., and Bsat, M. (2001). The cmu pose, illumination, and expres-

sion (pie) database of human faces, Tech. Rep. CMU-RI-TR-01-02, Robotics
Institute, Pittsburgh, PA.

Simon, N., Friedman, J., Hastie, T., and Tibshirani, R. (2013). A sparse-group
lasso, *Journal of Computational and Graphical Statistics* **22**, 2, pp. 231–245.

Smolensky, P. (1986). Information processing in dynamical systems: Foundations
of harmony theory, in D. E. Rumelhart, J. L. McClelland, and C. PDP
Research Group (eds.), *Parallel Distributed Processing: Explorations in the
Microstructure of Cognition, Vol. 1* (MIT Press, Cambridge, MA, USA),
ISBN 0-262-68053-X, pp. 194–281.

Sprechmann, P. and Sapiro, G. (2010). Dictionary learning and sparse coding for unsupervised clustering, in *Acoustics Speech and Signal Processing
(ICASSP), 2010 IEEE International Conference on* (IEEE), pp. 2042–2045.

Sroubek, F. and Milanfar, P. (2012). Robust multichannel blind deconvolution
via fast alternating minimization, *IEEE Trans. on Image Process.* **21**, 4,
pp. 1687–1700.

Sun, X., Qu, Q., Nasrabadi, N. M., and Tran, T. D. (2014). Structured priors for
sparse-representation-based hyperspectral image classification, *Geoscience
and Remote Sensing Letters, IEEE* **11**, 7, pp. 1235–1239.

Swain, P. H. (1978). Fundamentals of pattern recognition in remote sensing, *Remote sensing: The quantitative approach*, pp. 136–187.

Tenenbaum, J., Silva, V., and Langford, J. (2000). A global geometric framework
for nonlinear dimensionality reduction, *Science* **290**, 5500, pp. 2319–2323.

Tibshirani, R., Saunders, M., Rosset, S., Zhu, J., and Knight, K. (2005). Sparsity and smoothness via the Fused Lasso, *Journal of the Royal Statistical
Society, Series B* **67**, pp. 91–108.

Timofte, R., De Smet, V., and Van Gool, L. (2014). A+: Adjusted anchored
neighborhood regression for fast super-resolution, in *Computer Vision–
ACCV 2014* (Springer), pp. 111–126.

Tipping, M. E. and Bishop, C. M. (1999). Probabilistic principal component analysis, *Journal of the Royal Statistical Society: Series B (Statistical Method-
ology)* **61**, 3, pp. 611–622.

Tomasi, C. and Manduchi, R. (1998). Bilateral filtering for gray and color images,
in *Computer Vision, 1998. Sixth International Conference on* (IEEE), pp.
839–846.

Tropp, J. A. (2004). Greed is good: Algorithmic results for sparse approximation,
IEEE Transactions on Information Theory **50**, 10, pp. 2231–2242.

Tropp, J. A., Anna, and Gilbert, C. (2007). Signal recovery from random measurements via orthogonal matching pursuit, *IEEE Trans. on Information
Theory* **53**, 12, pp. 4655–4666.

Tropp, J. A., Gilbert, A. C., Martin, and Strauss, J. (2006). Algorithms for
simultaneous sparse approximation. Part I: Greedy pursuit, *EURASIP J.
App. Signal Processing* **86**, pp. 572–588.

van den Berg, E. and Friedlander, M. P. (2009). Joint-sparse recovery from multiple measurements, Tech. rep., Department of Computer Science, University
of British Columbia.

Vapnik, V. (1999). *The nature of statistical learning theory* (Springer).

Vincent, P., Larochelle, H., Bengio, Y., and Manzagol, P.-A. (2008). Extracting and composing robust features with denoising autoencoders, in *ICML*, pp. 1096–1103.

Wagner, A., Wright, J., Ganesh, A., Zhou, Z., and Ma, Y. (2009). Towards a practical face recognition system: Robust registration and illumination by sparse representation, in *CVPR*.

Wang, Y., Chen, S., and Zhou, Z.-H. (2012). New semi-supervised classification method based on modified cluster assumption, *IEEE Transactions on Neural Networks and Learning Systems*, **23**, 5, pp. 689–702.

Wang, Y., Yang, J., Yin, W., and Zhang, Y. (2008). A new alternating minimization algorithm for total variation image reconstruction, *SIAM J. Img. Sci.* **1**, 3, pp. 248–272, doi:http://dx.doi.org/10.1137/080724265.

Wang, Z. (2014). *Learning sparse representation for image signals*, Ph.D. thesis, University of Illinois at Urbana-Champaign.

Wang, Z., Nasrabadi, N. M., and Huang, T. S. (2014a). Spatial–spectral classification of hyperspectral images using discriminative dictionary designed by learning vector quantization, *IEEE Transactions on Geoscience and Remote Sensing*, **52**, 8, pp. 4808–4822.

Wang, Z., Nasrabadi, N. M., and Huang, T. S. (2015a). Semisupervised hyperspectral classification using task-driven dictionary learning with laplacian regularization, *IEEE Transactions on Geoscience and Remote Sensing*.

Wang, Z., Wang, Z., Chang, S., Yang, J., and Huang, T. (2014b). A joint perspective towards image super-resolution: Unifying external-and self-examples, in *Applications of Computer Vision (WACV), 2014 IEEE Winter Conference on* (IEEE), pp. 596–603.

Wang, Z., Yang, J., Nasrabadi, N., and Huang, T. (2013). A max-margin perspective on sparse representation-based classification, in *Computer Vision (ICCV), 2013 IEEE International Conference on* (IEEE), pp. 1217–1224.

Wang, Z., Yang, Y., Chang, S., Li, J., Fong, S., and Huang, T. S. (2015b). A joint optimization framework of sparse coding and discriminative clustering, in *Proc. of International Joint Conferences on Artificial Intelligence (IJCAI)*.

Whyte, O., Sivic, J., Zisserman, A., and Ponce, J. (2010). Non-uniform deblurring for shaken images, in *Proceedings of the IEEE Conference on Computer Vision and Pattern Recognition*.

Wipf, D., Owen, J., Attias, H., Sekihara, K., and Nagarajan, S. (2010). Robust bayesian estimation of the location, orientation, and timecourse of multiple correlated neural sources using MEG, *NeuroImage* **49**, 1.

Wright, J., Ma, Y., Mairal, J., Sapiro, G., Huang, T. S., and Yan, S. (2010). Sparse representation for computer vision and pattern recognition, *Proceedings of the IEEE - Special Issue on Applications of Sparse Representation & Compressive Sensing* **98**, 6, pp. 1031–1044.

Wright, J., Yang, A. Y., Ganesh, A., Sastry, S. S., and Ma, Y. (2009). Robust face recognition via sparse representation, *IEEE Transactions on Pattern Analysis and Machine Intelligence*, **31**, 2, pp. 210–227.

Xu, L., Neufeld, J., Larson, B., and Schuurmans, D. (2004). Maximum margin clustering, in *Advances in neural information processing systems*, pp. 1537–

1544.

Xu, L. and Schuurmans, D. (2005). Unsupervised and semi-supervised multi-class support vector machines, in *AAAI*, Vol. 5.

Yan, S. and Wang, H. (2009). Semi-supervised learning by sparse representation, in *SDM*, pp. 792–801.

Yan, S., Xu, D., Zhang, B., Yang, Q., Zhang, H., and Lin, S. (2007). Graph embedding and extensions: A general framework for dimensionality reduction, *IEEE Transactions on Pattern Analysis and Machine Intelligence* **29**, 1, pp. 40–51.

Yan, S., Zhou, X., Liu, M., Hasegawa-Johnson, M., and Huang, T. (2008). Regression from patch-kernel, in *Conference on IEEE Computer Vision and Pattern Recognition, 2008. CVPR 2008.*, pp. 1–8.

Yang, A. Y., Maji, S., Christoudias, C. M., Darrell, T., Malik, J., and Sastry, S. S. (2009a). Multiple-view object recognition in band-limited distributed camera networks, in *Proc. 3rd ACM/IEEE Conf. on Distributed Smart Cameras*, pp. 1–8.

Yang, C.-Y., Huang, J.-B., and Yang, M.-H. (2011a). Exploiting self-similarities for single frame super-resolution, in *Computer Vision–ACCV 2010* (Springer), pp. 497–510.

Yang, H. (1999). A back-propagation neural network for mineralogical mapping from aviris data, *International Journal of Remote Sensing* **20**, 1, pp. 97–110.

Yang, J., Lin, Z., and Cohen, S. (2013). Fast image super-resolution based on in-place example regression, in *Computer Vision and Pattern Recognition (CVPR), 2013 IEEE Conference on* (IEEE), pp. 1059–1066.

Yang, J., Wang, J., and Huang, T. S. (2011b). Learning the sparse representation for classification, in *Proc. ICME*, pp. 1–6.

Yang, J., Wang, Z., Lin, Z., Cohen, S., and Huang, T. (2012a). Coupled dictionary training for image super-resolution, *IEEE Transactions on Image Processing* **21**, 8, pp. 3467–3478.

Yang, J., Wang, Z., Lin, Z., Shu, X., and Huang, T. (2012b). Bilevel sparse coding for coupled feature spaces, in *Computer Vision and Pattern Recognition (CVPR), 2012 IEEE Conference on* (IEEE), pp. 2360–2367.

Yang, J., Wright, J., Huang, T., and Ma, Y. (2008). Image super-resolution as sparse representation of raw image patches, in *Proc. IEEE Conf. on Computer Vision and Pattern Recognition*, pp. 1–8.

Yang, J., Wright, J., Huang, T. S., and Ma, Y. (2010a). Image super-resolution via sparse representation, *IEEE Transactions on Image Processing,* **19**, 11, pp. 2861–2873.

Yang, J., Yan, S., and Huang, T. S. (2009b). Ubiquitously supervised subspace learning, *IEEE Transactions on Image Processing* **18**, 2, pp. 241–249.

Yang, J., Yu, K., Gong, Y., and Huang, T. (2009c). Linear spatial pyramid matching using sparse coding for image classification, in *Proc. IEEE Conf. on Computer Vision and Pattern Recognition*, pp. 1794–1801.

Yang, J., Yu, K., and Huang, T. (2010b). Supervised translation-invariant sparse coding, in *Computer Vision and Pattern Recognition (CVPR), 2010 IEEE*

Conference on (IEEE), pp. 3517–3524.

Yang, M., Zhang, L., Feng, X., and Zhang, D. (2011c). Fisher discrimination dictionary learning for sparse representation, in *Proc. ICCV*, pp. 543–550.

Yang, Y., Chu, X., Ng, T. T., Chia, A. Y.-S., Yang, J., Jin, H., and Huang, T. S. (2014a). Epitomic image colorization, in *Acoustics, Speech and Signal Processing (ICASSP), 2014 IEEE International Conference on* (IEEE), pp. 2470–2474.

Yang, Y., Liang, F., Yan, S., Wang, Z., and Huang, T. S. (2014b). On a theory of nonparametric pairwise similarity for clustering: Connecting clustering to classification, in *Advances in Neural Information Processing Systems*, pp. 145–153.

Yang, Y., Wang, Z., Yang, J., Han, J., and Huang, T. S. (2014c). Regularized l1-graph for data clustering, in *British Machine Vision Conference*.

Yang, Y., Wang, Z., Yang, J., Wang, J., Chang, S., and Huang, T. S. (2014d). Data clustering by laplacian regularized l1-graph, in *Proceedings of the Twenty-Eighth AAAI Conference on Artificial Intelligence*, pp. 3148–3149.

Yu, K., Xu, W., and Gong, Y. (2008). Deep learning with kernel regularization for visual recognition, in *In Advances in Neural Information Processing Systems 21*.

Yu, K., Zhang, T., and Gong, Y. (2009). Nonlinear learning using local coordinate coding, in *In Advances in Neural Information Processing Systems 22*.

Yuan, L., Sun, J., Quan, L., and Shum, H.-Y. (2007). Blurred/non-blurred image alignment using sparseness prior, in *ICCV*.

Yuan, M. and Lin, Y. (2006). Model selection and estimation in regression with grouped variables, *Journal of the Royal Statistical Society, Series B* **68**, pp. 49–67.

Yuan, X.-T. and Yan, S. (2010). Visual classification with multi-task joint sparse representation, in *CVPR*.

Zeyde, R., Elad, M., and Protter, M. (2012). On single image scale-up using sparse-representations, in *Curves and Surfaces* (Springer), pp. 711–730.

Zhang, G., Jiang, Z., and Davis, L. S. (2013a). Online semi-supervised discriminative dictionary learning for sparse representation, in *Computer Vision–ACCV 2012* (Springer), pp. 259–273.

Zhang, H., Huang, T. S., Nasrabadi, N. M., and Zhang, Y. (2011a). Heterogeneous multi-metric learning for multi-sensor fusion, in *Proceedings of the 14th International Conference on Information Fusion, FUSION 2011, Chicago, Illinois, USA, July 5-8, 2011*, pp. 1–8.

Zhang, H., Nasrabadi, N. M., Zhang, Y., and Huang, T. S. (2011b). Multi-observation visual recognition via joint dynamic sparse representation, in *IEEE International Conference on Computer Vision, ICCV 2011, Barcelona, Spain, November 6-13, 2011*, pp. 595–602.

Zhang, H., Nasrabadi, N. M., Zhang, Y., and Huang, T. S. (2012a). Joint dynamic sparse representation for multi-view face recognition, *Pattern Recognition* **45**, 4, pp. 1290–1298.

Zhang, H., Nasrabadi, N. M., Zhang, Y., and Huang, T. S. (2012b). Multi-view automatic target recognition using joint sparse representation, *IEEE Trans-*

actions on Aerospace and Electronic Systems **48**, 3, pp. 2481–2497.

Zhang, H. and Wipf, D. (2013). Non-uniform camera shake removal using a spatially adaptive sparse penalty, in *NIPS*.

Zhang, H., Wipf, D. P., and Zhang, Y. (2013b). Multi-image blind deblurring using a coupled adaptive sparse prior, in *CVPR*.

Zhang, H., Yang, J., Zhang, Y., and Huang, T. S. (2011c). Sparse representation based blind image deblurring, in *IEEE International Conference on Multimedia & Expo (ICME)* (IEEE).

Zhang, H., Yang, J., Zhang, Y., Nasrabadi, N. M., and Huang, T. S. (2011d). Close the loop: Joint blind image restoration and recognition with sparse representation prior, in *Computer Vision (ICCV), 2011 IEEE International Conference on* (IEEE), pp. 770–777.

Zhang, H. and Zhang, Y. (2009). Sparse representation based iterative incremental image deblurring, in *Proc. IEEE Int. Conf. on Image Processing*, pp. 1293–1296.

Zhang, H., Zhang, Y., Nasrabadi, N. M., and Huang, T. S. (2012c). Joint-structured-sparsity-based classification for multiple-measurement transient acoustic signals, *IEEE Transactions on Systems, Man, and Cybernetics, Part B: Cybernetics,* **42**, 6, pp. 1586–1598.

Zhao, B., Wang, F., and Zhang, C. (2008). Efficient maximum margin clustering via cutting plane algorithm. in *SDM* (SIAM), pp. 751–762.

Zheng, M., Bu, J., Chen, C., Wang, C., Zhang, L., Qiu, G., and Cai, D. (2011). Graph regularized sparse coding for image representation, *IEEE Transactions on Image Processing,* **20**, 5, pp. 1327–1336.

Zheng, X., Cai, D., He, X., Ma, W., and Lin, X. (2004). Locality preserving clustering for image database, in *ACM International Conference on Multimedia*, pp. 885–891.

Zhou, M., Chen, H., Ren, L., Sapiro, G., Carin, L., and Paisley, J. W. (2009a). Non-parametric bayesian dictionary learning for sparse image representations, in *Advances in neural information processing systems*, pp. 2295–2303.

Zhou, X., Cui, N., Li, Z., Liang, F., and Huang, T. S. (2009b). Hierarchical gaussianization for image classification, in *ICCV*, pp. 1971–1977.

Zhu, X., Ghahramani, Z., and Lafferty, J. (2003). Semi-supervised learning using gaussian fields and harmonic functions, in *International Conference on Machine Learning*, pp. 912–919.

Zontak, M. and Irani, M. (2011). Internal statistics of a single natural image, in *Computer Vision and Pattern Recognition (CVPR), 2011 IEEE Conference on* (IEEE), pp. 977–984.

Zou, H. and Hastie, T. (2005). Regularization and variable selection via the elastic net, *Journal of the Royal Statistical Society, Series B* **67**, pp. 301–320.

Zou, H., Hastie, T., and Tibshirani, R. (2007). On the "degrees of freedom" of the LASSO, *The Annals of Statistics* **35**, 5, pp. 2173–2192.